The Gilded Edge

The Gilded Edge

TWO AUDACIOUS WOMEN
AND THE CYANIDE LOVE TRIANGLE
THAT SHOOK AMERICA

Catherine Prendergast

DUTTON

Dutton
An imprint of Penguin Random House LLC
penguinrandomhouse.com

LIBRARY OF CONGRESS CATALOGING-IN-PUBLICATION DATA
has been applied for.

ISBN 9780593182925 (hardcover)
ISBN 9780593182949 (ebook)

Printed in the United States of America
1   2   3   4   5   6   7   8   9   10

BOOK DESIGN BY ELKE SIGAL

In loving memory

Nancy, Brigit, Katie

Contents

෧෴෨

The
Gilded Edge

Prologue

⌒〰〰⌒

NORA MAY FRENCH WAS TWO WEEKS LATE. SHE WAS TWENTY-FIVE years old and had never been late—not without a reason. She knew she was pregnant again. This time, she would need to act quickly; she could not afford a "therapeutic" abortion in a hospital even if she could convince a doctor to give her one. She would have to do this on her own.

She bought the pills on Friday night, easy to secure even though it had been not quite a year since the earthquake of 1906 leveled most of San Francisco. Her local drugstore boasted an array of cheerfully colored boxes on its shelves, advertised cannily as bringing on "suppressed menstruation," "regulation," or "the cure": Dr. Conte's Female Pills, Chichester's English Pennyroyal Pills, and Dr. Trousseau's Celebrated Female Cure. Chichester's, sold in small metallic boxes of red and gold, were advertised in the newspapers as safe, devoid of dangerous substances, and "always reliable."[1]

She knew—everyone knew—these compounds were not only unreliable, they were far from safe, containing undeclared noxious chemicals like turpentine. Even their advertised ingredients, tansy and pennyroyal, could kill a woman. Pennyroyal, a form of mint, could bring on the desired abdominal pains but could also deliver cardiovascular collapse, liver failure, and death. Tansy, with its deceptively benign yellow bloom, could induce convulsions and shortly dispatch her along with her fetus.

Nora paid for the pills, buried them deep in her bag, and walked back to her house. Her address, at 415 Lombard Street, was as good a one as any to have if your life was in shambles. Telegraph Hill shook regularly from blasts from the quarry on its eastern slope. She and her neighbors experienced unusual weather: a rain of rocks one day, a haze of smoke the next. Residents had complained, charging the quarry waving bats and brooms, and had even brought lawsuits against the owners, but to no avail. The city, needing boulders to rebuild the seawall, looked the other way, even as entire houses toppled.[2] Nora had now grown accustomed to being covered in dust by the time she reached her door. Mingled in with that dust were the ashes of those who had died in the great fire that followed the earthquake. Though she tried not to think about it, Nora could sometimes feel herself breathing in death with every step.

She got to her home and kicked off her shoes once she was inside the door. She loved this house. Her boyfriend, Harry, had constructed it from the quake's wreckage to lure her from Los Angeles to San Francisco. They were both poets who needed very little in the way of creature comforts to live. Together they decided there would be nothing artificial about this house. No wood would be painted or finished. It would be as close to nature as one could get in a city. They had been passionately in love with each other and with life then. She wasn't sure where she stood with him now.

She saw that a letter from Harry had arrived that morning. Nora looked around to make sure her sister, Helen, was not at home before she opened it. Helen had grown to hate Harry. Months before, Nora had implored her sister to leave a well-paid clerical job in Los Angeles and move north with her. Although Nora and Helen had weathered every step of their childhood of sorrows together, at first Helen flatly refused. How would moving to an earthquake-ravaged city to join its merry band of Bohemians and poets improve their lives? Because, Nora had responded, San Francisco was the seat of the cultural West, not a backwater farm town like Los Angeles. Harry was an editor of a literary journal and knew everybody. And all she had ever wanted to do was write. She needed to write.

So in September of 1906, Nora gathered up her few possessions, put on one of her rare suits without holes, and caught her train. She secured a room in a boardinghouse at 886 Chestnut Street on Russian Hill, not far from where the poet Ina Coolbrith lived and hosted her famous salons of Bay Area writers. But Nora had barely had time to unpack and explore her surroundings when she developed a cold that went straight to her chest. She wound up in Mount Zion Hospital for two days before being released by a condescending doctor who gave her a lecture about going out too much in the evenings.

Helen had immediately blamed San Francisco's clammy climate for Nora's ill health and used it as an excuse to delay joining her. More months passed. In the meantime, Nora had won *The*

San Francisco Call's contest for a poem celebrating the new year and had been featured on a full broadsheet of the city's paper. She had a new publication almost every month in literary journals. She was accomplishing what she had come to San Francisco to do. And yet she realized she could not live without her sister another day. When by mid-January her sister had still not arrived, Nora boarded a train for Los Angeles, determined to drag Helen back north with her—by the hair and shrieking if necessary.[3]

It hadn't come to that. Helen, no longer able to keep living without Nora, admitted defeat and joined her. But as much as creative, wild Nora loved chaotic San Francisco, calm, practical Helen hated it. And she had seen far too much of Harry's harsh words toward Nora and was beginning to worry about her sister. If Helen discovered Nora had gotten pregnant by him, she would pack her bags. The French sisters were the grandnieces of the great Henry Wells, who founded Wells Fargo and American Express, and on the other side of their family, they were granddaughters of the ninth governor of Illinois. They had their families' reputations to uphold. Nora's disgrace would be a stain on them all.

Her parcel of pills still unopened, Nora sat in the kitchen and read the letter from Harry. It was everything she had hoped it would be, sweet and passionate. She felt her will, so resolute earlier that evening, begin to falter. She tried to imagine a life with Harry and a child: Harry, walking their unfinished floor at 3:00 a.m., rocking their baby to sleep in his arms as she dozed. A beautiful baby perhaps with Harry's dark wavy hair but her own spooky eyes. She and Harry could be like Dante and Elizabeth Rossetti, living for beauty and art, while their child rambled happily around the house.

It didn't take long for this fantasy to collapse. Harry Lafler was still a married man, and despite his promises, Nora did not believe his separation from his wife would ever progress to divorce. In truth, she wasn't even sure if she wanted it to. She and Harry were bound by passion and recklessness, not responsibility and reality. She was his carefree muse, something ethereal and magical, not an ordinary woman who could get in ordinary trouble. He would recoil from the sight of a swollen belly and bolt from the rigors of fatherhood. She would be left raising a baby on her own—a complete disaster. Even if in 1907 women worked outside the home, rode bicycles, and published poetry, nobody looked favorably on an unwed mother and her bastard. Her child would be seen not as the product of love but rather as the punishment for sin.

She swallowed the pills on Saturday morning. Waiting for the cramps, she distracted herself by sweeping the floors and washing the dishes. After a flurry of activity, she still felt nothing. She tried to will a contraction, but her body showed no interest in complying. Her mind searched for a metaphor for her situation: She was like a rider astride a horse, fiercely spurring it to gallop while it refused to move to any impulse but its own.

Finally, early Sunday morning, a contraction deep in her lower abdomen woke her from sleep. Spasms soon came in waves. Nausea followed. As the pain intensified, she felt like screaming but clenched her teeth—she didn't want to alarm the neighbors—and let out a low moan.

So this is what it feels like, she thought. It was time to tell him.

Between contractions she went to her desk and took out a piece of Bohemian Club stationery she had filched from Harry (he belonged to one of the more exclusive businessmen's clubs in San Francisco). Returning to the commode, she placed it on a book balanced on her knee and began to write.

"Very dear," Nora wrote, "I have been through deep waters, and proved myself cowardly after all." She was never late, she explained, so she had gone to the druggist. His sweet letter had made her pause, she admitted, but in the end, she did not see another way. "I have gone through every shade of emotion. . . . It was as if we were walking together and my feet were struggling with some pulling quicksand under the grass. I would come near screaming very often."

A contraction interrupted her writing. She tried to moan only softly in case Helen, who was waking up, heard her. Too late. Helen was knocking at the door. She yelled back to Helen that she was just having one of her moods and desired only peace. It was a ready and believable excuse: Helen knew her sister's emotional turmoil all too well.

Nora continued writing. "Motherhood! What an unspeakably huge thing for all my fluttering butterflies to drown in! A still pool, holding the sky." The cramps increased. Her hands shook, but she continued the letter, her script uneven as she worked to steady the pencil. "I looked into it day after day, and sometimes I could see the sky, and sometimes only my drowned butterflies. Oh—"[4]

. . .

Oh. Oh, what?

I'm sitting at one of the broad tables in the manuscripts room of the Bancroft Library at the University of California, Berkeley, turning over Nora May French's letter, looking for a continuation, but there is none. Nora's letter ends mid-sentence. I have no idea what Nora wrote next, nor do I know what Harry had to say for himself, if anything.

There must be another page that fell astray, I think, rifling through the file, but nothing related is there. I search through more files of correspondence. Nothing to be found anywhere in the collection—which, I am annoyed to note, is named not after Nora May French but after her feckless boyfriend, Henry Anderson Lafler. Despite having been nationally known in her day for her poetry, her beauty, and her shocking death at the age of twenty-six, Nora May French doesn't have archives devoted to her papers under her own name. Lafler does—even though his main publications consist of an edited collection of Nora's poems (published after her death and against her family's wishes) and a real estate brochure showcasing residential lots in Alameda County.

Allow me to correct the record. It was Nora, not Harry, who was the sensation in her time. Less than a year after she wrote her letter about her abortion, French died from cyanide poisoning at the home of George and Carrie Sterling, whose bungalow was the center of the writing colony at Carmel-by-the-Sea on the Monterey Peninsula. Founded in the first decade of the twentieth century, the Carmel colony would become famous for hosting Jack London, Upton Sinclair, and Sinclair Lewis. The death of Nora May French—a beautiful, talented young poet of then national reputation—at the colony's height would make the news from Los Angeles, Chicago, St. Louis, and Boston to the *Twice-a-Week Plain Dealer* of Cresco, Iowa. Tabloid-style headlines such as "Midnight Lure of Death Leads Poetess to the Grave" and "Girl Writer Tires of Life" capped articles puzzling over the reasons why Nora, who left no note, might have killed herself.

After her death, it was said her friends in her Bohemian literary circle formed a suicide pact, some even carrying vials of cyanide on their person so as to dispatch themselves the moment the thrill of life had faded. Think of it as similar to 1960s California, a more recent period of youthful sexual experimentation, which devolved into violence (the lurid Sharon Tate murder). At the center of the

Carmel group was a love triangle in which all three members—Nora and her Carmel hosts, George and Carrie—died of cyanide poisoning. If that weren't morbid enough, a number of their friends also came to grisly ends, including one through decapitation and another via self-defenestration. Random strangers in New York died with Nora's poems in their pocket or under their pillow. Historically, Nora has been blamed as the pebble that started these ripples of death. With movie star eyes even before there were movie stars, Nora became history's most literary femme fatale, her most heralded legacy not poems but corpses.

When I first learned about these bizarre events, I felt drawn to Nora almost immediately. It takes some kind of woman to write a letter about an abortion to her boyfriend *while* she's administering it. But I soon became equally fascinated with the woman in whose arms she died, the hostess of the Carmel writing colony, Carrie Sterling. Carrie was born a go-getter. She left her mother's boardinghouse for a secretarial job in a Bay Area realty firm, becoming one of the first women in the West to work in an office instead of in a factory or a home. There she met George Sterling, a handsome young man whose connections within San Francisco's cultural, business, and political elite were surpassed only by his pedigree: A Yankee blueblood whose ancestors had founded several of the East Coast's early settlements. Riding his uncle's coattails, George was becoming rich selling East Bay realty, but he lived a double life as the "King of Bohemia," the head of a group of writers and artists who met regularly at an Italian restaurant on the fringe of the red-light district, reading poetry aloud and sketching the clientele till the wee hours. This group would soon move to Carmel, where Carrie would find herself tasked with feeding them nightly in her own house—hardly the life she had imagined for herself when she married George.

The popular legend of Carmel has it that George Sterling and his friends stumbled upon a landscape of unparalleled beauty, poked around for a few days, and decided that only there could they make great art. In truth, George was a seasoned land developer being cut in on an unusual deal: He had been hired by the Carmel Development Company as their resident Bohemian to lure his artistic friends down to Carmel, creating buzz about what was then only a square mile of nearly barren dirt next to a bay. Carmel thus became the first town to consciously use artists as the leading edge of gentrification of California's new frontier. The Sterlings were forerunners of what we call "influencers" today. Their jobs were to be seen and be written about.

And they certainly made Carmel seem like a lot of fun at first. The town captured the nation's attention as a place where women and men spent their evenings in literary salons discussing poetry and philosophy before heading down to the beach for bonfires and swilling beer from tomato cans. Despite the appearance of gender equity, behind the scenes, Carmel was a roiling pot of exploitation. Women's horizons were limited by the identities the men assigned them, namely scorned wife and elusive muse. Carrie was obliged to host her husband's endless guests while he ran around sleeping with the most attractive of them. "He bays in iambic pentameter," Jack London once remarked admiringly of his best friend Sterling's womanizing.[5]

Let's be clear: Carmel is just as much Carrie's legacy as it is George's—it would not have happened without her labor—but with the exception of a "thanks to my wife for typing" form of acknowledgment, she got none of the credit. Meanwhile, Nora May French, whose reputation was used to bolster the colony's image, was passed along a line of Bohemian men who treated her as a perpetual ingenue, co-opting her talent in an attempt to claim her as their personal discovery; they plied her with unwanted editorial advice while maneuvering her toward the bedroom.

Neither Carrie nor Nora went to Carmel anticipating such poor treatment. Quite to the contrary: Both women had every right to expect that life for them would be better than it had been for their mothers. They were both New Women, a name for women on the trailing edge of the Gilded Age who sought to enjoy the spoils of economic expansion. Factories needed their cheap labor. Magazines, then proliferating, needed their image. Novels of their day captured their experience through new heroines: the gambling Lily Bart of *The House of Mirth*, the lovestruck Edna Pontellier of *The Awakening*, the fallen Tess of *Tess of the D'Urbervilles*. These novels dangled the possibility of fulfilling lives outside the bounds of marriage and children before doling out hefty punishments for women who dared to dream.[6] Carrie's and Nora's real lives followed these plots, illuminating all the dilemmas of turn-of-the-century womanhood. Treated as mere accessories to male ambition, Carrie and Nora were set on a crash course against each other, one that resulted in their mutual destruction.

Considering this history, I began to wonder about the term "New Woman," so in vogue at the time, so evocative of freedom and limitless possibility. When in history, really, are women not "new"? When are they not enjoined to remold themselves to a world that has never bothered to change much for them? The truth is that when New Women emerged at the edge of the Gilded Age, there were no "New Men" to greet them. The phrase "New Men" didn't even exist—that's how entirely not "new" men were. As a result, despite all the progress on the labor or political front, the relationships between the genders remained largely unchanged. Women could strive to be suffragettes, Bohemians, or Gibson Girls (named after the glamorous but independent women sketched by popular illustrator Charles Gibson), but to men they were still only potential conquests or crones, a Madonna–whore complex on a national scale. Even when men claimed to want women who were more sexually liberated or allowed to work outside the home, all the negative consequences of the flowering of liberation were women's alone to bear.

zeugma?

I look back at Nora's letter with this in mind. As I hold it in my hands, I'm aware that it is one of very few early-twentieth-century first-person accounts of abortion, and it won't be around forever. It is already over one hundred years old. Wouldn't it be nice, I think, to see it amid a collection of other letters testifying to the length of women's struggle for reproductive freedom, rather than among the papers of an abusive ex-boyfriend?

But that's not the way archives generally work. Unlike libraries, archives are organized by the life of a person or organization, not by subject. Someone decided that Harry Lafler's life was significant, so his papers were preserved. I realize how lucky I am to be holding Nora's letter at all, considering its unlikely journey. It had traveled from her hands to Lafler's, subsequently landing in the closet of a friend or family member before being traded through collectors, to arrive in the 1950s at the marbled wing of the Bancroft Library at the center of Berkeley's campus, just ten miles as the crow flies from the Telegraph Hill flat where Nora, in agony, wrote it.

That particular flight path made Harry Lafler the de facto protagonist of his and Nora's joint history. But I want to push back on the archival logic that has elevated Lafler and many of his literary male compatriots beyond their rightful place in history. I was often asked in the latter stages of this project, Why are you writing about unknown women? This question rattled around in my head as I looked at Carrie's and Nora's faces splayed out on the front pages of century-old newspapers, as I read article after article that breathlessly followed their lives, their deeds, and their deaths. Neither of them was unknown at the time they lived.

Yet in the archives, I encountered a trail to their lives that had been deliberately wrecked. Letters written by them or about them had the top or bottom ripped off. Names or other incriminating information had been scratched out with pen and rendered illegible. Or—in the case of Nora's letter to Harry—pages had been deliberately held back. Carrie and Nora were not buried in the archives because they were dull women whose lives were of no consequence. They were buried because their personal histories exposed events and insights far too revealing of the flaws of the men who surrounded them.

Archives can resemble graveyards, with marked tombs for men that also contain the scattered bones of various women. You have to do a lot of searching to reconstruct women's lives. I traveled from New York to California to small towns in the interior of the country to find the documents that would connect the dots of Nora's and Carrie's stories. I found through these artifacts a very different story than the idyllic tales of Bohemian California featuring altruistic patrons and open-minded, progressive men. In this book, I take you with me as I read against the grain of archives, resisting the protagonists that the file headings offer, and instead look for the silences that have been carefully constructed around women. What I learned ultimately about Carrie and Nora is true of all women, potentially: One doesn't die but becomes an unknown woman, one mutilated sheet of paper at a time. I offer here a story within a story—on the one hand, the tale of the remarkable women in a Bohemian experiment that ended in disaster; on the other, the concerted efforts to make sure you would never hear about it.

Chapter One

᠙᠐᠙

Working Girl

I WILL NEVER HAVE CHILDREN, CAROLINE RAND DECIDED. CHILDREN destroyed a woman, physically and mentally. She had seen it happen to her mother. Her father, an Oakland police captain, had died before Carrie turned six, leaving five children for his widow to raise on an insufficient pension. Carrie had barely turned eight when her beloved eldest sister, Mary, died, leaving her with the responsibility of watching her little brother, David, a kicking terror. It was Carrie's job to keep David from running out of their house onto busy San Pablo Avenue and under a passing cable car. In her teens, her mother had moved the family closer to the docks and taken in boarders—a necessity to keep the money coming in. Carrie learned how to prepare bean soup; it was a cheap meal that could stretch to feed many mouths. She mopped the floors each evening and scrubbed the dirty shirts of the boarders. No matter how long she scrubbed, the house always smelled of the previous night's food and of that afternoon's dirty laundry. No matter how many hours she lost to chores, her mother would yell at her. Her mother found fault with everything she did, whether folding sheets, ironing tablecloths, or even making a blessed cup of tea. Carrie wanted to yell back but couldn't. Only her mother was allowed to raise her voice. So when her mother's back was turned, she performed impressions of the boarders—their ball-scratching, nose-picking, and farting. Her two older sisters acted shocked and nicknamed her "Cad," but they still laughed.

Reading was Carrie's escape. On weekends, she put on one of her sisters' hand-me-down blouses and headed to Oakland's public library. She spent an hour or so perusing books before choosing one or two to take to Lake Merritt, where she could sit and read. If she had a dime, she could buy the *Ladies' Home Journal* on the way home. The articles were on fashion and crafts, as well as advice from famous wives on the qualities that make for a good husband. Mostly she enjoyed the illustrations of sophisticated women. Sometimes they were depicted walking arm in arm on the street with their flowered hats, gloves, and sweeping skirts— in the midst of sharing confidences, she supposed. Other times they danced or boated with gentlemen. Despite their impossibly narrow waists, they weren't dainty but rather seemed equally comfortable in society or at sport. They looked down at people from atop their bicycles, which they rode without apology. And yet, with all their independence, they still captivated men.

Carrie knew she wasn't beautiful. Hers was a fit but not voluptuous figure. Her face lacked any particular charm beyond a youthful glow, but she noticed that the boarders flirted with her anyway. She could not have been less interested in those men. If they were poor enough to eat her mother's bean soup, they weren't for her. The man who would win her hand would have to show her his bankbook first.

She made a plan to get out of her mother's house forever. She would find a job to make her own income until she could marry and marry well. In the mid-1890s, more women than ever were finding work outside the home. But she wouldn't apply for a factory shift or to be a maid (those jobs were for immigrants or the truly indigent), and she didn't want to be a schoolteacher (looking after all those children). She wouldn't meet eligible men in those jobs anyway.

Carrie's older sister Lila had hit the jackpot, securing an office position as one of the Bay Area's first woman secretaries in a firm called the Realty Syndicate. She worked for a former stockbroker named Frank Havens, who was making a big play for East Bay land. Each weekday morning, Carrie watched Lila don a candy-striped blouse with puffy sleeves and a long black skirt and head out the door to San Francisco. Each evening, Lila came home and told Carrie of the growing financial district above Market Street—a maze of banks and law firms punctuated by the oddball psychic's office.

Mostly Lila talked about what a genius her boss was. An attractive glad-hander, Havens could sell anything, working a room with colorful stories drawn from his seafaring early life; he had captained a riverboat in Shanghai and sailed around Cape Horn, coming to San Francisco the long way. His vision was to transform the Piedmont, an area of depressed farmland in the hills above Oakland, into a residential community for San Francisco's elite. He and his capital partner, Francis Marion "Borax" Smith (of the popular 20 Mule Team Borax cleaning brand), were buying thousands of acres and mapping out residential lots. People would buy, Havens was sure, to get away from the opium dens, saloons, brothels, and gambling halls that made family life in San Francisco undesirable. The city's wealthy wanted bigger houses and open spaces where their children could play. They wanted the filth, the laborers, and their prostitutes out of view.

But knowing no one would buy unless they could commute quickly across the bay, the Realty Syndicate was also getting into the transportation game. They planned a three-mile pier— longer even than Oakland's "long wharf"—stretching from West Oakland toward Goat Island into the center of the bay. Their ferries would take off from the tip of the pier, shaving precious minutes off the existing commutes. Then they bought up and consolidated streetcar routes from the pier to all their developments. Via this unified system of transport, the Piedmont dweller could be deposited on busy Market Street inside of twenty-five minutes, a speed previously unheard of.

One day, Lila came home from work with great news. Business was going so well at the Syndicate that Carrie could join as an assistant to the bookkeeper. Carrie could hardly believe it. On her first day of getting ready with Lila for work, she gathered her brown hair into a smooth crown around her head and squeezed into a corset firm enough to approximate the proportions of the women in the magazines. With Lila nagging her to hurry, she laced her shoes and quickly grabbed her hat and ran out the door. At the waterfront, she followed her sister onto the ferry. As she looked across the bay, Carrie secured her hat to her head and gazed out at San Francisco's developing skyline in the distance.

Even before they docked, Carrie was pushed along by the swell of commuters. Down the gangway, through the ferry building's arcade, and under the clock tower exit she went, Lila already in front. Ahead, the pandemonium of Market Street. Horse-drawn carriages maneuvered around streetcars while pedestrians and cyclists and deliverymen and boys hawking newspapers jockeyed for space. The noise alone was disorienting. Carrie was nearly knocked off her feet by a produce cart emerging from a side street. Six blocks of this gauntlet until they arrived at 14 Sansome Street, shook the dirt off their shoes and skirts, fixed their hair, and entered the Realty Syndicate office.

Carrie's daily task involved organizing sales receipts and bills for the bookkeeper, George Sterling, who happened to be the boss's nephew. She loved the name "Sterling"—it had a nice ring to it. He was twenty-five, just two years older than she was. Tall and thin with dark eyes, dark hair, and a Roman nose, George had a noble air about him. Over time, she learned his ancestors were as close to noblemen as Americans could be: a combination of state congressmen and legendary Sag Harbor buccaneers on his mother's side and lawyers and doctors on his father's. Aside from his family's inexplicable turn toward Catholicism in the last generation, George was as eligible a bachelor as one could imagine. Carrie had never been all that religious, anyway, turned off by her pious mother, who would no doubt find something to complain about no matter what fellow she brought home.

George struck Carrie as lonesome. She found it took remarkably little to draw his attention—a brief smile or a brush with her skirt. He began asking her to accompany him to dinner in the evenings after work. He took her to expensive restaurants with French names to dine on oysters à la poulette. She tried to be poised and confidant in these new surroundings, but she had rarely eaten out much, never mind in such luxury. She remembered how the girls in the magazines looked, and she conducted herself accordingly. At her urging, George took her to the opera, which Carrie loved, but she could tell he only tolerated. On weekends, they went walking in the hills above Oakland that the

Syndicate owned but had not yet sold off. George, sitting with her beneath a tree, read her a sonnet he had composed to her beauty. He had studied poetry in college and was trying to get better at it. She often caught him writing lists of rhyming words when he should have been entering figures into the Syndicate's ledgers.

The poetry was nice, but the real clincher for Carrie was George's sheepish confession that as the eldest of eight, he felt no strong pull to have children. She accepted his proposal immediately, and Frank Havens blessed their union: The Sterling and the Havens families both only married Anglo-Saxons, and Carrie was, despite her poverty, purely that.[1] Her mother had certified all the girls as Daughters of the American Revolution.[2]

Carrie and George honeymooned in Hawaii.[3] It turned out to be an awful trip—George threw up the whole voyage over and then stayed in the hotel room writing poetry once they arrived, never wanting to go out dancing. After a few weeks of this "bliss," they returned to a Syndicate-owned house on the Vernon Heights tract of Oakland Avenue, where the smell from their neighbor's pink bougainvillea wafted over their fence. She could now invite her sisters to her own house. Nell, the middle sister, had married a businessman, Harry Maxwell. Lila, who had been circling around Frank Havens, waiting for his wife to die (which she finally did), pounced and became Mrs. Havens, married to a filthy-rich man two decades her senior.

The Rand girls had all escaped the dockyards of Oakland. They had made it out of poverty. But most importantly, they had evaded their mother's fate of a life of servitude to grubby strangers.

By 1901, five years into their marriage, George had risen to become auditor of the Syndicate, overseeing a capitalization of millions of dollars and bringing in more than $100 in salary a month. Carrie had a house large enough for a servant, but the Sterlings didn't have one: unlike Lila, who had a Chinese cook. Carrie knew she could cook better than anyone she could hire, and George appreciated her for it. Now she cooked and cleaned only for her husband. Every morning, she prepared George's breakfast as he donned his suit for his commute across the bay. Every afternoon, from the top of her front steps, she gazed down the hill toward the roof of her mother's house, and smiled.

. . .

In the Oakland Public Library where I had gone to reconstruct Carrie's early life, there's a 1905 photo on the wall of the Realty Syndicate's three-mile pier. It's quite impressive. To get to the main library from my San Francisco hotel, I essentially had to perform Carrie's commute in reverse. I started down Market Street—every bit as bustling as it was in 1895, with sidewalks still packed with pedestrians, even as automobiles have replaced carriages. Then I took the BART to Oakland and emerged at the Lake Merritt station, walking the several blocks toward the library, which has moved since Carrie's time. Now, of course, we take such routes for granted, but in 1902, when the Realty Syndicate constructed their pier toward Goat Island (now Yerba Buena Island) so ferries could take off from its tip, they were indeed creating the path that the Bay Area Rapid Transit system would follow in 1974 with a transbay tunnel. The East Bay as you encounter it today is largely a product of the Realty Syndicate's imagination. And Carrie's work helped make it happen.

The archivist of the local history room, a woman who knows her stuff, showed me what they had on early Oakland history: old city directories, photographs and tract maps, newspaper clippings, and even original correspondence from Jack London and other contemporaries of the Sterlings. An 1896 brochure printed by the Realty Syndicate demonstrates the atmosphere of heady entrepreneurialism that surrounded the young Carrie Rand. The Syndicate knew that to compete in the development game against the mighty Pacific Improvement Company—the development arm of the Southern Pacific Railroad—they were going to have to sell Oakland and its surroundings as more than just a railway terminus. The rhetorical job of the brochure was to convince the reader that Oakland, a city known for handling freight, was the next hot residential buy. The Syndicate pointed out that San Francisco had nowhere to expand that wasn't already drenched in fog. They bragged that the "death rate" of Oakland was only 11.85 per 1,000 inhabitants, the lowest of any similarly sized city in the United States. Tracts were advertised by the minutes it took to travel from there to the foot of Market Street. The brochure included land surveys showing a lot "Sold for $10,000"—certainly a fictional number given the actual sale prices of the lots as recorded on Syndicate company in-house maps. The capitalization of the corporation in 1896 was given as $5 million.[4]

I have no idea if that number is accurate. Because the Syndicate was as much a stock scheme as a realty company, peddling securities where investors could buy shares in the company's land investments, they inflated all their numbers. Who would know? *Moody's Manual of Industrial and Miscellaneous Securities* wouldn't be around for a few more years.

Frank Havens and George Sterling, aided by Carrie and her sister behind the scenes, must have been good at their jobs. The Piedmont, where Carrie and George began their married life, is now every bit as wealthy and exclusive as Frank Havens hoped it would become. Sprinkled with mansions, it became known in the

1920s as the "City of Millionaires." The area has achieved its goal of remaining overwhelmingly wealthy and white, with the median house price now $1.7 million. These days, a child growing up in the Piedmont can expect to live twelve years longer than one born in East Oakland. And the inhabitants haven't forgotten whom to thank for their excusive address; the elementary school is named after Frank Havens.

Even back when the Piedmont was just getting started, however, Carrie's move from her mother's house to the hills, only just a mile or so in distance, placed her a world away. Against great odds, she had made a leap from one social class to another by the only route available to women: marriage. Once Carrie wedded George Sterling, her prospects entirely relied on his; the percentage of married white women working outside the home in 1900 remained in the low single digits.[5] Her exhilarating career as a secretary was over. Her career as champion of her husband's ambitions had just begun.

Chapter Two

ᏃᎳᎳᎩ

Prodigy

Nora was so nervous she misbuttoned her blue silk shirt (newly acquired for a dollar—she kept meticulous account of her expenditures). She loved both the look and feel of silk, and it was now the best thing in her closet. Aged seventeen, she had been goaded by her father to pay a visit to the writer and editor Charles Lummis. Lummis had arrived in California on foot, through prairie and over mountain—a stunt so he could sell a story, but what a stunt. Since then, he had founded the literary journal *The Land of Sunshine*, which published Western authors writing on regional themes. By 1899, Lummis's salons had become legendary, his guestbook a real who's who of California's cultural elite.

A few months before, again after her father's relentless prodding, she had sent Lummis a few poems to critique. He encouraged her to keep writing, so now her father decided they should meet in person. But why appear at Lummis's doorstep, the eager prodigy, a marionette twitching on the strings of her over-proud father? This seemed almost cruel. Her father knew she didn't like to show her poetry even to her friends, yet here she was, asked to face the undisputed king of Los Angeles's literary set. Worse yet, she wouldn't have her sister, Helen, by her side. Helen was sick at home, waiting on the local minister their mother had called to come and lay hands on her.

· · ·

Nora and her father arrived at Lummis's home, the famous El Alisal, its stone walls rising from the sycamore grove bordering the Arroyo Seco.[1] The door was intimidating enough: rough wood reinforced with iron studs and hinges, as though the writer were expecting an attacking army equipped with a battering ram. Her father knocked. They waited. Nothing. He knocked again. They looked in the window. There was the desk where Lummis sat and edited poems. There was the living room where writers met and talked. Arrayed around the walls were tribal baskets and pottery, artifacts of Lummis's visits with Western Indian tribes. But Lummis never surfaced. Nora breathed a sigh of relief. Her father turned to her and said they would come back.[2]

Nora could see the determination in her father's face. He was desperate to get his daughters a leg up in the world. He could give them nothing—no dowry and no inheritance. Everything he had in life he lost on one bad gamble. Lured by brochures advertising cheap and fertile land in California, he had put their entire savings into a ranch in Glendale, just north of Los Angeles, joining thousands of other hopeful Americans swept up into the western land craze. It turned out to be their ruin.

The Frenches had previously lived in Aurora, New York, a town as good as built by Nora's great-uncle Henry Wells, that titan of the express industry, whose company Wells Fargo had long been trusted with transporting the nation's gold from coast to coast. Although Henry Wells had died a few years before Nora was born, he had left Wells College as his legacy. Nora's father, Edward, taught there and made a comfortable living. Nora grew up surrounded by young women pursuing higher education.

Her sister, Helen, had few memories of life in Aurora. But Nora remembered it well. Sledding down the hill in front of Henry Wells's mansion on crisp winter mornings. Boating on Cayuga Lake on warm summer afternoons. On weekends, their father took them for long hikes in the woods, during which he taught them the names and common uses of flowers or mushrooms. The girls and their brothers grew up as cherished children of the town's most beloved family. If there was a garden party at one of the mansions, they arrived with the boys in sailor suits, Nora and Helen in dresses with matching hats, their mother wearing an exquisite silk dress that showed off her perfect figure. At Christmas, her mother opened the house and guests stayed and sang late into the evening. The children fell asleep to the sound of their parents' joy.

At first the move to California seemed like a delightful adventure. On the train, Nora had watched America unfold its wild scenes before her eyes. Settling in at the ranch, her father got to work building the house. No more skating on frozen lakes, but they could run in zigzags between rows of apple, orange, pear, and olive trees, or hide behind shrubs of black raspberries. Life was harder. Her mother now did all the housework and mended their clothing. Nora's older brother Bert grew proficient with a rifle and hunted for food. In contrast, Henry, her other brother, failed to take after his great entrepreneurial namesake and was utterly shiftless.

They had one benefactor—their uncle Cassius Wicker back

east. Uncle Cash, as they appropriately called him, had married Edward's sister and was nearly drowning in money he made from railroads and mines. When Nora was eleven, Cassius wrote that he would buy each of the French children their choice of magazine subscription as their Christmas present. Nora chose *Wide Awake*, a children's periodical full of illustrated poetry and stories. Their mother asked Uncle Cash for one subscription to the city library so she could check out history books and keep up the children's education.[3] Subscriptions were $6 a year—nothing to Uncle Cash but far more than the Frenches could afford.[4] A mile from their nearest neighbor, all the French children became voracious readers.

As she grew older, Nora began to feel the family's precarious position in her bones. Her already thin parents were growing thinner. To escape the tension of the house, she explored the canyons of the San Gabriel foothills just beyond the ranch. One spot—her nook, she called it—became her secret garden. Angered or sorrowed, she would run there, her long blond hair streaming behind her, to lie on ferns. She spent hours building tiny castles out of twigs and sagebrush, filling them with the fairies of her imagination. Back home, she sketched the leaves she had gathered, copying the illustrations her father used to make but adding verses to her drawings. Soon she began writing poems on their own, unaccompanied by illustration. Helen watched her sister compose aloud in the middle of doing household chores, Nora circling the table she was setting as if in a trance, holding the plates suspended until she perfected a phrase.[5]

When she was eleven, Nora won a national contest for writing the best essay about school. The prize, a two-foot-high doll, came in the mail. It had on the kind of elegant dress Nora used to wear to garden parties at mansions she no longer visited.

When, in 1892, twenty-five inches of rain fell over the valley, her parents cried with relief. The orchard would flourish. But the next year, it rained only six inches. The next year, sixteen. The following year, eight inches. The creek where Nora played dried to a trickle. The green grasses of her nook dried and turned brown. Her father's exhaustive knowledge of seeds proved unequal to the task of designing effective irrigation systems. He wasn't able to keep up with the mortgage, and already strapped banks (there was a financial recession) were refusing to extend further credit. All their neighbors were suffering. The newspapers listed dissolution, creditor, and foreclosure sales daily.

Soon the Frenches could make more money renting the ranch house than they could growing fruit. They moved to a cramped apartment in Los Angeles at 791 Merchant Street. Nora's mother wrote to Uncle Cash, begging him to buy the ranch, suggesting that it would be an investment bound to pay off once it started raining again. The drought couldn't last forever, she argued. She sent brochures trumpeting the possibilities of Glendale— the same kind of brochures that had lured them out to California. He would double his money, she was sure.[6] But business-savvy Uncle Cash would not buy it. Then Edward wrote to ask if he could at least leverage a loan against a $2,000 life-insurance policy with Aetna, just so he could get through the summer. Or could Uncle Cash get him a job where he could earn just $50?[7]

Nora's mother, Mary, was hardly sleeping, wondering what would become of her daughters. Women could teach, but teaching was an invitation to lifelong poverty with no energy left for a creative outlet. Nora was not like other girls. Mary and Edward both believed she needed more specialized training than the diversions given to women to master in order to entertain their future husbands (Nora was awful at the piano anyway). Their eldest daughter's mind was like quicksilver, darting from one idea to the next. Nora could be an artist or a writer; she could pursue these crafts with the intensity of any man if she wanted to. They encouraged her to take art courses. She continued writing stories and poems. She met Lummis at last, spending a memorable evening in his courtyard under the sycamore trees, listening to his advice while her father beamed.

The April 1899 edition of *Land of Sunshine* arrived at the French house in the mail, containing on the very front page under the masthead a poem Nora had written while camping in the canyons of La Cañada:

By Moonlight

Here, where long grasses touch across the stream
That threads with babbling laugh on its narrow way,
My face turned upward to pale gleams, that stray
Through whispering willow boughs . . . I dream
     and dream.

Nora was in the midst of writing a verse on a scrap of paper when her father called to her, insisting she come read her publication. She ignored him. Once she had written something, she rarely read it again.[8] Her poetry lived in the moment of its creation, not for the applause of the reader. The poem she was writing was already better than the one her parents were reading in the next room. While her family oohed and aahed over "By Moonlight," she wrote the last lines of her newest verse and tossed the paper aside, where it landed on a pile of shopping lists.

. . .

That July, Nora's mother giddily called the girls to the kitchen table. She had just received a letter from Uncle Cash. He had offered to put up eighteen-year-old Nora in his luxurious West End Avenue apartment and pay her tuition at the Art Students League in New York. Their aunt, Edward's sister, had died the previous year, and Cassius would be happy to have some company while his own children were away at school.

For a moment Nora was so shocked she could say nothing. Recovering herself, she wiped her hands on her faded dress (a hand-me-down from Cash's daughter, Lucy, just as her mother's had been a hand-me-down from Cash's wife) and headed to the desk to write an ebullient note of thanks on one of their few sheets of stationery (her mother had been conserving paper by turning it ninety degrees to write her correspondence in a crisscross pattern): "New York—and Art!—a solid reality instead of a vague and tantalizing mirage! Good instruction, broadening of ideas in every direction, chance to find out if there *is* anything in me, and develop it if it's there!"[9]

But Nora could not bear the thought of going alone. Cassius agreed to her request that he also board Helen, just sixteen, and pay for her secretarial course. Helen wrote her own grateful letter, in her careful penmanship, thanking Uncle Cash. She understood that she would be benefitting from the genius of her older sister. "I look forward to the time when I have my own typewriter and can put Nora's manuscripts in shape for the editor. What fun to be the private stenographer of the future authoress of the family!"[10]

The girls set off in August on the cross-country train trip, arriving in New York tired and disheveled but elated. Uncle Cash and his driver picked them up at Grand Central Depot, and they never carried their own luggage again.

To be an artist in America as the momentous nineteenth century came to an end one simply had to be in New York. Robber barons, insecure about the relative youth of their wealth, threw their money into establishing cultural institutions to rival Europe's. Carnegie opened his hall. J. P. Morgan pooled his money with the Roosevelt and Vanderbilt families to build a house for the Metropolitan Opera—a coalition motivated by their shared desire to stick it to the Astors, who controlled all the opera boxes downtown. The most Bohemian way to be an artist in New York, however, was to take classes at the Art Students League on Fifty-Seventh Street. Emerging from a break with the old National Academy of Design, the League had no set curriculum; nearly a thousand students came in and out of its doors every year to take classes in painting, sketching, sculpture, decorative arts, and illustration. George Washington Vanderbilt, the flamboyant grandson of the Commodore himself, made the institution his pet project, dumping $100,000 of his family's steamboat fortune into its construction.

On her first day, Nora, running late, barely had time to admire the golden mosaic entrance to the League. She charged past the first-floor exhibition gallery and made for the stairs. Taking them two at a time, she arrived at the life-drawing studios on the top floor, where skylights perfectly illuminated the curvatures of the human form. She had taken a few life-drawing classes in Los Angeles, but they had felt silly and amateurish—the women in the class had all taken turns posing for one another in whatever old costumes were lying around. At the League, the models were nude, and often they were men. Nora looked around and saw the few easels had already been taken. She joined the other late students balancing their canvases on overturned chairs. Tying her hair in a loose topknot, she rolled up her sleeves above her elbows and stared at the young man on the platform. The only sound in the room was of charcoal softly rubbing against canvas. The room smelled of sweat.

After a few weeks she got to know some of the other women from the class. They weren't like Nora's girlhood friends from Los Angeles. They didn't spend all their time talking about boys. They cared little how they dressed or if their hair was in the style of the day. While sketching or painting, their faces wore the same look of concentration hers did. She had found her home.

By November, Nora had completed a solid portfolio of drawings, which Uncle Cash gushed over when she brought it home. Impressed by her progress, Cash told the girls they were welcome to stay as many years as necessary to complete their studies. Nora was delighted. She and Helen were finally putting weight on their frail forms, dining nightly on squab, oysters, or beef Wellington.

Christmas brought home Uncle Cash's daughter, Lucy, the cousin who had sent so many of her old dresses to Nora, and his nineteen-year-old son, Cyrus. As Nora watched her handsome cousin walk in the door, she felt a catch in her breath. Cyrus's eyes lingered on hers as he took her hand in greeting. Days later, the pair contrived to stay up after everyone else had gone to sleep. Their first kiss was furtive and nervous, wary as they were of passing servants. Cyrus sought her every night after. She didn't turn him away.

Cyrus went back to Yale, vowing to return to her in the spring. Nora threw herself back into her art and her writing. She wrote an essay about her experiences at the Art Students League and sent it to the *Los Angeles Times*. She had been writing stories for the newspaper for about a year by then, including a humorous account of being surprised by a snake on a camping trip with friends, and a fable of a king who searched for a shirt that was said to grant happiness, only to find it on a poor boy's back. By the turn of the century, the *Los Angeles Times* boasted a circulation nearing twenty thousand a day, providing Nora a step up in visibility from publishing in Lummis's literary journal. Her account of the Art Students League, entitled "Pencil and Brush," appeared in the *Times*'s illustrated magazine.[11]

She also wrote more poems and mailed one to her father to forward to Lummis for criticism. Entitled "Answered," it drew upon a repetitive theme in her writing: that of a young girl whose death reinvigorates the land. The girl of "Answered" dies unappreciated, as if her life is of no consequence or importance, but when her friends visit her grave, the earth reveals her true depth.

> For there above the girlish heart
> With upturned faces, Pansies grew.[12]

In the spring, she watched the trees sprout new leaves along Riverside Drive. Uncle Cash motored them across the Hudson to walk in the woods of New Jersey. The girls gathered lilacs, which Nora weaved into a chain for Helen's hair. She shelled peanuts for Uncle Cash on the drive back.

Cyrus returned. Nora greeted him too ardently, and Lucy caught them embracing. Seething that Nora had replaced her as the household's favorite, Lucy told her father about the affair. Cassius felt betrayed. The French girls might be family, but they were the poor cousins, not to ruin his son's trajectory through society.

The end of the term found Nora packing her bags, pausing occasionally to stroke the head of her sobbing sister. Uncle Cash was sending them back to California. They would not be returning in the fall to finish their schooling. They said their goodbyes at Grand Central Depot, thanking their uncle again for all his kindness. Helen was so angry at Nora that she barely talked to her the whole way home. Nora comforted herself by gazing out at the astounding world. She wrote a story of their journey and sent it to the *Los Angeles Times*.

Once back in California, Nora got a job in a leather factory sewing together scraps to make boots and mittens eight hours a day, bending over a table where a glint of sunlight fell. At the end of each week, she took home $5.

. . .

In 1960, Helen French Hunt made a trip back to Aurora, New York, with her husband to see the town where she was born but that she never really knew. By then in her seventies, she had questions about her family she needed to answer. An archivist from Wells College working on the history of the school had written to ask her why her father had moved them all to California. Helen had written back that she couldn't remember. Her curiosity piqued, she made the trip from Los Angeles. Seeing the beauty of Cayuga Lake, the grandeur of the mansions lining it, and the now co-educational college, the question of why her father left it all behind to propel them toward ruin became an even greater mystery to her than it had been before. She wrote the archivist, "From my impressions of the college and Aurora I am wondering why he ever decided to leave it. But I believe his health was not good and the winters severe."[13]

You have to love the nineteenth century. Enough people then

met their deaths through disease that "health" made a ready excuse for any otherwise inexplicable decision. It was replaced in the late twentieth century by "family reasons." Edward's decision to trade teaching for farming does seem suspicious. Imagine this: You have four children, a steady job, and your house is given to you to live in for free. Would you give it all up to buy a patch of dirt in California? When you don't even know how to farm? No, you would not. Even taking into account Edward's spectacularly bad timing—a three-year drought beginning in 1893, the same year the stock market crashed to an unprecedented low, causing hundreds of banks to shutter—one has to wonder how the son of an Illinois governor, married to the favored niece of the founder of the express industry, could fall into poverty so quickly. When the ranch failed, why didn't the wealthy Wells clan help their own?

This nagging question prompted me to follow Helen French's path to the Finger Lakes region of New York State and the archives of Wells College. Not coincidentally, the college is situated across the lake from Seneca Falls, where the Declaration of Sentiments was forged in the summer of 1848, kicking off America's first official feminist movement. Modeled on the Declaration of Independence, the Declaration of Sentiments made the revolutionary proposal that all men and women were created equal. It charged that men had usurped God's authority by rendering women nonentities, morally irresponsible and "civilly dead" when married, deprived of education and employment, and subjected to a life of abjection. The final document was signed by sixty-eight women, including Elizabeth Cady Stanton and Lucretia Mott, and thirty-two men, including Frederick Douglass.

Across the water from these developments, Henry Wells was beginning to contemplate his legacy. He decided that the best use of his money would be to counter what he saw as a dangerous radical movement among American women. Wells, a strict Presbyterian, believed that women working in any kind of job for money was akin to prostitution. This was personal for him. His father, the noted minister Shipley Wells, had preached in Seneca Falls. Henry's brothers, including Nora's grandfather, were all ministers with the unshakable belief that Providence had assigned women their gifts as the "better half" of the human race to be exercised in the home, not in an office.[14]

Wells decided to build a college to educate ladies to fulfill their roles as wives and mothers. In 1868, he opened the Wells Seminary for the Higher Education of Young Women and soon after invited Edward French to join the faculty. Edward took the job because he was unable to attract enough clients to his law practice in southern Illinois, and his wife, Mary, was suffering in the humidity. Edward's annual salary at Wells of $1,000, while not a terrific sum by the standard of the day, was much more than any woman instructor was offered, especially as Wells provided the French family with a house as part of the bargain, while the single women instructors were put in the dorms.

In Aurora, every mansion porch faced the lake except Henry Wells's Tuscan-style villa, Glen Park. Henry wanted it to face campus so he could sit on his porch and wave to the students—he very much thought of them all as his "girls"—as they crossed the footbridge over a shallow ravine to the buildings where their classes were held. Every year on Wells's birthday, students were excused from instruction to prepare the hallway of the main building with boughs of evergreen. At the appointed time, a bell would ring, and Henry Wells would enter under cages of canaries to the strains of "Hail to the Chief." He would be greeted by students who, dressed head to toe in white, sang hymns to their snowy-bearded patron's generosity. Though Henry died a few years before Nora was born, Wells College continued to celebrate Founder's Day. She would have grown up thinking of her great-uncle as nearly a god.

When I arrive at Wells College to look through its archives, I find the campus is almost a postcard-perfect example of what a liberal arts college should look like: brick buildings, sprawling green lawns, and lots and lots of trees. I explain my mission to the college archivist, who brings me the Edward French file. French's personal papers are sparse but provide enough context to conclude that he was not in ill health at Aurora.

I find a photograph of Edward in his late twenties. This is the first time I've seen his face. He's quite handsome. Sexy, even. I'm sure he could have arranged to seduce his students if he felt so inclined. Maybe that was why he left.

Or maybe not. As I look through the file, I see the typical signs of faculty overwork. A high course load. Too many administrative duties. He was not only the registrar handling the tuition of incoming students; he was also the curator of apparatus, buying all laboratory and science supplies. Wells College in its early years struggled to attract students. There were no raises for faculty but always plenty to do. It must not have been easy for Edward French, the son of a governor, to accept this lowly position teaching in a women's college in a town where he lived in the immense shadow of his wife's family. His own lineage included men who had settled Salisbury, Massachusetts, in 1640. He must have felt underappreciated, even as Henry Wells welcomed him to go sailing with him or to take light hikes in the woods.

Just as I'm mulling over Edward's stable but circumscribed life, the archivist brings me a file marked "Misc. Wells." It contains notes from a previous scholar who had been pursuing information about Nora. Within these loose papers are a few sentences divulging that Edward French had been let go from Wells in 1887 for embezzling $20,000.[15] That would be more than a half million dollars in today's money, a major blow to any college, never mind one that was struggling to establish itself. A theft of this amount would have been more than enough to send Edward French to prison for a long time, but the trustees had decided that the scandal would be an even worse blow to the college's fortunes. They let him go without prosecuting him for the theft. Only three short lines on the bottom corner of page 2 of New York's *Evening World* publicly recorded his crime.[16]

Spare a thought for Edward French. He had been working three jobs for one salary paid by one of the richest men who ever walked the earth. When Henry Wells died, Edward no doubt imagined a large payout for all his years of devotion. But outside of provisions for immediate family, Wells left everything to the college. Edward was suddenly not family but rather a lowly employee whose job was to teach young women how to be just educated enough to attract a rich husband but not so educated as to scare him away. Surely, as he traveled to Aurora to go Christmas shopping each year and could barely afford a piece of striped candy, Edward contemplated the injustice of it all.[17]

Embezzlement is a crime of intimacy. A crime of trust. As a relation to Henry Wells himself, Edward had been trusted with the institution's financial health, handling both student and supplies accounts. Padding expenses by a dollar here and there without getting caught, he would have found it too hard to resist increasing the amounts. When he hired governesses for his daughters and bought silk dresses for his wife, people in the town would have given him the benefit of the doubt and assumed that family money was supplementing his modest salary. Somewhere along the line, however, someone noticed, and he and his family were excised from the Wells family like a malignant mole off an otherwise pristine face.

Nora only ever wrote about the trauma of her family's move to California and subsequent ruin obliquely. Among the stories she sent the *Los Angeles Times* from New York was a fable about a family fleeing "misery and trouble and their own kind and seeking solitude." They head to the hills, where there is not another human being in sight and the air smells fresh. The father of the family decrees that it is there they will stay. While memories of their former lives fade away, the daughter grows up, "a strange, wild creature, hardly more human than the rabbits that peeped at her as she passed." She comes to know all the plants of the woods but loves the maidenhair ferns best—"her sisters," she calls them.

But then a drought descends, through the summer and beyond, and the brook that runs through her favorite glen dries up: "Day after day she kept her precious ferns alive with water from the scanty home supply, but soon even that began to fail." Crying over the browning fronds of her ferns, she hears the voice of Pan, the guardian spirit, who offers a trade: her life for the life of the brook, to keep the glen the most lovely place in the land. In recompense, her own beauty will become one with the water.

Called "The Brook's Story," the ending reveals that Nora dreamed all this next to the stream where the most enchanting ferns grow.[18] In essence, it is a parable of a daughter who sacrifices herself to save her sister. Nora always believed that the weight of the family rested on her shoulders. And it did, because the family put it there. Edward French never told his daughters the real reason why they had to leave Aurora. Neither Helen nor Nora knew why a once-fond family cut them off. By lying about why he had to leave Wells College, Edward preserved his daughters' adoration of him; they idolized him their entire lives. But the result of his deceit was that when his daughters returned from Uncle Cash's house to a life of poverty and hard labor with no clear end in sight, there was no one but Nora to blame.

Chapter Three

ᖕᙡᖇ

Homemaker

December 1904. George Sterling sat across from Carrie, his heavy-lidded eyes cast downward, his long fingers gliding backward and forward, working a knot of wood in the dining room table. Carrie regarded him steadily. He looked like a cornered rat—one begging for the quick kill or at least a drink. But she would give him neither. She had discovered that the apartment on Montgomery Street that he claimed was a writing studio he most often used as a love nest for a mistress.

Their marriage, she decided, had been going to hell ever since George met the reprobate Jack London in 1901. Before London appeared, their associations had been respectable. They spent much of their time with two families who represented the cultural elite of the Bay Area: the Bierces and the Partingtons. The Bierces were the extended family of Ambrose Bierce, the famed author of gruesome Civil War stories who had, along with Mark Twain and a handful of other writers, founded the West's literary scene. Since then, Bierce had moved back east, sent by William Randolph Hearst to cover the lobbyists who worked for C. P. Huntington, the great railway robber baron. Bierce's satirical talents had caught the attention of the entire nation. He derided Huntington as a "promoted peasant" and "inflated old pigskin" in the press. "Of our modern Forty Thieves," he declared, "Mr. Huntington is the surviving thirty-six."[1]

George had met Bierce in 1892 through Ambrose's brother Albert (all the Bierce names in that generation began with "A"), while camping in the hills above the Piedmont. George later roomed in an Oakland boardinghouse with Ambrose's son Leigh. Although Leigh would too soon die in a romantic duel (souring Ambrose forever on women and romantic poetry), George kept up the correspondence with the old writer. He sent Ambrose a poem entitled "Memorial Day," inviting critique. Bierce passed it on to *The Washington Post*, which printed it. Buoyed by this success, George started on a longer poem whose theme was the stars, which he considered his first major work. He wrote Bierce nearly daily, convinced that Bierce could make him a major poet.

The Bierces were closely intertwined with the Partingtons, a group of British-born siblings whose father founded an art school in San Francisco. All the Partingtons were creative: Blanche was the culture critic for *The San Francisco Call*; Dick, a painter like their father; Phyllis, an opera singer; and Gertrude did etchings. Carrie and Blanche, similar in age, had become fast friends. But as a couple, George and Carrie spent most of their time with the youngest Partington sibling, Kate (or, as George called her, "Lits," short for "little"), and her husband, Fred. Together with some subset of the Partingtons and Bierces, George and Carrie spent their weekends hiking, camping, or going to operas and galleries.

Long evenings would be spent playing cards or charades. These families replaced Carrie's own too-critical one. They changed her nickname from "Cad" to "Madame Rabelais," a more refined name for someone who was clever, quick, and funny but could be cutting when the situation required.[2]

These had been wonderful times for Carrie. Occasionally, the men drank too much, but they always came home.

Then George met Jack London.

From Carrie's point of view, Jack London was an unfathomable connection for her husband to cultivate. A fatherless man pulled from the dregs of Oakland society. A nobody who had worked in laundries, swept up sailor spit in the saloons lining the docks, and pirated oysters from fishing company beds along the coast. And yet for all his odd jobs, Jack never seemed to have two pennies to rub together. He was a stocky brute of a man, a sloppy drunk who poured the last sixth of his drink down his crooked, poorly knotted cravat. When Carrie looked at him, she saw the worst specimen of boarder in her mother's house.

But what George saw in Jack was a writer who sold his first book, *The Son of the Wolf*, to a major publishing house and a drinking partner whose thirst for alcohol had no limit. He eagerly took Jack, seven years his junior, under his wing to mentor him just as he, George, had been mentored by Bierce. Jack needed tutoring not only in vocabulary and meter, George decided, but also in the ways of society. So George took Jack to a private room at Marchand's, the five-floor French restaurant that had opened up on Union Square. He taught Jack what fork went with which dish and when to order claret and not scotch. In return, Jack took him to socialist meetings so George could appreciate the weight of his forefathers' sins against the working class.

Jack called George "Greek" for his love of wine and resemblance to Dante. George called Jack "Wolf"—a reference to Jack's time in the Klondike, and his untamable nature. The two men quickly became inseparable.

Carrie thought Jack was playing George for a sucker, draining his wallet on a regular basis. Not content with picking up every bar check, George saved the entire London family from starvation by renting one of the Realty Syndicate's houses to Jack for well below market rate. It was, conveniently enough for George, right down the street from the Sterling house. George then spent each Wednesday evening there, attending Jack's popular literary salon, and stopped by most weekends when Jack hosted quoits, bare-chested fencing with the men, and co-ed boxing bouts.

Carrie had joined George on a few visits to the Londons and watched Jack box with the singularly unattractive Charmian Kittredge. Carrie could not fathom what men saw in her. A few years older than Jack, Charmian was reputed to be sexually experienced, but she was plain-faced, wide-mouthed, narrow-eyed, and squat in stature. Yet there Charmian and Jack were, grinning at each other over their boxing gloves: jab jab feint giggle giggle. Other frequent guests at the Londons' included the lovelorn socialist writer Anna Strunsky and Carrie's own dear friend Blanche Partington, who had yet to perceive the limits of Jack's attention span. And in the background there was the poor wife, Bessie London, juggling Jack's child and baby, having to watch her husband flirt with his female guests.

All these women were trying to show how evolved they were—how modern, how unconstrained by social convention—when in fact all they wanted, evidently, was Jack London. Blanche plied him with help on his vocabulary to make up for his poor schooling. Charmian lent him scandalous books like *Tess of the D'Urbervilles*. Anna Strunsky corresponded with him for months on the philosophical nature of love. Jack then published these letters, completing Bessie's public humiliation.

Carrie made the mistake of expressing to George her concern about Jack's growing harem. George told her she was being bourgeois.

She couldn't put her finger on why, but she found Charmian Kittredge the most irritating. Such a feeling surprised her, because they shared a great deal in common: Charmian had lost her mother at the age of six, almost the same age Carrie had been when her father died. Charmian had done office work in the 1890s, just as Carrie had. Both were well-read. But Carrie perceived in Charmian a hunger for Jack London that would conquer every obstacle. Also, Charmian never seemed to stop smiling, which was unnerving. Nobody could be that happy all the time. No, Carrie identified most with Bessie London, who was, like her, having to receive, in the middle of the night, a husband smelling of drink and sometimes other women.

Carrie dubbed Jack London's penis "the blonde beast."[3] Untamed. Always ready to pounce. She hated him.

She waited patiently for George to notice Jack's true colors, but he would not, even though London's inability to conduct himself in polite society became apparent shortly after he moved to the Piedmont. Jack's name had appeared in the local paper in connection with an argument with a local grocer. The grocer had called at the Londons' to collect a $35 debt and threatened to blacklist them with other tradespeople if they didn't pay up immediately. Jack took great offense at being reached at home over what he considered a minor matter. He fired off five paragraphs to the grocer, telling him he would pay every other debt he had (and he had many) before he would pay him: "I have never had to treat but one other person as I am now treating you. I gave that person the same terms I am now giving you. But he preferred to kick over the sand and play rough with his mouth, so he never got a cent."[4]

Shocked by the intensity of this response, the grocer, a vital member of the nascent Piedmont development, made good on his threat. He read Jack's letter aloud at the next meeting of the Oakland chapter of the Retail Grocers Association. *The San Francisco Examiner* printed Jack's letter in its entirety under the headline, "To Man He Owes Jack London Writes." Rather than take his debts quietly like a gentleman, Jack London had created an embarrassment to Frank and Lila Havens, sullying the image of the Piedmont as a place for "good people." George could teach Jack when to order claret, but he couldn't restrain his pen.

In the end, none of that mattered. Jack London published an astonishing three books in 1903. Of those, *The Call of the Wild* was an immediate hit, its first print run of ten thousand copies selling at $1.50 gone in days. "A big story in sober English," *The New York Sun* crowed. A story that would "stir the blood," promised the *Brooklyn Eagle*. "A tale that is literature," *The New York Mail* declared, awkwardly.[5]

George longed for such recognition and considered his relationship with Ambrose Bierce the key to achieving it. He pursued Bierce with the fervor he had honed going after high-profile realty clients. He paid for the publication of some of Bierce's works. He sent cases of vintage wine. But when George offered Bierce the hand of his sixteen-year-old sister, Marian, Carrie thought he might have gone too far.

George had always had a weird infatuation with this particular sister, which made Carrie dislike her. When he walked up and down the street with Marian, arm in arm, George preened like a cock showing off his prize hen. Marian, contemplating a stage career, seemed more than happy to be exhibited. So George sent a photo of Marian to Bierce as though he was auctioning her to the highest bidder: "She is sixteen years old now, weighs about 150 lbs, and is *perfect* in face, form and health."[6] He then tried to arrange a meeting between her and Bierce, but even Bierce, forty years older than Marian, thought that premature. He did send his photo to her, his graying beard on full display.

After all this flattery, when George asked Bierce how his long poem "The Testimony of the Suns" compared with Rudyard Kipling's "Recessional" and William Vaughn Moody's "An Ode in Time of Hesitation," the old writer naturally responded, "It is *your* superiority to the *authors* of those poems—your superiority as a poet—there is no question of that. You can beat them in a canter."[7]

And yet while Jack London was collecting royalty checks, George had to pay up front for publication of six hundred copies of "Testimony." And then he couldn't sell them. A chest full of unsold books sat cluttering up his office, despite the dedication poem to Ambrose Bierce that George had written to show that he was the heir to the throne of American literature: ("Ah! glad to thy decree I bow, / From whose unquestioned hand did fall, / Beyond a lesser to recall, / The solemn laurels on my brow").[8]

Success and family both unnerved Jack London. He took the first opportunity to run away, accepting a job to cover the Russo-Japanese War for the papers. Seen off at the dock by his friends for his voyage to Asia in early 1904, Jack was welcomed back the following June by a gentleman serving him divorce papers. The revelations in the documents, republished widely by the press, were brutal. Bess had accused Jack of cruelty and alleged that he had given her gonorrhea. In the divorce papers, Bess identified Anna Strunsky as the reason for the marriage's dissolution. This was a smart pick from among Jack's mistresses; Strunsky, the daughter of Belarusian Jewish immigrants and an outspoken socialist, presented the least sympathetic face to name in a very public suit. Bess was using whatever ammunition she had to get cash from Jack, who, for the first time in his young life, actually had some.[9] Reading the divorce charges in the papers, Carrie felt vindicated at last.

Yet Jack proved more shameless than even Carrie had imagined. Even before the divorce was finalized, he organized a yacht trip for the Partington sisters (Kate, Phyllis, and Blanche) and Jack's socialist comrade from Los Angeles, Cloudesley Johns. Jack had written Blanche that she would get her own cabin on the boat, which Blanche had naively interpreted as confirmation that she was to be favored with his special attention.[10] Yet during the voyage, Jack spent more time looking at Kate, photographing her straddling the mast, swinging from the rigging, lying on the deck, or with her skirt pulled up around her knees. He deliberately steered too close to a ferry wake in order to soak all the women and make their clothes cling to their bodies.

George and Carrie had been invited on the yacht trip, but Carrie refused to go. The less time George spent with Jack, the better. Unfortunately, by 1904, George seemed to have already adopted Jack's ways as his own. He hardly came home, spending most of his evenings at an Italian restaurant around the corner from the Realty Syndicate offices. "Coppa's," as the locals called it, occupied space on the ground floor of the Montgomery Block, affectionately dubbed "the Monkey Block." A four-story building that took up the entire distance between Washington and Clay Streets, the Block's upper stories were a warren of artist and writer studios. Fifty years earlier, the area had marked the edge of the red-light district, where drunken sailors teemed in and out of topless bars and brothels, but by the turn of the century, the neighborhood had cleaned up and was now frequented by bankers, lawyers, and real estate developers.

Carrie had agreed to visit Coppa's a couple of times after the theater, though the food was not good. But the food, George repeatedly pointed out, wasn't the attraction of the place. The attraction was themselves. George's artist friends had made it their home. They had covered the upper ten feet of the restaurant's wall with colorful murals of naked women, crouching devils, and a giant lobster entertaining a quadrille over the quote from *Alice's Adventures in Wonderland*: "Curiouser and curiouser." Quotes from the greats of classical and European literature were so numerous on the walls that the reader would have to possess command of seven or more languages to comprehend them all.

Behind the bar, a mural depicted all of George's friends at their regular table like a modern-day Last Supper. The mural's painter, Xavier Martínez ("Marty" to his friends), put himself at the far end, generously mustached. At the other end, the writer Harry Lafler raised a glass. Behind Lafler stood Bertha Newberry, or "Buttsky" as she was called, smoking a cigarette, one hand on her hip, her other hand draped over Lafler's shoulder. Lafler and Buttsky's affair was the worst-kept secret of the place. The satirist Gelett Burgess approached the table with his papers under his arms. Next to Burgess, George himself was rendered in profile, a wreath of laurels atop his head. A ghostly apparition of a naked woman—supposedly Sterling's muse (it certainly wasn't a likeness to herself, Carrie noticed)—hovered over him, casting into his head the genius of Dante, whose name appeared on a frieze below the ceiling. The frieze displayed the names of the "greats" alongside those of Coppa's Bohemian regulars: Martínez next to his idol James Whistler, Lafler squeezed in between Whistler and Sappho, and so on.[11]

George claimed he was making connections in the literary community with the time he spent at Coppa's, but Carrie had met the regulars and was not impressed by most of them. There was one writer, Jimmy Hopper, with a wife and two kids, who never seemed to have enough money for the check. Short of stature—barely an inch over five feet—Hopper had quarterbacked for the football team at UC Berkeley (where he met Jack London) before dropping out of law school to write for the newspapers. In between assignments he wrote short fiction. George considered him an even better short story writer than Jack, but his stories hadn't sold much.[12] Carrie was most leery of Harry Lafler—a ladies' man if ever there was one—whose claims to literary rank seemed inflated. Carrie far preferred George's friend Arnold Genthe, a wealthy German gentleman with a doctorate who took photos as a hobby.

None of these men had anything near the established reputation of Ambrose Bierce, and even Bierce seemed limited in his powers to advance George's career. Carrie was beginning to think Mrs. Havens (her sister Lila—she always called her Mrs. Havens now) had been correct in questioning George's claim to be a serious poet. She called him a "false alarm." George spat back in private, calling Lila a gold digger and a "vicious cat." He said she possessed the mind of a peasant, a charge that made Carrie wonder what George thought of her own mind. Though softer on his uncle, George felt neither Lila nor Frank knew anything about "Art."[13] He had even written Bierce melodramatically, "*No* salary advantage can ever compensate me for the misery of working for ignorant and presumptuous bourgeois, who abuse my friends at one breath and insist that I bring them to their home at the next."[14]

Carrie defended her husband whenever her sister attacked him, no matter what her doubts of the moment were. She always felt it was her duty to support George in whatever he aspired to do. If he wanted to write poetry, she would help him succeed. But when she learned that George and Lafler were teaming up to seduce women at Coppa's—often descending on the tables of unsuspecting ladies and reading them poetry until they succumbed to their charms—something in Carrie snapped.

Now as they sat together at their dining room table, George cowering, Carrie glaring, she wondered if it would be better to leave him. Finally, he raised his eyes and told her he didn't want to work in an office anymore. He was tired of selling real estate, tired of the long hours, and had more than once contemplated throwing himself over the rails of the ferry on the daily commute. He was meant to be a poet full time. Bierce had read his latest work and declared George to be a poetic genius. A genius! If he could only give up his glorified clerical position at the Syndicate, he was sure that he could be the world's next Keats. It was the frustration of lowly work that had driven him to his excesses.

Carrie listened but felt herself growing irate. Did he realize how lucky they were to have a steady income? Did he know what bean soup tasted like, night after night after night? She watched as he methodically refilled and then emptied his wineglass. His tone became more emphatic as he talked about the soul-killing mundanity of work, the higher calling of art, how he yearned to devote more time to his craft.

He did (finally) admit that he had failed her. He knew he was powerless against the temptations of the city. But he had an idea, a way to make sure he stayed sober and faithful. They needed to move. A business acquaintance had approached him about some property adjacent to Carmel Bay, just a few miles south of the popular Hotel Del Monte resort on the Monterey Peninsula. This man would give them a five-year lease on easy terms if George would use his connections to build a literary colony in Carmel. Something that would generate publicity and draw in buyers.

George looked into Carrie's eyes and reached for her hand. He explained that they could live off potatoes and peanuts they grew themselves and devote their vast spare time to each other. The simple life would restore his health and their marriage. If only she would consent to the move, if only she would believe in his talent, he would be true to her and never drink again. Would she please, please, please say yes?

. . .

This might have been the moment Carrie decided to stop having sex with her husband. The chronology is about right. In 1911, George confided to Bierce that Carrie "never cared for the physical side of love, and we gave that up years ago."[15]

I'm not about to take George's word for Carrie's interest. Painting his wife as a prude served to legitimize his extramarital flings. Yet I can well believe that Carrie's sense of self-preservation may have kicked in when George's affairs multiplied. After all, Jack London, George's best friend and fellow brothel trawler, had already given his wife a well-publicized venereal disease.

But based on the primary documents, I can't divine for sure the state of George and Carrie's marital relations. People speak little enough about their sex lives, record even less, and lie about all of it anyway.

What is clear is that during the time George was philandering, Carrie forged closer connections to women in her midst. She had been Kate Partington's stalwart friend during a series of tragedies. When Kate's first husband, Fred, took ill with pneumonia, necessitating the couple's move to a sanatorium in Arizona, Carrie wrote her long letters of support. Kate, who always joked with Carrie about her aversion to children, sent a postcard of a "Pima baby" swaddled into immobility, on which she had written, "This is something you have always wanted."[16]

Fred succumbed to his illness, choking on his own blood while Kate cradled his head.[17] When Kate returned to the Piedmont penniless, Carrie placed her dislike of children to one side to offer Kate and her toddler, Helen, a room in their house. Once the Londons' marriage had dissolved, Kate and her daughter moved into their house down the street. Then, another tragedy. Little Helen died in 1904. Kate spent more nights back at the Sterlings' house, crying herself to sleep, clutching an urn of her daughter's ashes.

In a pattern that would be repeated over their married lives, the Sterlings invited the younger woman to their intimate acquaintance to serve very different needs: Carrie wanted companionship, and George wanted to ogle. He confessed his attraction to Kate to Bierce, "She is getting much too attractive for my nerves, and should be moved from Piedmont or marry."[18]

Of course, Carrie and George were in denial when they blamed their marital problems on San Francisco and its available distractions. But they were also in denial about George's potential as a poet. His "Testimony" was an ornate and labored try at an epic poem, overlarded with obscure references and unnecessarily rarified vocabulary, and littered with "thees," "thous," and "thines."

> Altair, what captains compass thee?
> What foes, Aldebaran, are thine?
> Red with what blood of wars divine
> Glows that immortal panoply?[19]

And so on. George's lyrics are, to modern readers, a slog. Even in 1903, when he was trying to market "Testimony," poets were moving away from such ornamented verse. Americans didn't want this pomp and gentility. They wanted raw, intimate works—Walt Whitman's "I Sing the Body Electric" and ripping Yukon stories such as Jack London offered. They wanted literature to be democratic, something a person without a college degree could read and enjoy. They wanted Jack's "damn dog tales," as George once called them, and would show it by making Jack London the first millionaire author in the country.

George Sterling remained convinced that he was offering a more refined product that would stand the test of time. He truly believed he was as good as Rudyard Kipling. The issue of merit aside, there is no way Sterling could have eclipsed Kipling in the literary canon. Kipling's "Recessional" was commissioned by Queen Victoria and thus guaranteed its audience; it also earned its place in history by foreshadowing the British Empire's demise. When Queen Victoria died in 1901, so did the use for these lyrics, but George had failed to take note.

How seriously did Carrie entertain leaving her husband? Probably not all that seriously. In 1904, she knew divorce wasn't really an option. By the turn of the century, only a handful of every one thousand American marriages ended in divorce, despite the arrival of the much trumpeted "New Woman." Divorce remained a humiliating and public exercise, particularly for women. Carrie had already frustrated the traditional gender script by declining to have children. If she sued for divorce on top of that, she risked complete dismissal as unnatural. So when George suggested she pack up her comfortable home and move to the undeveloped outpost that was Carmel-by-the-Sea, she really had no choice but to say yes.

Chapter Four

⌖

Ragged Robin

LEE, HER FIANCÉ—HER *EX*-FIANCÉ—WAS REFUSING TO GO QUIETLY. He stood in her apartment—she sat—and informed Nora that she was insane. Abandoning his sweet Southern drawl, he shouted the list of what she lost by breaking off their engagement. She had given up comfort. She had no inheritance. Her parents were paupers. Her aspiration, to be a poet, meant she would be even poorer than they had become. She worked in the lowliest profession—that of seamstress—so low that it was often used as a synonym for prostitution. Already in her twenties, she would in a few short years reach the age where men began to pass her by.

Nora sat and listened to it all, his words flying over her head and crashing against the wall behind her, leaving nothing but whiffs of pale smoke.

He had every right to be angry. She had made a promise, but

it had been made in desperation, she realized, and contrary to her true nature. The last four years had been one continuous plummet from her dreams since her inglorious expulsion from New York. Working in the leather factory had taken its toll on her body and spirit. Her fingers had grown dull from working the needle into the leather, her eyes strained in the low light, and she found herself too tired at night to think of lifting a pen. Her mind began to slow down, sitting among women who had nothing better to talk about than when they would get married and leave. One morning she woke up and realized that she had become one of them. She couldn't wait to get married and leave.

Then Lee proposed. At first, she hesitated. She told him everything about herself, how she was happiest wandering in the woods, how she lived to write poems, and how she would never be just an ordinary girl, if that was what he wanted. He assured her, absolutely assured her, that he loved her just the way she was and didn't want her to change a bit. So she said yes. Her parents cheered the news of her engagement. Helen was thrilled. Uncle Cash, who had long forgiven Nora's past indiscretion with Cyrus, sent his blessing, along with $200 as an engagement present. The black sheep of the family had been sheared and was growing a full and fluffy white coat at last.

It made Nora happy that they were happy. But no sooner had she accepted Lee's proposal than he, heedless of his former promises, launched a crusade to make her a respectable woman. Nora would soon be a wife and mother, he reminded her. She should prepare for her new role. He complained about how much time she spent on poetry (she was picking up speed with her poems and brimming with ideas). She should cook more—things other than spaghetti. Her letters should be shorter and not "run to nonsense."[1] She should be less impulsive and more judicious. She should be more like his stepmother, a soft-voiced Southern woman with a cameo pin who believed that a man was the lord of all creation, and that that included women.

When his stepmother failed to get through to her, he sent in his aunt Betsy. The aunt's lectures on Nora's forthcoming duties were interminable, like a river flowing for eternity to the sea. Nora set her face in a neutral expression, but the moment she was free of her, she felt like running down the street screaming.

She delayed the wedding for six months and then another six, claiming to be torn over silverware patterns. In fact, she knew exactly which pattern she preferred—she had a background in design, apparently never to be used to earn a living again. But silverware of any kind seemed like poor compensation for a life dedicated to the dullest pursuits of beautifying a home she now knew she would never be allowed to leave. What would be the point of freeing herself from factory life if she was to be forbidden to write? Why trade one prison for another?

In March 1904, a month before their announced wedding date, she broke it off. Her parents begged her to consider her circumstances. Even Helen scolded (Helen had become the family's breadwinner, having landed a secretarial position with the city that paid $15 a week). Lee dropped by periodically to try to persuade her by yelling at her. But she had uprooted from her mind the image of a future with him, and she could never envision it again.

She had one last person to tell. Uncle Cash. It would be unfair to keep his $200 gift, she decided, now that there was no wedding. On a quiet afternoon when everyone else seemed at last exhausted from berating her, she sat down with pen and paper to explain the situation to him and promise to repay the gift (some of which she had already spent).

She began, "You know, from your experience of me, that I am a kind of crazy freaky thing, without much idea how to behave and likely to do unexpected things. Well I reckon I was made that way."

From that rough start her pen began to move more freely, describing how a once-promising relationship had turned so sour. "There has never been perfect sympathy, but at first we were enough in love—was it love? Enough infatuated with each other, perhaps, not to realize that. But a long engagement is a sure test. One has to reach out all the tendrils of character and personality and find if there are projections to hold them up, or if they must slip away from a smooth wall."

She knew that Lee loved her, but that had become beside the point. The only way to make him happy as his wife would be to turn herself into a different girl entirely, "corked up and hammered down." In the end, it seemed that it was more important to remember that his ideal was not her, and never could be her: She told Cash she concluded not that she loved Caesar less, but that she loved Rome more, "by Rome meaning peace and freedom. It was just a month ago, after a more-than-usually-full-of-good-advice letter from him, that I simply felt I could not marry him. I was plumb tired and frazzled out with harrying and being re-formed. . . . I hate to be reformed. I know I need it, but it doesn't seem to do any good, and the process is so uncomfortable."

Any attempt to change her into a conventional woman was doomed, Nora explained. "He might as well try to talk a ragged robin into a pansy."[2]

Uncle Cash wrote her back that she shouldn't worry too much about the money. He expected that by the time his letter reached her, Lee would have made it up to her, and her engagement would be back on.

How little did any of them understand her.

. . .

At the age of twenty-three, Nora embraced spinsterhood with enthusiasm. Freedom from marriage was freedom to live one's own life. She would devote herself to her writing. No more light ditties like the "Ode on Aunt E.'s Bloomer Bathing Costume," which had made Helen laugh for hours.[3] No more stories to distract the readers of the Sunday *Los Angeles Times*. She would focus only on poetry and set goals to challenge herself. That year she published four poems in Lummis's journal but decided to shoot for journals with more national reach. In March, her poem "In Empty Courts" appeared in *The Smart Set: A Magazine of Cleverness*.[4] A new publication out of New York, *The Smart Set*'s circulation had shot up to well over one hundred thousand in four short years by printing national names like Jack London.

About a man's inconsistent attention, "In Empty Courts" had been inspired by a muse of sorts who had recently entered her life. Captain Alan Hiley had two main qualities that recommended him: He was already married, and he lived far away, in Santa Cruz. A tall, handsome timber magnate and retired British Army captain, Hiley considered himself an established author; he had published his memoir of distinguished service in the Boer War. They had met at a poetry reading (Hiley's wife was also a poet) and started an on-and-off affair.

On the weekends, Hiley sailed down the coast on a yacht to take Nora to dinner in fine restaurants. He asked her about poetry, though she noticed he rarely listened to her answers.[5] As she talked, he seemed engrossed by the cuisine, the wine, and calling upon the waiter for this and that. She was just another element of a scene, carefully constructed for his appreciation. And then he sailed back north and left her to her drudgery at the leather factory.

Lately, however, Nora had started using her hours of sewing mittens to spin her brain through meter and rhyme combinations for a cycle of verses she was planning. She drew upon her usual Spanish Old West themes but added a subject closer to her present life: love and its perils. She called it "The Spanish Girl."

> José may journey, never I.
> In all the lonely hours I spend
> He bids me tell my beads and sigh . . .

When Hiley came next to Los Angeles, she took him walking in the foothills of the Verdugo range, showing him the canyons where she had spent so many happy hours dreaming. She wore the leather gaiters she had made at the factory to protect her legs as she wandered off path. But he had no eye for the subtle beauty of sun-drenched grasses. No appreciation for the little succulent clinging for its life to the side of the hill. The only part of nature that engaged him appeared to be the killing of it: Men mastering the towering redwoods of Santa Cruz. The struggle between the snake and its winged predators (an account of which, copying her, he published in the magazine of the *Los Angeles Times*). Oblivious to all the wonders that inspired her interior life, he spent much of their hike reviewing his more memorable battles in Africa.

> Across José's unending drone
> (Some ancient tale of arms and doom)
> There came a poignant sweetness blown
> From sleeping leagues of orange bloom.

At last, she was able to take some vacation time. He sailed her up north to see the majestic trees he owned and would soon fell for money. She wore her hiking suit, beret, and wide cravat and posed for a photo in front of redwoods, unsmiling, as stiff as the tree behind her.[6] She kept her guard up around him, wary when she occasionally felt herself warming to his attentions. When he sang instead of talking and looked deep into her eyes, she felt herself begin to yield. She wished he wouldn't sing.

> The doorway gleams, the pleading magic charms,
> Step after step, with fluttering breath and will—
> Step after step . . . at last . . . into his arms.[7]

. . .

Her body betrayed her. She was pregnant.

They debated too long what to do. He would leave his wife. Of course he would. Then, no, a divorce would take too long and be too public. In her distress, she made the dreadful mistake of telling Helen everything. Helen, scandalized, was even more distraught than Nora. She must get Hiley to marry her, Helen counseled, or the whole family would be ruined.

But marriage was not in the cards. Instead, the eminently respectable Captain Alan Richard Hiley secured a doctor and money enough to pay him. What at first had seemed to Nora like a vexing process—coming to the decision, finding the willing physician—turned out to be the easy part compared to what came next. She experienced the procedure itself as a surreal horror, the doctor's cold, pointed, metal tools contrasting with the soft warmth of her flesh mingled with that of the fetus. Only partially sedated during it all, she glanced down and saw the aftermath.

Recovering in bed she asked for a pen and paper and wrote a short poem:

> We saw unpitying skill
> In curious hands put living flesh apart,
> Till, bare and terrible, the tiny heart
> Pulsed, and was still.[8]

She added four more lines and titled it "Vivisection." She didn't publish it.

. . .

After her "illegal operation," as Helen termed it, Hiley kept coming around, but Nora noticed his eyes no longer followed her when she moved.[9] Where she had once kept herself from him, she sought him and found him talking more wistfully than ever of his life abroad. She had entered the gloom, but he seemed as happy as before.

> What alters with my changing? Not José,
> Content in little duties that he loves.

Nora's daily life had no such ease. Her father's cataracts had rendered him nearly blind and unemployable. Her useless brother ran off with the insurance money after the ranch burned. The other brother escaped to the army. The sisters were left holding up what remained of their shattered family, financially and emotionally. Nora had barely an hour to think, much less write.

Her beautiful mother stopped singing; then she took to her bed. Helen and Nora took turns fixing dinner, emptying chamber pots, applying moist towels to her forehead. They exchanged frightened looks, furtively, while their mother awaited her peace. The daughter of a minister, Mary French had assured her children of her belief in the hereafter and the sure reward for a virtuous life, however short hers might be cut at the age of fifty-six. She was a Wells, and none of the Wellses ever doubted: not Shepard Wells, their grandfather, nor Shipley Wells, nor Ashbel, nor Ebenezer, nor Ichabod (who put his own wife on trial to answer the charge of fornication prior to marriage), nor any of them going back to Thomas Welles, the seventeenth governor of the Connecticut Colony, and the first Wells to step foot in the country, when they still spelled their name with a second "e."[10] They were all born with God's word on their tongues. American Express and Wells Fargo owed their existence to Henry Wells's stutter; only that impairment had prevented him from following his father and brothers into the clergy.

Every time her mother spoke of her expectant reward, wide-eyed and hopeful, Nora could only see her own punishment. Oblivion, burning, eternal damnation—no reward, not for her, not after what she had done. She added a third and final part to "The Spanish Girl," revealing her sin without naming it:

> I tilt my hollowed life and look within:
> The wine it held has left a purple trace—
> Behold, a stain where happiness had been:
> If I should shatter down this empty vase,
>
> Through what abysses would my soul be tossed
> To meet its judge in undiscovered lands?
> What sentence meted me, alone and lost,
> Before him with the fragments in my hands?

She had never found comfort in a notion of God as a white man with a beard who held grudges. Her solace was in a feminized deity, incarnate in dirt, wind, and sky. She added another verse:

> Better the patient earth that loves me still
> Should drip her clearness on this purple stain;
> Better my life upheld to her should fill
> With limpid dew, and gradual gift of rain.[11]

Chapter Five

൭ᚉᚉᚏᎧ

Poet's Wife

Carrie sat with George atop the Carmel stagecoach through three dusty, bumpy miles from the Monterey train station, wondering what kind of mistake she had made. The driver—a disgusting man who chewed and spat tobacco—continually egged the horse, Pet, up the steep hill. It took nearly an hour to reach the crest, whereupon Carrie was pitched sharply forward. She rearranged her hat as Pet plodded down the long slope to reach Carmel-by-the-Sea.

When George took her hand to show her to their new address, she stumbled over a tree root, unable to see for the fog. Her husband led her to the back of the property to the tent where they would live while the bungalow was under construction. It was July 11, 1905, and Carrie's life in Carmel had begun.

She awoke to dense fog again on July 12. Fog again on July 13. All through the next week—as the builders laid the house's foundation and began to put up its walls, and as Carrie struggled over a camp stove to provide them with three daily meals—she could barely see ten feet in front of her face. George's diary of the weather, kept on a tiny lined notepad, had become distressingly repetitive: Fog all day. Fog all day. Fog all day.

The sun came out in the first week of August, to their great joy. As they exited their tent, they were treated to views clear to the Carmel River and the hills beyond. They walked to the beach and sat together on the white sand, gazing at Carmel Bay, sapphire and dazzling. But then the sun disappeared once again and Carrie was back at work, scrambling to keep the builders fed and their clothing washed. Carrie had lost so much weight, she had at last achieved the Gibson Girl willowy frame. Her white blouse, though frequently soiled, narrowed dramatically at her cinched waist. But was it worth it? Carmel was beginning to feel much like her life in Oakland, minus an oven, a sink, restaurants, theater, dress shops, and any of her friends. The only "society" was an assortment of earnest older women at the Arts and Crafts Club who hosted the occasional talk on dreary subjects. For "the elevation of the mind," she supposed.[1]

Mid-August, their friends arrived with the furniture. Carlton Bierce (Ambrose's nephew) and Jimmy Hopper unloaded chairs, tables, artwork, and other cherished possessions from the stagecoach and dumped them in a pile on the bare living room floor. George rolled up his sleeves to help. As the men arranged her furniture into a semblance of a living space, Carrie thought that surely domestic stability must be on the horizon. True, her best dishes were still in boxes, and the windows took on all the dirt of the constant construction. But she forced herself to look on the bright side. At least she and George would have more time together.

When, a week later, George spent the evening down the street to "help" Mrs. Kaplansky, a so-called aspiring poet, Carrie sank to her knees in front of her unfinished chalkstone hearth and began to cry. In a town nearly devoid of women—devoid of any people, even—George could still find a mistress. He had taken her to the middle of nowhere and left her shivering, her clothes stuck to her skin, another blanket of fog descending, while he warmed the bed of another.

She and George fought every night for the next month. Rather than admit his behavior, George denied that his time with Mrs. Kaplansky was spent on anything but poetry and blamed Carrie for not embracing the adventurous change. She had agreed to it, yes? And did she understand that their income now depended upon recruiting others to buy in Carmel? Could she at least try to cheer up?

George had been writing to all of his friends, and some prominent California authors he had never met in person, putting the hard sell on them to move to Carmel. One, Mary Austin, an eccentric writer of Western life, said she had already bought a place, having been reached directly through the Carmel Development Company. Mrs. Austin looked promising to Carrie; she had mentioned in her letter doing her own housework. She had also shown herself to be no fan of Jack London, either the man or his work. She boldly wrote to George that London's writing revealed his immaturity, "as for instance when he tries to draw what he thinks other people think a good woman is."[2]

No. Best of all was that Mary Austin had sent a portrait of herself, and she was plain—ugly, even. A thick face, pug nose, and wiry hair. The perfect neighbor.

Next on George's list of top recruits was their friend Blanche Partington, whose move to Carmel he believed would sway the entire culturally powerful Partington clan to follow. The Partingtons had money enough to buy anywhere they wanted. As Carrie was closer to Blanche, George enlisted her help with the sale. So in between cooking meals from the scant provisions available at Carmel's one store, Carrie was tasked with writing Blanche letters extolling Carmel's scenery. She was living in paradise, she affirmed to Blanche, as she looked at the piles of dirt still in mounds around her yard. Paradise!

After weeks of watching George trot off to help Mrs. Kaplansky after dinner, the pretense of bliss had become an insupportable burden to Carrie, and pointless besides. Blanche had already intuited that Carrie was unhappy. As Carrie picked up a pen to write to her friend the truth, she knew George would be angry, yet she could no longer bring herself to care.

"Of course I haven't been the same this summer, both mentally and physically," she told Blanche. In fact, it had been the most miserable summer of her entire life. George had not fulfilled his promises. He wasn't faithful, or sober, or productive. Rather than write, he frittered away his time chasing just about the only other woman in town.[3]

Blanche would understand heartbreak and disappointment. For the past year she had been nursing her grief that Jack London's separation from his wife had not resulted in the marriage proposal she had expected. Instead, Jack seemed to have chosen the squat and calculating Charmian Kittredge. It was a shocking development. Charmian had been positioning herself as a staunch ally of Bessie London, visiting her constantly when Bessie was in a state over Jack's presumed affair with Anna Strunsky. Chipper Charmian fired a line of assurances toward Bessie, telling her that she shouldn't worry about Jack's wandering eye and that all would be well.[4]

The mendacity of this woman. Now they knew it had all been an act. Charmian had intended to steal Jack the entire time. Carrie and Blanche decided that Charmian should be exposed and expelled from their society. They told all the women in their wide social network how conniving Charmian had lured Jack London into her bed.[5] Their campaign worked. Charmian, humiliated, fled to her relatives in the Midwest and stayed there for two months.[6] And yet it was only a partial victory, as the more Jack and Charmian were vilified, the closer they were driven together.

Blanche, still much in love, continued to write Jack under the pretense of warning him that his continued association with Charmian would tarnish his reputation. Carrie thought this was only making matters worse. Imagine, she begged Blanche, the delight Charmian would take in knowing her former rival was so desperate. Even worse, George stood fast in support of Jack and Charmian's union. It benefitted him to do so. By refusing to condemn Jack, George excused his own behavior with women. He even went so far as to write to Blanche that it didn't matter whether Carrie or Blanche liked Charmian: "So far as I am concerned, *I do*; and if it turned out that she had been a very whore in a 'house,' I should think none the less of her, nor believe that her nor any of her sisters, was not good enough for any man living, did he treat her with loving kindness."[7]

He could not have said anything worse in Carrie's view. All the time he had told her that his dalliances meant nothing, that the other women in San Francisco had been just sex, that what he and Carrie had was so very different and so very sacred—it had all been lies. He saw no difference between whores and wives if he thought one capable of becoming the other.

Crassly, in the midst of all this, George continued to press Blanche to buy in Carmel, even using Blanche's heartbreak to leverage the sale. Carmel's tall pines, the beach, the mild climate, would all be a healing balm to Blanche, easing her sorrow. Blanche ignored his pitches. She demanded that George read her letters from Jack, which would reveal how Jack had strung her along, how irresponsible with her feelings he had been. What about that trip on the yacht where Jack indicated flirtatiously that he would make sure Blanche had her own sleeping quarters? What about Jack's letter in which he had written, "The thought of you was a tonic. It seemed to clear my brain and steady me. You had strength, you were brave—and, believe me, the thought of you has more than once shamed me"?[8]

George responded that he would, under duress, read London's letters, but that they wouldn't change his opinion. Perceiving that Blanche was not moved by the pitch of Carmel's therapeutic properties, he tried the angle that she should buy in Carmel because it would make her rich: "I've a great investment here for you,—a lot on Carmel's one business street, a block from the hotel. It's 25 x 130 feet, with a rather nice cottage on the rear of the lot, which cost the owner, a man in San Jose, $1100. He will sell lot and all for that amount. I only wish *I* had the money. . . . But this offer will have to be accepted without delay, so wire me *if* you accept it."[9]

George had tried a version of this pitch on Jack months before. In response, Jack had given an exhaustive and nearly insulting reckoning of his accounts to explain his decision not to buy into Carmel. It only seemed like he had a lot of money, Jack explained, but what he had coming in amounted to nothing when one also considered his obligations to three households—his mother's, Bessie's, and his own—and the servants in all locations, dentist and doctor bills for the children, not to mention the couple hundred that Bessie's lawyer was gouging out of him. And then life insurance. And his philanthropic obligations. And ten bucks for a socialist paper in Toledo. Another thirty to fund an ex-convict's appeal to the Supreme Court.[10]

It was all equivocation. The real reason Jack wouldn't move to Carmel was because of Carrie's treatment of Charmian. George was furious with Carrie, blaming her for ruining his chance of recruiting America's top writer to Carmel. Indeed, Jack had become so famous it stunned even Carrie. *The Sea Wolf*, his adventure novel pitting men against Nature's brute forces, was climbing the best-seller list. Whether she liked Jack London or not, the world had decided that it did.

She and George fought every evening now, not about Mrs. Kaplansky—what could really be said there?—but about Jack and Charmian, who had since reunited in Oakland and were waiting for the finalization of Jack's divorce so that they could wed. George enumerated the ways Carrie had spoiled his chances to capitalize on Jack's success. Because of Carrie, Jack had declined to join him that August for the Bohemian Club's annual campout by the Russian River, where George had been looking to flaunt his friendship in the faces of fellow club members. These were important meetings for making connections with the kind of people who could underwrite one's literary work, he explained. It might look to a woman like men sitting together around a fire circle, pushing one another off rowboats, and drinking all night under the redwoods, but important work was being done.

Their final battle was over George's desire to visit the sprawling ranch the Londons had just bought in Sonoma County. Over Carrie's strenuous objections, George was determined to go. How could she see this other than as running away from her and toward Charmian, a woman who had validated adultery? Fearing she really could lose George completely, Carrie began to back down from her attacks on Jack. She proposed a bargain: If George agreed that Carrie would never have to entertain Charmian at their new home, she would write Blanche and try to reverse the damage she had done in maligning Carmel.

Early in September 1905, as George got on the morning train to head up to Jack's ranch, Carrie settled down to her meal of crow. She wrote Blanche that she now thought of Carmel as a place of great solace that would attract only the finest people. The celebrated photographer Arnold Genthe was building his house nearby and expected to entertain on most weekends. She had seen the error in her ways, she wrote. She had caused enough trouble to George and would henceforth always remain neutral in fights between friends. Perhaps Blanche could see that she really had not been wronged by Jack after all. He had simply fallen for another woman. The best course would be to accept it and move on: "I am glad it is all over . . . how time flies—Just about a year ago you went yachting, was it not?"[11]

. . .

"You know, George Sterling had to leave town because he got a teenage girl pregnant?"

"Really?" I look up from the papers. "Is that written down somewhere?"

"I don't know. I'll look." Ashlee, the local history archivist of the public library of Carmel-by-the-Sea, adds my query to her list of unanswered questions to pursue when she has a free moment, which, I have observed by sitting next to her desk for two weeks straight, is not often. Walk-in visits are common to the library's history room from patrons seeking genealogical records or the backstory on one of the town's many artistic cottages. In her early thirties, Ashlee strikes me as wise beyond her years: preternaturally patient, scrupulous about maintaining records, and very curious about Carmel ancient dirt. She's thrilled that I'm digging into slimy George Sterling's love life, and every so often throws me a bone, like this tidbit about George's tryst that sent him packing out of town.

I soon learn that Ashlee has her own reasons for uncovering the truth of Carmel's founding. Nothing frustrates her more than the constant evocation of Carmel's Bohemians as grounds for decisions that are made a century later. Carmel is quite the town for civic participation, and the sanitized origin story of poor writers and their altruistic corporate patrons is routinely cited in city council meetings over issues like, for example, whether the only bike store in town should be permitted to conduct cycling tours. Or whether to remove a tree on public land—one of the more controversial issues, as Carmel's founders were said to have loved the trees.

Yes, modern Carmel-by-the-Sea does love its ordinances. Several pages of city rules cover the placement of coin-operated news racks. There are no vending machines. It is unlawful to kick a ball in Devendorf Park, named for the first manager of the Carmel Development Company (the ball might damage a shrub). Perhaps one of the weirdest ordinances forbids the public wearing of shoes with heels over two inches in height and under a square inch of bearing surface. If you must wear high heels, you can apply for a permit, but you have to assume liability for tripping over the odd tree root along darkened side streets (darkened because streetlights there are forbidden—of course).

Perhaps the most anachronistic Carmel tradition is that mail is not delivered to houses. Carmelites of today, like Carmelites of yore, collect their mail at the central post office. Houses are identified not by number but by name, like "Sticks and Stones." The Pine Inn is still located officially at "Ocean Avenue between

Lincoln Street and Monte Verde Street." While quaint, this form of signage has become an increasing problem as package deliveries now threaten to exceed the capacity of the town's post office to store them until they are retrieved. Carmel residents recently opted to spend tens of thousands of dollars on their own opt-in local courier service to deal with the backlog.[12] They can afford it. The median price of a little house in Carmel is well over a million dollars.

And yet, beyond the service industry, which feeds and otherwise sustains the current population, no one seems to work. In coffee shops, a lapdog is a more frequent sight than a laptop. The only people who seem to visibly labor are retail personnel and waitstaff. Perhaps sensing that I, too, am out of place, they begin talking to me. "Look at them," the weary retirement-aged woman working in the shoe store says, pointing to the two ladies who had come in ten minutes before closing time and were now leaving. "I knew they wouldn't buy anything, but they made me get everything from the back anyway." That night, the hostess of the Mexican restaurant does me a big favor by warning me off sitting at the bar to eat, explaining that the three old men in golf attire have been drinking there all day and will definitely bother me. She gives me a small and secluded table in the back, and both the service and the food are delightful, as they are everywhere in town. Carmel sometimes feels like a one-square-mile, land-tethered cruise ship.

John Steinbeck noticed this on his visit to Carmel in the 1960s. "If Carmel's founders should return, they could not afford to live there, but it wouldn't go that far, they would be instantly picked up as suspicious characters and deported over the city line," he wrote in *Travels with Charley*.[13] What Steinbeck didn't know was that the whole job of those "suspicious characters" was to turn Carmel into what it is today. Maybe this was preordained. When the wandering novelist Robert Louis Stevenson stumbled upon the Carmel Mission in the late 1800s, enchanted by the sound of what he imagined to be happy Indians singing in Latin with passable pronunciation, he wrote to *Fraser's Magazine* that the wondrous landscape would soon be destroyed. A nearby railway and hotel in Monterey indicated that the "millionaire vulgarians of the Big Bonanza" would wring further wealth from the area, flooding it with vacationers.[14] Stevenson couldn't have been more right. But he could have said the same of any number of spots in California, which, once reached by the Southern Pacific Railway, were touted as the next mecca for salubrious living.

Ashlee gives me the complete file on the early years of the Carmel Development Company, the for-profit corporation that coaxed the Sterlings to town. I like trolling through corporate records. I find that fiscal accounts, maps, meeting minutes, and correspondence between shareholders make for dry reading but often reveal things that diaries and memoirs conceal. And what these documents show is that young attorney on the make Frank Powers, president of the Carmel Development Company, chose to fill Carmel with writers not primarily because he loved the arts but because he had already tried every other way to sell this land.

Powers's original plan to turn Carmel into a playground for the rich had seemed foolproof, at least on paper, following a model that appeared successful elsewhere on the Monterey Peninsula. The biggest land developer in California, the Pacific Improvement Company, had already built the sprawling Tudor-style Hotel Del Monte (the hotel to which Robert Louis Stevenson referred) and 17-Mile Drive, which snaked by the water and through the trees. Visitors would take the Del Monte Express train from San Francisco to Monterey and arrive at the grand hotel. There, they'd be encouraged to tour available residential lots at adjacent Pebble Beach and urged to buy. Carmel, sharing a border with Pebble Beach, seemed the next likely place the wealthy might want to settle.

In 1902, Frank Powers figured that all he had to do to turn a profit was lure the money a little farther down the peninsula. He had been assured that the railway line was planning a three-mile extension from its current terminus in Monterey down to Carmel. Once that connection was complete, San Francisco dwellers could make the trip with ease, and the land Powers had bought on the cheap would rise exponentially in value.

Certain of this railway extension, he invested heavily in developing the land. He had pine and cypress trees planted along the coast of Carmel Bay to give the place a Mediterranean feel. He loaded the town's only hotel on logs and rolled it closer to the beach. He published illustrated brochures trumpeting the natural splendors of the region. All these efforts succeeded in drawing only a smattering of uncharismatic professors and teachers, who were accustomed to discomfort. Although roughly two thousand visitors passed through Carmel each summer to enjoy the scenery, most didn't buy, even when prices on lots dropped dramatically.

And small wonder. Whereas Hotel Del Monte's guests would step off the train under the shelter of a portico, the Carmel-bound passengers would face a long, grueling horse-and-buggy ride over a steep hill, through the mud when wet or dust when dry. They would arrive at Carmel's Pine Inn, but if the small inn was full to capacity, they'd unload their baggage into adjacent tents. There, the Carmel Development Company would furnish them a bed, a table and chairs, and a two-burner oil stove on which to cook.[15] People who could afford to pay upwards of $10 each for two nights' ac-

commodation in the Hotel Del Monte—inclusive of train travel—
would never suffer through this welcome.

By October 1904, Powers had sold roughly $63,000 worth of
the smallest parcels of land, but as yet had collected under $30,000
for them. And he'd spent far more than that in improvements. In
a month, he would have to bring these numbers to his fellow
stockholders at the Carmel Development Company's November
meeting, which he dreaded.

But then he had a fortuitous encounter with the ad man from
the Pacific Improvement Company's Pebble Beach development.
They were both in the lavish club car of the Del Monte Express
heading south from San Francisco. Powers learned from the ad
man that Pebble Beach wasn't doing much better than Carmel
when it came to moving residential lots. Many people visited, but
few bought. The whole peninsula was in a slump.

Powers considered the situation. If traditional advertising
wasn't working any better for the Pacific Improvement Company's land than it was for Carmel, they were all wasting their
money. Then he remembered one development that had turned
around its bad luck. In Pasadena, a dusty land development scheme
west of Los Angeles, residents had created a New Year's festival
featuring a parade of the roses grown in the area and organized a
letter campaign to implore their friends in the East to come see
it. These direct petitions to personal associates, together with a
novel attraction, had worked where traditional advertising had
failed, turning a nondescript valley of orange groves and straw-
berry patches into a resort town boasting an opera house and a
scenic railway.

If Pasadena, with no seacoast in spitting distance, could pass
itself off as the "Mediterranean of the West" simply by loading a

bunch of bouquets on rickety wagons and dragging them down its main street, then Carmel, with its enviable ocean views, could create its own local attraction. Frank Powers struck a deal with the Pacific Improvement Company: If they would give the Carmel Development Company five hundred acres of land on their shared border, he would lure a group of writers to move to Carmel. He would have those people write to their friends and publish stories and poems in literary journals about the beauty of the area. As part of the deal, visitors to Carmel would be taken to lunch at the Hotel Del Monte and driven down 17-Mile Drive past Pebble Beach. Both developments would benefit from this arrangement.[16]

By the spring of 1905, George Sterling had signed on to be the anchor of the writing colony Powers had envisioned. The exact terms of the deal George struck with the Carmel Development Company are occluded in the records—and unusually so. The minutes of the August 1905 board meeting describe Arnold Genthe's deal in detail; for example, revealing that Genthe paid $1,740 for six lots, with interest forgiven on the mortgage for three years provided he erect "an artistic house." In contrast, the agreement between George and Powers is only vaguely described in the board meeting minutes as "a five year lease covering a portion of the 80 acre tract, with the privilege of buying same at the expiration of five years."[17] Beyond that, the minutes note only that the specific terms of this contract were read aloud to the other stockholders. Powers must have wanted to keep the baldly transactional nature of Sterling's move to Carmel off the permanent record.

What the minutes do reveal is that all the time George Sterling was pressing each of his friends to buy lots in Carmel—telling them that he had forsaken the rat race of the city to embrace the simple life by the seashore—he was merely renting, just in case the whole scheme failed and the land became worthless.

And while he "moved" to Carmel, he retained his position as vice president of the Realty Syndicate, so he personally risked nothing.

To be fair, Carmel these days sells itself. The main thorough-fare, Ocean Drive, runs at a sometimes steep pitch past gift shops, galleries, and restaurants before ending at a curving shore of white sand. There you can sit and look at the sunset to the accompanying sound of gentle surf. Behind you at the back of the beach, a winding street shaded by cypress trees meanders past the town's most ex-quisite houses, including a Frank Lloyd Wright, before reaching the mouth of the Carmel River. To the south is the beginning of Point Lobos and the mountains behind. To the north is Pebble Beach, now a wealthy residential community attached to a world-class golf course. Certainly there must have been moments Carrie was dazzled by the beauty of it all. But for a woman with a philan-dering husband, far from friends, tasked with creating the illusion of a happy marriage so the Carmel Development Company could prosper, the wide open vistas of sea and sky must have only mag-nified feelings of loneliness.

Chapter Six

⚬ᴍᴍ⚬

Dear Heart

Iᴛ ᴡᴀs 10:00 ᴀ.ᴍ. ᴏɴ ᴀ ʙᴇᴀᴜᴛɪғᴜʟ Sᴀᴛᴜʀᴅᴀʏ ᴍᴏʀɴɪɴɢ. Nᴏʀᴀ sᴀᴛ at her bench, plunging her needle through leather. Her coworker not four feet from her made the same motion at her bench. Nora knew when her coworker was going to sigh before she sighed, so accustomed had she become to her movements. They had all become parts of one large machine, interchangeable with one another. Nora stopped for a moment and looked down at her work. The mitten she was sewing was half-done, but another pile of half mittens waiting to be conjoined lay beside it. She glanced at the clock and watched the second hand go around for a whole minute: tick, tick, tick. She got back to work when the second hand returned to the 12.

By 11:00 a.m. she could bear it no longer. She was sick of her sighing coworker, sick of the smell of so much desiccated cow, and very, very sick of mittens. She put down her work, grabbed her bag, and ran out the door. She knew the second after the door closed behind her, that her coworker would murmur something disapproving about "that girl." Let them talk. There was nothing more heavenly than leaving work early to spend what remained of the day in the sun.

She went home to the apartment she shared with her sister on Marmion Way so she could change into her hiking shoes. The house they lived in was one of a few in the sparsely populated strip bordering the Arroyo Seco, only a ten-minute walk to Charles Lummis's El Alisal. A group of like-minded artists and writers had settled in this section of town. There she felt she could walk around without being stared at for how she dressed or the casualness with which she pinned up her hair.

Nora plopped an old cap on her head, considered and then rejected a warmer jacket. Instead, she took the most recent letter she had received from Harry Lafler off the desk, folded it, and tucked it into her leather gaiter. She let the door slam and started down the front steps, but something stopped her. Harry would caution that she'd get hungry later and regret heading out for a long hike with no sustenance. What would happen if she became faint and lost her way? Back inside the house she rummaged through the icebox and found a leftover chicken drumstick. She wrapped it in a paper napkin, slid it into her blouse, and headed back out the door toward the San Rafael Hills.

She brought Harry with her on these walks. The idea of him anyway. Harry, the man she had never met but felt she knew better than any other. She could envision him encouraging her tiny rebellion against work and industry. She needed an absolutely useless day from time to time. She would not gather ferns, or cress, or berries, or do any other purposeful thing that would cause her to miss the million accidents of divine beauty that nature provided. If she ran into holly on the way back home, she'd pick some, but she would commit to nothing more.[1]

She couldn't say exactly when Harry Lafler became so much a part of her emotional life. Right after her mother died in July, she had sent a poem to *The Argonaut*, where Harry was serving as an editor. He accepted her poem, and their correspondence quickly became romantic. They fell in love through words.

How perfect, she thought, that the body was not there to intervene. Since the abortion, she had a nickname for herself: the "Hands Off" girl. Except for a date here or there, she kept men at arm's length—especially Alan Hiley, who, in an irritating reversal, *now* wanted to marry her. She spent most of her time hiking with Helen or reading. She had just finished Edith Wharton's *House of Mirth*, a book whose heroine's story was uncomfortably close to her own life.[2] Lily Bart, a society girl, plummets through the social ranks because she fails to secure a husband. With several eligible men swirling around her, Lily soon becomes the object of everyone else's speculation—will she, won't she marry this man, or that one. By rejecting them all and deciding to live a life according to her own code, she becomes poverty-stricken and falls into that most disparaged of all women's professions: seamstress.

Like Lily, Nora had felt the lingering burn of disinheritance, and with it the sense that her fate was all her own fault. *The House of Mirth* felt like a book she could have written, but possibly with more rounding out of Lily's character. Lily's weakness was gambling. Nora's had been sex. But both she and Lily declined the transactional bargain that marriage presented. Because Lily "refused to sacrifice herself to expediency, she was left to bear the whole cost of her resistance," Edith Wharton had put it.[3] That perfectly summed up Nora's engagement to Lee and her now nearly moribund relationship with Alan Hiley.

In her darkest moments, Nora believed she had worsened her mother's health by refusing to marry. She believed she deserved this humiliation: the long hours in the factory, the drying fingers, the languishing brain. She became numb to all but pain.

Then Harry Lafler entered her life. He seemed to offer a window into another world. He was one of the writers who frequented Coppa's, the restaurant at the center of San Francisco's thriving arts scene. Poets and painters gathered at a table near the back, dining on sand dabs and green salads and drinking cheap red wine while talking into the night. Everyone in California had heard of Coppa's. Every artist or writer who visited San Francisco stopped there. And Lafler was painted onto the very wall.

He had told her about the artist Xavier Martínez, or "Marty," who sat sketching the crowd, a cigar protruding beneath his long, black mustache. And Arnold Genthe, the photographer who would come to Coppa's after capturing the life of Chinatown with his camera. Harry was at Coppa's almost every night, writing and then reading his sonnets. He was most often in the company of George Sterling, whom they all called "The King of Bohemia" because he had defined Bohemianism for the world: "There are two elements, at least, that are essential to Bohemianism," he decreed. "The first is devotion or addiction to one or more of the Seven Arts; the other is poverty."[4] All of this reminded Nora of the intensity of the life she had experienced at the Art Students League. During her long, monotonous working day stitching mittens, she often fantasized about sitting around the table at Coppa's, laughing into the wee hours.

She knew it was ridiculous that she had developed such strong feelings for Harry when they had never looked into each other's eyes. He was as yet only a literary abstraction. At one point she pointed out that she didn't even know what he looked like. Harry responded by sending her a photo of himself, his dark brown curly locks framing his face. It accorded with the image she had formed of him in her head. He looked like a latter-day John Keats.

Then they got to the edits of her poem. Nora opened his letter to find with horror that he had changed her "wind" to "wynd."

Her next letter began, "Dear Critic." She wrote about her latest hike, on which she watched a trail of ants for an hour, and then described a dinner with a condescending man who wanted to marry her (she wouldn't name Hiley yet) at which she molded "dropsical bears from the bread" to keep from going mad. She confessed that besides the "marriage question" imagined to be every girl's ambition, her chief trouble was an occasional "hideous depression" during which she would entertain dark thoughts of suicide, but that such "evanescent difficulties" passed much more rapidly than her "insistent joys." And then she got down to business:

> *We will disagree violently on the subject of wind or wynd. I know wynd is the approved version, but I don't know it personally, it isn't wynd I love but wind—wind. A wynd is something that crawls around moated granges and sends chills up Mariana's spine, a wind whoops through the sage-brush and sings in the pines and tries to take you with it, right off the top of the hill.*

She liked expression to be uncluttered and as raw and forceful as her own life had been. And in case he was considering exercising his editorial prerogative, she informed him, "I will have wind, with a short 'I.'"[5]

She had discovered he had lied about his age; he had told her he was forty-two but was really only twenty-six. "Not even old enough to have an opinion," she added. She stopped calling him "Critic" and began her next letter "Dear Boy," which he had encouraged. She asked him to stop calling her the fussy nickname he had decided on for her: "Carissima"—as bad as "wynd." The nickname she preferred was "Phyllis," but he also could address her instead as "Girl," which seemed to fit best with "Boy."

She had already told him why she took his letters with her on her hikes. "You belong to a very private little world of visions and impracticalities, where there are no ugly streets or distressing, harsh voiced people," she wrote. "Everyone else I know I must draw through my fingers shrinking from rough beads until I find a pleasant one, but the little string of your letters—which sums my knowledge of you is of varying sizes, but similar smoothness. I like to touch it," she teased.[6]

Harry claimed that he had revealed to her a great deal about himself while she had told him so little about her own life. She relented and gave her history. She had been born in Aurora, New York (the same state he had been born in, she pointed out), then had come out west to tumble around on a ranch, followed by a year at the Art Students League—the best of her life. The rest she summed up as hard work and "various heart complications."[7] Why say more of the past few years than that? Now her heart was uncomplicated. It had one desire. "I love you," she wrote him. "All of you—Boy, Harry, Henry Anderson Lafler. . . . I can't do things by halves. The outer self loves to play pitch and toss, but the inner self loves you with every drop of her blood."[8]

They planned a meeting. He would come to see her in Los Angeles and consummate the relationship. But they had last spoken of that weeks before the day she abandoned work early to walk in the hills. On that hike, she had been thinking that Harry was drifting away from her. In a recent letter, he had suggested that she didn't really understand him as he needed to be understood.[9] This stung. She screwed up her courage and confessed her fears, ending the letter with a verse from "In Empty Courts," the poem she had written first about her uncertain days with Hiley:

> To you my heart must turn for all its light—
> Alas, the grudging taper that you give!
> So small to make the inner temple bright,
> So dim to give the glow by which I live.[10]

After Christmas, she received a very long letter from him with an alarming confession. Yes, her sense of his having held some love in reserve—the "grudging taper" she had called it—had been accurate. For the last year he had been in love with Bertha Newberry (or "Buttsky," as apparently everyone at Coppa's called her). He assured Nora that the Buttsky affair had gone no further than caresses and kisses. Could Nora not pity poor old Buttsky, whose life was so dismal that the affair with Harry had become "the flower of her life"? Were it a young woman he had been involved with for a year, he would have felt no guilt about throwing her over for Nora. "But this is so unfair. On your side are youth and beauty. You are a poet. The years have set no mark upon you. You are tall and strong, and slender—dear. That is why it is so unfair. You have so much, she so little." He loved both of them, he declared, and thought that they would love each other if they ever were to meet. "In many respects you are alike. Perhaps this is why I love you both and can't bear to think of having neither of you in my life." He ended the letter, "I may have robbed myself of much. Perhaps, now, you will hate me, I do not know. Boy."[11]

Nora felt as if she had been slapped. A very different man had written this than the man she had held in her heart. That man had been passionate but tender. This man had put on boxing gloves and dared her not to duck. But hadn't she asked for this? She had wanted to be consumed by drama, by life in all its colors. He had offered her "wynd" at first, and she told him she preferred "wind." Well, here was forceful, chafing "wind."

She considered her response carefully before she wrote back. She would disarm him first with a little teasing: "Don't expect any more sugar. If I had known what a fat, spoiled animal you were I would have given you dog biscuit from the very start." She said he didn't need to rush to see her; she would be waiting for him with an irrepressible smile and nails sharpened. As to whether she hated him, she wouldn't give him the satisfaction. "Why I'd have to love you, actually intensely love you, to hate you! And it's only a dream love."

That was sharp from her, but hurting him wasn't what she wanted. She wanted to be the one in pain. She wrote him he could have both her and the other woman. "Oh, I dare you, I dare you to hurt me! It sets my feet dancing to think of the fun it would be. Hurt me. I like it."[12]

. . .

I hope you already despise Harry Lafler. Lest I leave any doubt that he is a rake of epic proportions, his papers at the Bancroft Library include his correspondence with the other women he was involved with while courting Nora in 1905. These letters paint a picture of a remarkably busy man.

Lafler's wife, Alice, a former teacher who had separated from him and moved back east, wrote him for money in June. He had strenuously objected to her resuming her profession, yet since their separation he had not sent her an allowance she could live on. In a letter I'd have to call a clinic in sarcasm, Alice explained to Harry how she had calculated what she was owed based on what he should be able to provide: "The lowest figures I could well put upon your literary efforts would be an average of $35 per week. . . . Since September 2nd 1904 there have fortunately been 42 weeks at $35 per = $1470; of which amount I have by your kindness received $315!! $315 divided by 42 = $7.50 per week—a very good showing were it not that clothing, illness, and several extravagances have come out of this amount. Pardon my going over these dry details and taking up so much of your time at the minimum of $35 per."[13]

As it turns out, just hours before Harry wrote Nora confessing his affair with Bertha, he had written to Bertha about his increasing interest in Nora. Harry had been at Coppa's that evening with the "Crowd," as Jack London liked to call this group of George Sterling's friends, celebrating a late Christmas. After Buttsky left, Harry stumbled back to the office of *The Argonaut*. Pitching himself toward the writing desk, he took out a piece of Bohemian Club stationery:

"Dear Heart," he began. "There is something very crude and careless about me." He never imagined anyone could come between them, he explained, but someone had. He was going to Los Angeles to visit Nora as soon as he had pulled together enough money. "And yet it is you I love—I know that—while all about the girl is vague—I do not know. Isn't that rotten?"

He continued. "Oh dear—I almost hate myself now; but tomorrow when I receive from Phyllis"—Nora's nickname, he had been talking about her a lot with the Coppa's crowd so Buttsky already knew it—"a beautiful letter from a tall, young, slender, supple creature, beautiful as the dawn, with yellow hair, with temperament and a poet, I will want to go where she may be since the passionate love of such a one is too dear a thing to lose out in life, even if I cannot give her everything." One presumes that by not giving Nora "everything" he meant marriage, as he was still married to Alice. He concluded, "*Dear*, you were beautiful tonight; you were beautiful all yesterday (Sometimes, you know, you are beautiful, and sometimes not) and I wanted you." He signed it "Boy."[14]

It was Buttsky, you see, who had first nicknamed him Boy.

Harry Lafler fell asleep in his clothes on the office couch and awoke, freezing cold, at 6:30 a.m. He grabbed another piece of Bohemian Club stationery and wrote to Nora about Buttsky. Smooth, huh?

Buttsky responded to Harry with a long and, even for her, melodramatic letter, her anger unmistakable: "Should Phyllis not be God's own one for you—be careful. There is a sort of curse attached to me for men who love me. Five men there are who walk the world in wistfulness—one died—you are the seventh—Perhaps the seventh number will ease you—(Good heavens I am about as conceited as you)."[15]

He didn't need to hear the number, nor did he doubt her. Realizing he was about to lose access to his local mistress, Harry delayed his trip to see Nora. He tried to woo Buttsky back, but Buttsky had other plans. Surprising him, she took another lover and rejected him flat.

Incredibly, neither Alice nor Buttsky was the cause of the reticence Nora had sensed in Harry earlier that fall when she feared she was losing him. His "you don't understand me" letter to her was written fewer than two weeks after he had received a shocking letter from a former flame. It is unsigned, yet it was clearly not authored by any of Harry's writing acquaintances, judging by the multiple spelling errors in routine words. It begins, "My Dearest Sweetheart" and continues: "I have tried to keep from doing this but it is imposable [*sic*] for me to keep still any longer."

In wild scrawl that goes down one side of a long, narrow sheet of paper and up the back, the writer informs Harry he will soon be a father: "Do you remember Harry 'Darling' when we were together the afternoon I left your City and you said I could call on you for help any time? If ever I got into trouble you would be my friend and help me?" She begs Harry to take her back but admits she knows that he probably won't. "Now Harry if you can't do that won't you promise me you will love the little one (who I swear to be yours) if I am able to bring it in to the world. 'Boy' or 'girl'?"[16]

.   .   .

After the revelation about Buttsky, Nora wrote to Harry less frequently. Her letters were shorter, more perfunctory. It seemed to drive him crazy. He began to whine that the pages he received from her were so few and so bare. Before, every sheet had been filled to the margins with her scrawl. Now, almost nothing. Her soul, once open to him, she now sheltered. He pressed her for more. He wanted to know every detail of every day as if he were in the room with her. Was she reading her letters at her table? Was she taking tea or coffee? Was she staying home in the evening? Who was calling to her home? "I am like Oliver," he begged. "I want more."[17]

Nora received these letters at her new address, an apartment she shared with her sister on Olive Street in downtown Los Angeles. They lived a few blocks from the new Angels Flight funicular railway up Bunker Hill. She continued to freeze him out with only short notes for all of January.

In early February, for his birthday, Harry was in Carmel for a visit with the Sterlings. After an early rain, they had hiked for the rest of the afternoon, Harry beating a new path through brambles to a perilous cliff near Point Lobos that had so far eluded even George. Harry had a limber body and a knack for sticking to the rock without slipping. That evening he and the Sterlings returned to the bungalow to dine on bread, honey, and tea. They relaxed by the fire, George reading from his poetry drafts. Harry read a poem by Nora that George thought very good, though he seemed overly curious about who this new girl was in Harry's life.

As the playing cards were brought out, Harry crept away to write a letter to Nora, which he'd done each night, walking in the dark to deposit it in the slot at the Carmel-by-the-Sea general store that served as the post office. "Love o' Mine!" it began. He described his hike, the beautiful mission, the treacherous climb. He had discovered paradise, he told her. There was nothing, nothing like Carmel in her bleached canyons. She had to see it for herself.

But Harry could never write in praise of anything without also writing in praise of himself:

> *Today we were coming along the deep trodden trail by which for a hundred years men have come through the green valley of Carmel to the great door of the yellow mission, when, where the trail curves to a little stream, we saw a wonderful lily soaring from the wet lush grass, and George quotes, 'An amorous golden mystery / a lily shadowed from the sun.' I said 'Good! Whose?' and then it dawned on me that I wrote the thing myself. Oh, I have to take you along these black rocks and white beaches and trails—just you and I, no one else, not even George.*[18]

Harry was threatened by Nora's talent and needed to show her that the great King of Bohemia, George Sterling, had validated his work. But he was also threatened by George.

"Not even George." He could too easily envision what would happen were George to lay his eyes on Nora even once.

Chapter Seven

⌒ΠΠ✇

Homewrecker

CARRIE DISLIKED NORA IMMEDIATELY. THE GIRL BOUNCED INTO the house after Harry Lafler (notorious for having a new girl every week) and plunked herself down in a chair after perfunctory greetings. George made straight for the wine and gave Nora a glass. After one drink, she never seemed to stop talking. Everyone said she was intelligent, but Carrie found her wearying. Nora's mind seemed comprised of dozens of gears and wheels, all moving at once and in every direction.

Carrie excused herself, saying she needed to prepare dinner. She expected Nora to follow her into the kitchen with an offer of help. But Nora just stayed in her chair, yapping away. She seemed blind to other women. She could see only men.

And they saw only her. George hung on her every numerous word. Downing a third glass of wine, he poured Nora a second, maintaining his face in profile as he so often did, because he thought it made him look more serious. Nora swung her one leg over the other and held her glass aloft, nattering on about the bungalow Harry was building for her on Telegraph Hill.

George soon moved from wine to whiskey. He'd been taking advice from a Dr. Abrams in San Francisco, who massaged his liver, squeezing it like a sponge, supposedly enabling George to outdrink his companions. The treatment was supposed to cause the liver to evacuate poisons that caused intellectual fatigue, sleep disorders, and neurasthenia—all of which George was prone to. Carrie felt sure that most of his problems concentrating on his writing would be cured by cutting down on drink, yet George's consumption had only escalated since their move to Carmel. And this summer had been so filled with refugees from the earthquake in San Francisco, George had endless excuses to lift his glass.

In the kitchen, Carrie enjoyed the relative quiet. She thought about what she would tell Blanche about Nora's visit. Blanche had described Nora as delightful once you got to know her and had embraced Nora as a sister. Typically inclined to follow Blanche's recommendations on interesting women to get to know, Carrie nonetheless balked at entertaining a brazen adulteress in her home. Did no one care that Harry Lafler was still married? Social propriety had been perhaps the last casualty of the earthquake. Quietly but surely, the rules had changed. Affairs that would have been a scandal before the quake now barely registered. Who cared about a homewrecker now that nearly every house lay in ruins?

Although the Sterlings had been safe in Carmel on April 18— a date none of them would ever forget—most of their friends had been in San Francisco and had only narrowly cheated death. Lafler had woken up just in time to avoid being crushed by the skylight above his bed. He descended what was left of his stairway and looked for the front door but it wasn't there anymore. Once in the street, he joined a crew of survivors heading for safety in Portsmouth Square, stepping carefully around live wires as they went. Once in the square, though, Lafler became anxious that precious manuscripts in his home would be completely destroyed. Sensing a narrow window of opportunity to collect his belongings, he talked his way past a soldier guarding his street and retraced his steps up his destroyed stairway. He filled a trunk with poems, clothes, and books and grabbed some paintings by Marty before heading back to Portsmouth Square.

Later that day, encroaching fire from Market Street forced Lafler to abandon his possessions again and seek higher ground. He wandered the city all night observing the disaster unfold. He saw the mansions of the railroad robber barons crumble atop Nob Hill. He watched throngs of people on the docks clambering over one another to board ferries to the East Bay. Families, he noticed, had saved their dogs and canaries, but not their cats. Turning toward the refugee camps in Golden Gate Park, he mused that the Chinese seemed to camp more nonchalantly than white people; not even twenty-four hours after the quake, they were cooking tea over portable stoves, almost like they were at a holiday picnic.

After two days, the fires subsided and Lafler returned once again to Portsmouth Square. He was astounded to find his trunk and Marty's paintings unscathed by the blaze; there were only a few charred spots on some of his typewriter's key bars. He set the typewriter on his trunk just to the side of a growing trench of graves. The fresh dirt was still in mounds, a shovel nearby indicating its frequent use. He had been awake for sixty continuous hours. As he typed up his first-person account of the devastation to send to *McClure's*, he was oblivious to both the living and the dead.[1]

Jimmy Hopper, who had in the past couple of years replaced Jack London as George's most frequent companion, had awoken in San Francisco's Neptune Hotel to the sound of the walls grinding. He had slept only a few hours, having spent half the night writing up Enrico Caruso's appearance at the Grand Opera House for *The San Francisco Call*. He rose from his bed to open the window, but the window fell to the ground outside. Then the greater portion of the hotel joined it, crushing a small wooden house below. Jimmy held fast to the wall that stayed up. After the dust settled, silence. And then, from somewhere down below, he heard a woman's soft moan.

Jimmy carefully made his way down the stairs and headed into the street, taking a pad of paper with him. He started taking notes for *The San Francisco Call*—this would be some story—but then he saw limbs sticking out from a pile of rubble. He threw his pen aside and began pulling bricks off a woman. She wrapped herself around him as he carried her to a clear part of the street and set her down. He turned back to the rubble to where the arm of another woman was sticking out, her hand dangling like a white daffodil planted haphazardly in a mound of dirt. He touched her fingers to let her know that someone was there and she would soon be freed. But this hand was cold.[2]

Arnold Genthe had also been in San Francisco at the Caruso concert, and stayed that night in his city home rather than return to Carmel. He woke up to hear his collection of precious Chinese porcelain crashing to the floor. His servant, Hamada, came in to tell him it was an earthquake—a very bad one. A veteran of several quakes in Japan, Hamada knew there would soon be a rush on the food stores; he ran out to scavenge what he could before they were all looted. Genthe went first to get one of his cameras, but they had all been damaged by falling pieces of ceiling. He ran to his camera dealer and borrowed a Kodak 3A Special. Heading for his beloved Chinatown, he worried he would find only devastation.

While he was gone, his house, studio, library, and a life's worth of negatives burned to the ground.[3]

Compared to what their friends had survived, the Sterlings, fortunately in Carmel that day, experienced nothing. Carrie first felt a jolt to the house. She leapt up, running from her bedroom to the porch in just a few seconds. George followed from his own bedroom, and they both clung to the whole-pine porch supports of their veranda, listening to their chimney crumble. They looked toward the bay and braced for a tidal wave. None came. George recorded the events in his diary: "Fine weather. Hard earthquake, knocking out both chimneys and smashing bric-a-brac and crockery. Chimneys down all about town. Monterey isolated by break-down of telegraph and telephone."[4]

A week later, George embarked northward to rescue his mother and sisters in Oakland. He wanted to be helpful, but he had also sensed opportunity. Although a disaster for the Bay Area, the earthquake could be a boon for Carmel. A waterless cabin on a quiet beach compared favorably to a city now in ruins and under martial law. The bumpy three-mile carriage ride from the Monterey train station to Carmel was a picnic compared to navigating San Francisco's split streets, where only insurance adjusters moved unmolested by soldiers.

The northbound train George was on moved haltingly, stopping often for emergency freight to get through. It took him twelve hours to get to Oakland, a trip that usually took no more than four. Stepping into the street, he was at first stunned by all the people. It was as if the population of Oakland had doubled as refugees had landed there from across the bay. His uncle Frank had allowed people to camp in a Realty Syndicate–owned gated amusement park. This bit of generosity displeased George's mother, who complained that "10,000 Chinamen" had invaded; she yelled at George for failing to bring his revolver to protect her.[5] George completed his filial duties by inviting her and his sisters to Carmel and then swiftly departed to catch the ferry to San Francisco, where he hoped to find his friends.

He told Carrie that his former commute by ferry and foot—which he had never enjoyed even under normal circumstances—had been transformed into a ghoulish parody of itself. Halfway across the bay, he could already see the dust. As he stepped through the cleared parts of the docks, he smelled lime. Where Market Street had only the month before been crowded with people moving purposefully about in every direction, now ragged survivors picked through rubble or stood staring into space, as if trying to orient themselves by a sun they could no longer see. The city had been leveled for acres. The beautiful nineteen-story domed *San Francisco Call* building at Third and Market Street, completed only the decade before, was a hollowed-out shell. Fire had consumed the opera house.

Moving around the city was still perilous. Saloons had been raided of their booze. Hungry residents scuttled in and out of destroyed storefronts clutching whatever goods they could carry. George heard that a woman's corpse was found in the street, her fingers amputated to remove the rings. In response to looting, Mayor Schmitz had issued a "shoot to kill" order to police.[6] Reportedly, a man had been gunned down for stealing a loaf of bread. Despite the lime, the stench of decaying bodies still wafted up from under toppled buildings; to George, it smelled like sour pork.[7]

The house where most of the Partington clan lived, at 1822 Fell Street, had a condemned sign on it, so George went around the corner to 851 Masonic Avenue, where Kate and her boyfriend, Toddy, lived. He found all the Partington siblings with their mother cooking dinner out in the street (indoor fires had been banned under San Francisco martial law).[8] George extended the invitation to them to join him in Carmel. For once, even Blanche seemed mildly interested.

He returned to Carmel and told Carrie that they were going to have to make accommodations for their friends and family. George found a cottage for his mother and sisters to rent. Kate and Toddy moved into the cabin in the Sterlings' backyard. He put a tent up for his eldest sister and her husband and children. Blanche and her mother took the guest room in the house, though they didn't stay long.

Soon others followed, some Carrie barely even knew. She hosted a Miss Cotton and her mother, who were weighing Carmel; they said they would "buy in" to an acre if only they could convince Blanche Partington to share it. A Miss Bonner arrived, whose company Carrie actually found enjoyable.

By the end of July, Carrie was exhausted from running a makeshift refugee camp. And deeply saddened. George, who had barely written anything aside from fifty lines of blank verse that didn't even approach his best effort—not that her opinion mattered to him—had rekindled his interest in Mrs. Kaplansky.[9] The time that he didn't spend with his mistress, he spent at Point Lobos gathering mussels and abalone. He'd grown proud of his physique and started sunbathing nude on the veranda, displaying himself to the town's increasing population.

By August when Lafler rolled into town, bringing his friend Nora from Los Angeles with him, Carrie had run out of patience with guests. As Carrie watched Nora take up all the oxygen in the living room with her patter, she wondered to herself: What kind of woman plans to move to San Francisco *after* an earthquake? One perhaps just deluded enough to think that Harry Lafler could be capable of anything approaching love.

After they left, Carrie wrote Blanche to report on the visit. Nora was "a freak," she declared. "I'd rather read her poetry than have her company."[10] She doubted she would ever see Nora again. Lafler would certainly forget her within a month.

. . .

As the summer waned, the weather turned from clear and warm to clear and cold, and then to fog. The surf rose, throwing huge pylons of kelp onto the rocks, making George's attempts to dive for abalone perilous and leisure swimming unappealing. The summer dwellers began to leave Carmel. George's mother had determined that the place was far too rustic for her tastes, and so had decamped for the St. Helena Sanitarium near Napa. None of the Partingtons who visited opted to buy. Only Kate and Toddy stayed on in the Sterlings' backyard, living rent-free.

Too few of the refugees from the earthquake had actually opened their wallets and bought land. The Carmel Development Company resumed its pressure on George to attract a big name in American letters to Carmel. The writing colony needed a heftier anchor than him to secure its success.

George realized that if they couldn't get Jack London to buy in Carmel, they could at least make it seem like he had. He arranged for the Londons to visit in early November. It would be their last chance for a while. Wounded by bad press over his hasty marriage to Charmian (they had wed almost immediately after his divorce had been finalized), Jack was looking to get out of the country. Most of his money and time went into the building of a yacht, the *Snark*. He was planning a cruise around the world. It seemed like madness, but Charmian was going along with the plan. Whatever Jack desired, Charmian would give him, even if it killed her, which, Carrie suspected, this foolhardy trip just might.

Jack London had only extended and cemented his place as America's foremost writer in the past year. *White Fang*, London's tale of a half dog, half wolf scarred by the pack, had been serialized and the book bought by Macmillan. Carrie thought it was diverting enough, though not as good as *The Call of the Wild*. It was the first work of Jack's that Charmian had more of a hand in editing than George. Jack had started writing it during the time he and Charmian were pretending not to be lovers. Charmian had even been written into the book as a shaggy sheepdog who seizes White Fang's attention. Carrie couldn't help but be impressed that Jack had captured Charmian's big teeth and unkempt hair in a dog. White Fang and the female sheepdog wrestle in the backyard instead of boxing, but despite these minor changes, this was the fictionalized courtship of the Londons in canine form. In the end, the sheepdog settles down with White Fang and bears his pups. Except Charmian didn't seem to be bearing any pups.

George had spent the spring urging Carrie to make up with the Londons now that they were legally married. He felt she should drop her objection to Charmian visiting Carmel, as Jack would never come without her. And so Carrie had choked down her pride, writing Charmian to extend a hand of friendship. Charmian wrote an effusive response confirming that of course they must be friends.[11]

That September, Carrie made her first visit with George to the London ranch in Sonoma. Charmian received them enthusiastically. Jack was obviously delighted to show off the property. Whereas the Sterlings had but a few acres in Carmel, the Londons had well over a hundred, with plans to buy adjacent property as it became available. They were constructing a barn for Charmian's riding horses. They had plans for fields of corn, hay, and grapes. Having had more than twenty different addresses in his life, Jack planned to build a ranch so vast and unwieldy it would tie him in place.

Looking around, what made Carrie most envious was not the land the Londons had, but the help. Charmian had people to cook and people to clean. She complained they had endless visitors to entertain, but unlike Carrie, she hardly had to do anything but smile while they were there. In between games of whist, Carrie watched the ranch manager, Eliza, fit Charmian for a petticoat of white Havana lace, all the while Charmian exclaiming, "Booful, booful!"[12]

To Charmian, everything was "booful": "Booful sky!" "Booful flower!" It was like spending time with an infant.

On the visit, George knocked back glass after glass of whiskey with Jack (who, as a joke, gave him a special tumbler with a hole drilled into the bottom). There was no hiding what a mess George had become. In a weak moment, Carrie confided to Charmian about his continuing interest in Mrs. Kaplansky. She regretted mentioning it instantly. It clearly gave Charmian immense satisfaction to see how miserable Carrie had become.[13] Charmian put her arm around her waist on walks through the fields and tut-tutted sympathetically. It had been a humiliating trip.

Now it was Carrie's turn to host. Charmian and Jack arrived in Carmel on November 4, having spent the day before at the baths of the Hotel Del Monte. Carrie put them in the guest room. The next morning, she got a mountain of housework done while the Londons slept until 11:00 a.m. After breakfast, Charmian took off on a horse from Carmel's livery while Jack wrote. She came back wet with surf, brimming with delight over her discoveries along the coast. Jack exclaimed his pride at "his Mate's" independence, or more likely her ability to leave him alone when he was working.

The next morning, while Carrie was making breakfast, she heard the steady knocking of the wooden headboard against the guest room wall.

The Londons were having sex.[14] In her house. On her bedsheets. That she would have to clean.

It was the morning of the planned photo shoot with Arnold Genthe at which Jack London would be passed off as the center of the Carmel group of writers. Carrie watched George choose his attire with care, concocting through great effort the appearance of the Bohemian at ease: dark cap, billowing white shirt tied off with a cravat, and tall socks. The Londons also had made an effort, Jack wearing a suit jacket over his own billowing white shirt. The Hoppers and Mary Austin came over, and they all moved down to the beach.

Genthe spent ages setting up the shot. He had George, Jimmy, Mary, and Jack sit on the beach with the bathhouse beyond them. Everyone else—Carrie and the other women and children—were shooed out of frame behind a long log. George sat, turning his face so the camera could get his profile, his eyes cast down. Across from him sat Jack, who—cigarette in hand, bare feet in the sand, hair tousled by the wind—appeared to be making some argumentative point. A primly dressed (for once) Mary Austin also sat in the sand next to them. None of her Native American headdresses and neckwear that she usually preferred for this particular occasion. Her long hair, neatly braided, was done up on the crown of her head, her knees tucked under her long skirt. She, too, faced Jack, listening intently. Jimmy Hopper sat in the sand to Jack's left, his high leather boots laced around his thick calves, his curly blond hair tucked under his light cap, one ear tilted in London's direction. Four California writers, deep in conversation at Carmel-by-the-Sea, Jack London the center of it all.

The whole scene was ridiculous. Jack had never bought even a square foot in Carmel. And yet here the Londons were, pretending to be full-time residents, when in two days they would get back on a train and leave, and the Sterlings would go with them so that George could put in his hours at the Realty Syndicate.

George wanted to quit the Syndicate but he and Carrie still needed the income. Despite Ambrose Bierce's efforts to use his publishing contacts, George's next major opus, "A Wine of Wizardry," had been rejected by most of the major magazines in New York. Bierce still buttered George up regularly, calling his poems the best he'd ever read in the world, and George still believed him. But Carrie was starting to think that marriage to a poet, however lofty in repute, paled in comparison to a full larder.

After the scene on the beach, Genthe urged the women to join the men on the rocks for a more domestic, yet still highly constructed, tableau. George Sterling posed standing, his arms crossed, turning his face to the sea (profile, again), squinting against the wind. Jimmy stood on a rock behind George, to make him look taller, perhaps, but it only accentuated his jockey-like form. Jack London, open-collared, jacket gone, leaned on a rock in the center, radiating self-confidence and raw masculinity. The others were arrayed around and above him—a panoply of saints attending to the word of Jesus Christ himself: Charmian, with her broad, manic smile, sitting over Jack's right shoulder; the MacGowan sisters—writers and friends of the now stratospherically famous author of *The Jungle*, Upton Sinclair—over his left, and on the fringe of the group, Carrie with the cuddly pup Skeet on her lap. Genthe might have caught her in mid-eyeroll.

During the break between shots, Carrie got to work feeding everyone. She sat on the sand cutting up food on the picnic basket between her legs. She was among them, yet they scarcely noticed her until she offered them a plate. George balanced a bottle of seltzer on one knee and a bottle of whiskey on the other, listening to Jack, who was still talking. The men were clearly only interested in each other, but Charmian kept trying to nose in. She thought just because she fixed Jack's grammar that the men saw her as one of their own, but actually they thought of her as Jack's typist.

Maybe the whole literary colony experiment would fail, Carrie thought hopefully to herself as she passed the plates around. She longed to move back to the Piedmont permanently. George would probably be at the Realty Syndicate through at least the spring.[15] If she could, she would move all her furniture back up to the Piedmont with her. She had gained nothing by moving to Carmel. George had broken every promise he had made, including the one promise that she truly thought he could keep: that she would never have to entertain Charmian Kittredge London. And for that she would never forgive him.

. . .

It is impossible to overestimate the impact of the photo shoot on the beach in making Carmel-by-the-Sea what it is today. The photo of London, Sterling, Austin, and Hopper in front of the beach house is simply *the* shot on which the Carmel myth is made, reprinted often in books about Carmel's founding and turn-of-the-century Bohemian California. And it is a masterpiece. It really does seem as if these writers are engaged in spontaneous conversation. It has accomplished exactly what it was intended to: forever ensuring that when Carmel was mentioned, Jack London would be mentioned, too, even though he only ever spent a bare few weeks there in all his life.

The other photos from that day, while not as widely circulated, give context to how contrived the original shot was. There's one photo of Genthe setting it up (taken, presumably, by an assistant), which reveals the artistry involved in creating the illusion of autonomous Bohemians. Carrie, Charmian, and Mattie Hopper, Jimmy's wife, are apportioned off from the four central writers by a good twenty feet, positioned behind the log. The women appear to be busying the children so they don't run around and destroy the shot. The writers look like actors waiting for their cue.

The women were necessary extras, though, for the shot on the rocks. Carmel needed to attract families. The Carmel Development Company didn't want a town of only artists, because the endgame was a town of upper-middle-class folks who liked the idea of living near creative types, as long as they behaved themselves. People want to go slumming, but nobody wants to buy into a slum. So the Bohemians had to show they were family folk, just like bankers and lawyers. The message was clear: Carmel is Bohemian but not a free-love commune! Look at these respectable women! It is safe to bring your children!

Mary Austin, tellingly, was left out of this shot. She drew attention through her eccentricities and for writing in her "wiki-up" (Genthe had taken a photo of her and Hopper in her tree house on this day as well). But she otherwise didn't fit the script of what Carmel women were for. She had left her disabled daughter in an institution and her husband in Inyo County, California, so she could wander the world wherever her spirit determined it should go. Her absence in the shot on the rocks perhaps demonstrates the extent to which Carmel wanted Mary disassociated from the domestic side of the development. She was in actuality more Bohemian than any of the men.

When not needed to display domesticity, the wives were tasked daily with performing it out of view and largely unappreciated. Mattie Hopper, whose English was shaky (she had emigrated from

France), minded the children so Jimmy was free to write and swim for mussels with George. Carrie fed the visiting artists just as she had the year before fed the men who built her house.

In recompense, the men treated their wives as symbols of the bourgeois conventions they were escaping, writing to one another suggestively about their escapades with other women.

Notably, Jack London would profit from Carmel just as much as the land developer through their mutual association. Frequently drawing his plots for his books from his life, Jack would write several novels featuring his relationship with a fictionalized version of George Sterling. One, *The Valley of the Moon*, finds two wandering laborers, Billy and Saxon (Jack and Charmian), searching for government land to settle and happening upon Carmel:

> Dropping down through the pungent pines, they passed woods-embowered cottages, quaint and rustic, of artists and writers, and went on across wind-blown rolling sand-hills held to place by sturdy lupine and nodding with pale California poppies. Saxon screamed in sudden wonder of delight, then caught her breath and gazed at the amazing peacock-blue of a breaker, shot through with golden sunlight, overfalling in a mile-long sweep and thundering into white ruin of foam on a crescent beach of sand scarcely less white.[16]

The first Carmel dweller Billy and Saxon encounter is the spitting image of Jimmy Hopper: "smooth and rosy-skinned, cherubic-faced, with a thatch of curly yellow hair," but with a body "hugely thewed as a Hercules." The next day they meet the image of George Sterling, dark wind-swept hair, high cheekbones, and a lean nose. Jack names this character Mark Hall and gives him a businessman father in San Francisco for a backstory. Hall, however, is an ardent socialist who holds gatherings in his living room to preach about how capitalism is a rigged system.

Hall suffers from depression, and it falls to Mrs. Hall, a drastically underwritten version of Carrie (her main talent is making good coffee), to remind him to stay chipper. London also wrote a small revenge against Carrie by having "Mrs. Hall" admire Saxon's superior figure on a swim, and then, like a frigid busybody, "look inquiring" at the pair when they return from a midnight stroll.

Billy and Saxon eventually reject Carmel, just as Jack and Charmian did. Billy realizes he would have to again be a wage slave to afford to live in town. And Saxon had seen a downside to the merry Carmelite crowd: They would not age well, if they managed to grow old at all.

Jack London must have wanted the world to know that he didn't believe in the Carmel experiment. He and his wife had nobler plans. But as the novel was first serialized in *Cosmopolitan* and later became a movie, London made a good deal of money off Carmel, enabling Charmian to maintain the Japanese servants that Jack gave to Mr. and Mrs. Hall in *The Valley of the Moon*. The servants that Carrie saw waiting on Charmian at Beauty Ranch? They were to become hers, fictionally, while Jack and Charmian's fictional selves wandered into the sunset unaided and unspoiled.

Remember this, because it's going to become very important later.

Chapter Eight

༆

Hello Girl

EACH DAY SHE JOURNEYED TO WORK IN MAY 1907, NORA STEELED herself. As she approached the Pacific Telephone office where she operated the switchboard, she could hear her striking coworkers even before she could see them. They lined the sidewalk in front of the building, holding signs aloft, a blockade of puffy blouses. As she neared, they fixed their gaze on her. Two walked up to block her path. "Are you going to scab today, Blondie?"[1]

Nora squared her shoulders and kept moving forward, even as they grabbed her arm, screaming that they would win. One woman kicked her. Another one grabbed at her hair, but Nora had made it almost inside. The policeman posted at the door stood unmoving as an egg sailed past Nora's head.

She had known when she applied to be a telephone operator a few months before that it was difficult work. Even worse than sewing leather mittens. Telephone operators had a notoriously high suicide rate, their nerves shot from long hours and constant surveillance. Only twenty minutes for lunch was permitted, and there were few other breaks. Their supervisor, the "chief operator in pants," monitored their every move, so fearful were the company directors that the women would write down snippets of conversation to extort important callers.[2] After operators left for the day, their ears buzzed for hours.

Even the application process was an exercise in humiliation. They were invited into an office to undress, a cold stethoscope was put to their chest to gauge their heart and lung capacity, and their jaws were pried open to check the soundness of their teeth. They were weighed. Finally, a vision test was administered to determine if they could distinguish red lights from green.

"Hello Girls" they were called. In the papers, they were depicted as empty-headed young women who trawled the wires in search of rich, single men to woo and eventually marry. The rare operator who managed to wed a millionaire became an instant cover story. More frequently, the operators were sexually harassed during work by their superiors and after it by any other man. But Nora, desperate for money, applied for the job knowing its challenges, passed the degrading physical, and began work on the wires.

The Pacific Telephone Company required neither Nora's substantial design experience nor her facility with language. She learned the arrangement of the switchboard, memorized the stock phrases for saying the line was busy, and got the hang of tallying her "pegs." Her brain, previously brimming with poetic verses, now filled up with numbers for the police, fire department, and hospital. She felt assaulted by blinking lights and cords, confused by the protocol of when to collect from the nickel phones and when to refund. Always sensitive to sound, she cringed when callers shrieked into the lines. And a supervisor would read a list of her mistakes aloud to her coworkers at the beginning of the next shift.

The women who worked at the exchange had given her an icy welcome, sensing her incompetence. When she asked her co-workers a question about the circuits, they said they didn't have time to break in the "new girl." She noticed that these women had an informal uniform: the Gibson Girl pompadour—some dyed red—breasts pushed up under a white blouse, corset tilting the pelvis backward. Nora wore the prescribed color skirt and shirt but otherwise dressed as she did every day, her hair loosely pulled up and only the lightest restriction for her breasts. She felt marked by her refusal to conform. Whenever she tried to get to know the other women, they looked at her as if she had three heads. They wouldn't eat with her, instead sitting at the next table and talking in loud voices about their "fellows." Some of them even unplugged her board when she wasn't looking, forcing her callers to hang on the line.

She soon learned that the real reason that they distrusted her was that she hadn't joined the union. Hoping to mollify them, she agreed to go to a meeting. There she listened to a man from the butchers union urge the operators to strike. San Francisco was on its knees, he said. The city needed their work to rebuild. The electricians had gone on strike. The launderers had joined them. The women of the phone company should be next, declared the man from the butchers union. Attorney General Francis Heney's anti-corruption investigations had revealed that Mayor Schmitz had accepted bribes from corporate bosses, including their employer, the president of Pacific Telephone.[3] The spring of 1907 would see the victory of the laboring class.

The operators stood and cheered in response. Nora looked

around at her coworkers. These women had sabotaged her day in and out and now yelled at the top of their lungs in the name of solidarity. She decided right then and there she wasn't going to chant their chants any more than she would adopt their hairstyle or wear their corsets. So when 575 operators walked off the job, Nora joined the twenty-four others who stayed on.

Aside from having to cross the picket line to get to work, Nora's life improved dramatically from that moment. The bosses, grateful that anyone was willing to work, treated the scabs well. Suddenly the break room had the latest magazines. Suddenly there was fresh fruit at each table. Nora began to improve at her job and even started to enjoy it. She put through a call to an ambulance that a man had lost both legs in an accident. She mobilized the fire department to respond to an emergency. She felt useful.

Sometimes, sitting on her stool, she could tap one key after another, listening in to the intimate conversations of a city on the brink. She became a spider, traveling a tangle of wires, moving from voice to voice, drama to drama. It was almost poetry.

The strikers were right about one thing: The telephone company really didn't pay enough to live on. To support herself, Nora needed to write something that would sell. Walking by the newspaper stand, she noticed that *The Saturday Evening Post* had a series of long-form articles featuring women disclosing the routines of their ordinary jobs. In February, they featured "The Diary of Delia," a tell-all from a woman in domestic service promising a peek into the lives of her wealthy employers. Well, if the intimate thoughts of low-wage women were what men desired, Nora could provide them—publishing anonymously, of course. She didn't want her name to be associated with the piece. She just wanted the money. *The Saturday Evening Post* reputedly paid quite highly and boasted a circulation nearing a million. She started formulating her ideas on the way home from work and picked up a pen the minute she got through the door.

> I sat down between two of the girls that had been oper- ators for years. A soft-shelled thing enough I was between those two hard, spiky creatures. I felt like Alice between the Red Queen and the Gryphon. They were simply horrid to me. The board was a little different from the practice-board I was used to, and the "call circuit keys" puzzled me. I asked the girl at my right about them.
>
> "You go take a sneeze; your brain's dusty!" was all she said.[4]

As she wrote, she realized how deeply she had been hurt by being shunned, even by women whose passions and preoccupations were so alien to her own. The truth was, she had never felt more in need of female friends and never less capable of finding any. Her move to San Francisco to be with Harry had left her more iso- lated than at any other time in her life. The more she had wrapped herself around him, the more she had lost her sense of herself.

She and Harry had made their second visit to Carmel that Christmas. The cabin in back of the Sterlings was taken by an- other couple, so they stayed at the Pine Inn. That was fine with Nora. Carrie, she knew, didn't like her—or maybe she didn't like Harry. She couldn't quite tell. But she hoped Carrie would warm to her over the weekend. The Carmel market was out of turkeys, so George and Harry had driven into Monterey to try the stores there, but even those were sold out. It would be a primitive feast of popping corn and boiling chestnuts over a fragrant pitch pine fire in the hearth. They exchanged some presents. Nora had ex- pected nothing—she barely knew the Sterlings—but George gave her a gift. It was his volume of poetry by Keats. She opened up the first page and read aloud the dedication to her: "When you meet Keats in the poet's Elysium, may I be there to see."[5]

The look on Harry's face after Nora gave George a thank-you kiss on the cheek. It had been just a flash, but she saw it. Harry pretended to be fine the rest of the evening as they drank and played charades with the Sterlings. But the moment they got back to the Pine Inn, he charged her with flirting with George. They quarreled. He wouldn't let up. As the sun was rising, Harry packed up their bags and marched her to catch the early stagecoach to the train. He refused to even send the Sterlings a note to say they had left.[6]

A year earlier, Harry's forcefulness—his sadism, really—had been attractive to Nora; it had jolted her out of her grief after her mother's death. At that time, she had felt as if she was at one edge of a dark tunnel, and the rest of the world was at the faraway end, making faint murmurs and whispers she could hardly discern. It took Harry Lafler, the fuzzy-haired, erratic youth with his spates of hot and cold and his petty cruelties, to shock her back to life.

She could see now she had too much craved to be under his power.[7] Helen had spotted it right away, warning her against the relationship from its very beginning. But Nora didn't understand how much danger she was in until after the abortion. It changed everything. Sex lost its power to bond her to Harry as it once had. He grew increasingly suspicious of her, and angry, as if she had done something to him deliberately. He kept asking her how she could have known she was really pregnant that early.

She soon learned he had fanciful ideas about maternity. Once, while camping with a Shoshone Indian family, he had witnessed a woman give birth quietly, with no assistance.[8] The woman went back about her business the next day, he recalled admiringly. He had no regard for women's pain. The sight of it only seemed to anger him.

When he finally hit her, he looked almost proud of himself, as if he'd done something manly, something he could brag about later. No longer her "Boy."[9] When Nora finally confessed everything to her sister, including the abortion, Helen stood on the front steps and told Harry that she didn't care if he owned the place, he was no longer to enter the house. Harry, always a bit frightened of Helen, obeyed.

By March it was all over. The men of the former Coppa's crowd, sensing a vacuum around her, moved in quickly. The satirist Gelett Burgess, just then finishing a novelization of the lives of the San Francisco Bohemians, was first out of the gate. Months before, he had helped Nora with the wording of a poem that she then entered into *The San Francisco Call*'s contest for best poem to greet 1907. "Says the Old Year to the New" was written from the standpoint of the devastating year of 1906:

> They were stately walls and high—as I felled
> them so they lie—
> Lie like bodies torn and broken, lie like faces
> seamed with scars[10]

Awful fluff, she thought, but it won her $50 and got her a full front-page spread in the culture section of the *Call*.

She moved on from Burgess to his friend Will Irwin, a former managing editor of *McClure's* who had returned to San Francisco to study discrimination against the Chinese. Irwin spent his days wandering Chinatown with Genthe and his evenings writing captions for a book of photographs Genthe was working on. He was more earnest than Burgess and worlds more handsome. But he was also single, and single men might one day want more from her than she was willing to give.

Then, one day, she found herself in the arms of George Sterling.

He had been consoling her over the breakup with Harry. He, who knew Harry better than anyone, had affirmed her decision to stay away from him. Harry had always feared George would charm her away from him. Perhaps he had been right after all. She could tell George wanted her, but then again, he wanted every woman in his vicinity. Yet she was drawn to his sadness, which seemed to match her own.

During the spring of 1907, both she and George were swept up in the workaday world—he at the Realty Syndicate and she at the telephone company. George had been separated from his usual entourage. Jack and Charmian London had sailed off in April to circumnavigate the globe. Jimmy Hopper was frequently on assignment or busy with family. And Carrie seemed happy enough going to the theater with her sisters.

So, on a predetermined evening, Nora left the telephone exchange, made her way through the picketers, closing her ears against their curses, and headed for the Embarcadero to catch the ferry to Oakland. Disembarking, she walked to the Realty Syndicate offices, which had moved after the earthquake to the tenth floor of the Union Savings Bank Building. High up in the tallest building in downtown Oakland, George's office commanded splendid views of the bay.

Nora relaxed in a lounge chair while George finished up the day's work. It was strangely comforting to watch George do something he pretended to hate but was clearly good at. Every entry in the ledger was recorded in meticulous penmanship. Letters that began "Yours of the 12th at hand" or "Referring to your purchase of" and so on were written with ease. It was a different side of him, and she loved seeing different sides of people. Every so often he looked up at her, as if he couldn't believe she was still there, before he turned back to his work.

She asked him if he could spare a scrap of paper. She had been asked by their friend, the playwright Porter Garnett, to compose a poem for his wedding in early June. She was an odd choice for this assignment, she thought. What did she know about commitment? But she was honored to have been asked and so took the job seriously. She had worked out the lines in her head on the ferry on the way over and needed only to write them down before she forgot them.

George stood up, walked to the shelves, and took down a ledger from the year 1893. He opened it to the middle and tore off half a sheet from the date Monday, May 22, and gave it to her. She took the paper back to the lounge chair and wrote:

> Ay pluck a jonquil when the May's a-wing.
> Or please you with a rose upon the breast,
> A sweeter violet chosen from the rest,
> Your mood with blue caprice of Spring
> Leave windy vines a tendril less to swing.
> Why, what's a flower? a day's delight at best,
> A perfume loved, a faded petal pressed,—
> a whimsey for an hour's remembering.
>
> But wondrous careful must he draw the rose
> From jealous earth, who seeks to set anew
> Deep root, young leafage, with a gardener's art—
> To plant it queen of all his garden close,
> And make his varying fancy wind and dew,
> Cloud, rain, and sunshine for one woman's heart.

Turning on the conceit of a gardener who cuts several flowers before he finds one to dig from the ground and nurture as his own, the poem told of a once flighty man who had found his true love. Perfect for a wedding. She was pleased. When she finished it, she wrote her signature sideways in the dollars and cents columns of the ledger paper to gently spoof George's formal Syndicate tone: "as witness my hand, Nora Phyllis May French."[11]

At his desk, George finished his correspondence, set his pen aside, and crossed over to her. He brushed a lock of hair from her shoulder and bent down to kiss her neck. As she felt his lips touch her skin, she leaned back and closed her eyes.

. . .

Full disclosure: I have no idea if George kissed her neck. Of course I don't. How could I? No letters between George and Nora exist to testify to such intimacies. This is unsurprising, since it was a clandestine affair on both sides; Nora was terrified that Helen would discover that she was dating yet another married man, and George hid the affair from Carrie.

In order to tell this story at all, I've had to fill in some cracks with my imagination. I felt bad about this until my colleague Dana Rabin, a historian of eighteenth-century Britain, told me that we have a choice when we write about women's lives: Either we connect the dots to make sense from the sparse records available, or we get silence. Or we just wind up writing about men, over and over and over, because their records are the ones that get preserved.

As a case in point, the Huntington Library in Pasadena, California, where I find Nora's handwritten "Rose" poem, has no other manuscripts of hers. I was lucky to find this one. It was tucked away in the George Sterling Papers but was not on the finding aid's list of "notable items." In fact, it was not on the finding aid at all.

Sterling himself is a mere sideshow at the Huntington, which holds 666 documents under his name in twelve boxes. (Most of his papers are elsewhere.) To compare, Mary Austin has a respectable 6,698 items in 148 boxes at the Huntington. The African American science fiction writer Octavia Butler has more than eight thousand. But none of these collections can compare with the jewel in the Huntington's gilded crown: their collection of Jack London's manuscripts, correspondence, and photographs, totaling over a mind-boggling sixty thousand items. Most of these were sold to the library by Charmian after Jack's death—she was trying to keep the ranch afloat and settle his many debts. So if you want to write (another) biography of Jack London, you are well supplied by the Huntington. But if you're trying to resurrect the life of poet Nora May French, you're out of luck.

It is ironic that the life of the socialist Jack London is now preserved in a library founded by the fortunes of Henry Huntington and his second wife, Arabella, who herself was the widow of Henry's uncle and business partner, C. P. Huntington, one of the "Big Four" rapacious railway magnates. Jack London, here, is merely one more piece of history that conspicuous, multigenerational wealth could afford. In the reading room there's an enclosed bookcase made from centuries-old wood harvested from different venues where Shakespeare's plays were performed. It was purchased for $10,000 in 1916. There's an 1874 Rose Steinway piano down the hall from the reading room. Above it, a painting of Benjamin Franklin before the Privy Council in London, by the renowned American artist Christian Schussele.

At the Huntington, the Gilded Age still feels gilded. Behind the library, 120 acres of gardens welcome tourists year-round. The splendid rose garden containing more than one thousand varieties boasts a tearoom where you can nibble on salmon and caviar finger sandwiches while sipping the Huntington's signature blend of tea. Right out the library's front door, the visitor is met with exquisitely cultivated plant specimens from around the world: *Urginea maritima*, or sea squill, from the Canary Islands; *Justicia californica*, or hummingbird bush, from Mexico; and a *Quercus suber*, or cork oak tree, from North Africa. These plants, too, are evidence that the Huntington is carrying on where Jack London tried and failed; London devoted his later years to a passionate but half-cocked attempt to turn Beauty Ranch into an experiment in sustainable agronomy. With Luther Burbank, he manufactured a strain of spineless cactus, only to see the spines grow back.

The best part about the Huntington for researchers, however, is that its archives are spectacularly run. Scholars are treated like honored guests. Knowledgeable staff quickly retrieve your materials and speak in whispers so nothing disturbs your work save the occasional rustle of shuffling papers. Collections are in good order. Rarely is a sheet out of place. Staff welcome rather than resent scholar insights to dating manuscripts or identifying authorship. In short, the Huntington runs a tight ship, and researchers appreciate that even more than the array of succulents or the finger sandwiches.

When I found Nora's handwritten "Rose" poem on my first trip to the Huntington in 2015, I hypothesized immediately that the ledger paper it had been written on belonged to the Realty Syndicate. It was, after all, archived in the George Sterling Papers. I also knew that Nora never used ledger paper for her correspondence. Of her few available handwritten poetry manuscripts, none are committed to ledger paper. The paper would have been used in accountancy for the year 1893. In 1893, Nora was only thirteen, hardly old enough to do accounting, nor did it likely belong to her parents; many of her family's possessions had burned in the fire on their ranch.

George Sterling, however, had been keeping the books for Frank Havens since 1891. I turn the paper over. Smudges of black and red crayon on the back—both of which were regularly used to mark sold and unsold property on Syndicate maps—further suggest this ledger book was George's. I jump online to look at other examples of ledger paper from the period. Numerous varieties of ledger paper were available in the 1890s (in the Gilded Age, there were a lot of books to keep), but this one is similar to the kind George preferred: broad middle section to describe the transaction, divided down the middle, with only a couple of vertical columns on the right to enter the sums.

Archival documents frequently have a smell. For example, some of London's manuscripts reek of the tobacco he smoked. I sniff the paper of Nora's "Rose" poem. It smells musty, like an office.

I try to reconstruct the timeline of Nora and George's affair. George practically lived at the Realty Syndicate offices in the spring of 1907. Frank Havens was trying to shift out of the land game as there was no more money to be made there. Real estate was entering a bear market. The Dow Jones had peaked early in 1906 and had been trending downward steadily since. The earthquake accelerated the decline. Just when money was needed to bolster the markets, England raised its interest rate, making it more expensive for American banks to borrow from abroad. How could Havens create a city of millionaires if millionaires were disappearing?

The Piedmont also had suffered from a spate of bad press. In January, a night watchman employed by the Syndicate had shot his sister and then himself on a hillside.[12] The city of Oakland was fighting the Piedmont's plans to incorporate as a separate municipality. Havens's hold on power in Oakland was slipping.

Ever looking for the next big play, Havens began buying water utilities but had failed to watch the bottom line.[13] He needed another loan to keep his multiple companies afloat, but the bank would no longer take Realty Syndicate stock as collateral. Having no other options, Havens gathered together deeds for real estate in the Piedmont and turned them over to the Oakland Bank of Savings to secure a $150,000 loan.[14] His partner, Borax Smith, the capital side of the operation, balked at the mounting debt and wanted to buy his way out. Mortgages, contractors, ferry accounts, water accounts, capital stock, bonds, real estate—all had to be valued, bickered over, and divided. It fell primarily to George to calculate it all.

Havens emerged from the split worth about seven or eight million on paper. He settled a large income on his sister, Mary Havens Sterling, moving her out of the Piedmont house and sending her back east.[15] Then he bestowed $9,000 in company stock upon George and Carrie. With this largesse coming in, Carrie would have been more than happy to let George work late. Ample time for an affair.

But I'm not happy with circumstantial evidence. So I make a return trip to the Huntington in 2019, looking for a smoking gun. I again comb through the George Sterling Papers, this time looking for any confession of his illicit meetings with Nora during the time both of them were in the Bay Area. Surely he confided in his best friend, Jack London. After two days of reading their correspondence, however, the only thing I can find is a reference to Nora's first visit to Carmel with Harry in August 1906. George had written

Jack immediately afterward, referring to Nora as "Nora May French (the poet—and a peach.)"[16] He had added the presence of Lafler as a marginal notation in the letter, as if he were the least important feature of the visit. But I can find nothing from the spring of 1907 that implicates meetings between Nora and George alone.

I give up on the George Sterling Papers and go to the Jack London Papers in case there is anything in there. Nothing in correspondence. I turn to a box labeled "Manuscripts," which contains poems George signed and sent to Jack or Charmian, sometimes accompanied by handwritten notes as to what he was thinking about at the time of composition. I'm hoping for any mention of Nora in the margins, however oblique, but for three-quarters of the box, I find nothing.

Then I open the file for his poem "In Extremis." George wrote it in 1906. This work is handwritten on ledger paper, seemingly the same kind of ledger paper on which Nora wrote her "Rose" poem. It, too, is torn out, but from the middle of the sheet, so the year that should be at the top is missing. The only visible date is Friday the 19th, but no indication even of what month.

I return to the fragment of ledger paper on which Nora's "Rose" poem is written. Though the date on top of the side she wrote on was marked Monday 22nd in the month of May, the date at the top of the back of the sheet is Thursday the 18th. I position Nora's "Rose" poem above George's "In Extremis" poem so I can compare tear marks in the paper. They line up exactly. I lift "In Extremis" to my nose, and a familiar musty odor wafts up.

Gotcha.

How unlikely is it that these two pieces of paper—once one sheet—would wind up in archives only yards from each other more than one hundred years later? Although they started and arrived together in the same rooms, these scraps of paper have had very different journeys in the meantime. George sent "In Extremis" to Jack for review, but only after it had already traveled through several pairs of hands. A letter from George to Ambrose Bierce shows that he had already shown the poem to Garnett, London, and Lafler (none of them liked it) before sending it to Bierce, who sent it back. This piece of paper has made the rounds.[17]

Nora's "Rose" poem also went on excursions through the post. Just after Garnett's wedding in June 1907, at which Nora presumably read it, George sent it to Ambrose Bierce, but without telling Nora. This wasn't an unusual move for him: If he wanted to get a gift for a girlfriend who was a writer, he could think of nothing more meaningful than securing Ambrose Bierce's approbation of their work. But he also knew that Bierce could be a harsh judge, and if he didn't like Nora's poem, George didn't want to be in the position of bearing bad news.

"Dear Master," George began. "Just as a partial return for all you have done for me, I'm enclosing the MS of a poem by one Nora May French, a San Francisco girl about twenty-three years old—a blonde and beauty." (Nora was actually twenty-six.) "If it's not the real Tennysonian crystal may I become 'popular.'"[18]

It's telling of George's limited understanding of Nora's nature that he thought Bierce's opinion would even matter to her. Her reputation was by this time established. She had published in every West Coast literary journal of note. George could have sent Bierce any one of her published poems, or mentioned her many publications to date in his letter, but he did not. Instead, he treated her as an unknown poet whom he had discovered. He never considered that by 1907, Nora didn't need anyone to tell her she was good. She knew she was good.

Bierce returned the poem within two weeks with a scathing and patently misogynistic review. He admitted that it had some desirable qualities, like clarity, but that it hadn't quite "hit" him. The chief problem, he felt, was that the author herself lacked maturity and experience. "My guess is that she never loved, sorrowed, suffered nor sinned. It would be a God's blessing to seduce her—can't you undertake it? The work drags a little owing to the equal number of feet in lines rhyming alternately—a meter not very tolerable in a long poem."[19]

I'm getting to know George fairly well by this time, and I can tell that this response from Bierce upset him. He usually answered Bierce's letters immediately, but this time he waited two weeks before writing back. This gap is particularly notable as he was in Bierce's debt at the time. Bierce had finally secured publication for Sterling's epic poem, "A Wine of Wizardry," in *Cosmopolitan*—no small feat as over the years "Wine" had been rejected by *Harper's*, *Scribner's*, and *The Atlantic*.[20] Editors had returned the verdict that the lyric was too Victorian, too cluttered, too ornate for modern sensibilities. George had been livid that his genius had not been recognized by the top journals of the East but was also well aware that Bierce had eased the poem's acceptance into *Cosmopolitan*. To fend off potential bad reviews, Bierce was even penning an essay to accompany the poem, in which he would certify George as the greatest living American poet.

So if George was upset by what Bierce said about Nora's poem, he would have been loath to say so directly. Instead, when George did write his response, he chose his words carefully. He allowed that yes, Nora's poetry might be "pure" and "undefiled"—not compliments, he knew—and yes, perhaps his personal fondness for the authoress affected his judgment. But as for Bierce's supposition that she had never loved, George assured him that she had, adding the half lie, "not me—fortunately."[21]

Chapter Nine

⌒⧓⌒

La Bohème

CARRIE WAS THRILLED TO BE BACK IN THE PIEDMONT. BACK TO the land of regular transportation, plentiful grocery stores, and butcher shops. No more living on snails, quails, and the occasional potato. The Sterling calendar soon filled up with teas in the afternoon and theater dates in the evening. They had been invited to attend so many formal parties that George was obliged to get fitted for a tux.[1] Carrie soon gained twenty pounds to top the scale at 140—more than she had ever weighed in her life—and was forced to buy new dresses. She sighed into the mirror at the dressmaker's. She used to be so effortlessly thin, but her age was starting to catch up with her.[2] She even noticed a few more strands of gray in her hair.

They purchased Mama Sterling's Piedmont house with everything in it for $10,000—all money given to them from Frank Havens.[3] Thanks to Frank's generosity, they would own it absolutely debt-free. Carrie set to work designing the interior. Mrs. Havens gave her a few pieces of cast-off furniture that were of the very best quality, as everything bought by her sister had to be. Carrie placed the Steinway grand piano in the front room in anticipation of hosting concerts. At Carmel, music was what she had missed most. She was bored to death of literary salons every night. Writers never seemed to tire of the sound of their own voice.

And she could now go back to the opera, her greatest love. She went as often as possible, even though she missed the old opera house, which had burned along with everything else. In March, the Sterlings joined the Hoppers and Xavier Martínez to hear the San Carlo Opera Company perform *La Bohème* at the enormous Chutes Theatre at Tenth and Fulton Streets. The Chutes, one of the few theaters to survive the earthquake, now showed everything from boxing to vaudeville. For this night of the opera, however, the theater hosted the elite of San Francisco. *La Bohème* had already been hailed as Puccini's crowning achievement and was the hottest ticket in town. Carrie bought a new dress for the occasion and took her seat, pressing her skirt to her sides carefully so as not to crease it. Looking around at the audience felt like a dream: rows and rows of finely dressed women on the arms of gentlemen.

As always, when she brought George with her to the opera, she had to ignore his irritation with it. She focused on the music, closing her eyes to hear Alice Nielsen in the role of Mimì, the seamstress, sing, "*Sì. Mi chiamano Mimì.*" Carrie felt herself almost lifted into the sky as Nielsen hit her high A.

The performance was not without flaw. Afterward they agreed the tenor, reputed to be the equal of Caruso, disappointed. But George had nothing good to say about any of it. He couldn't stand the acting; he wondered why people didn't just stand there and sing the songs. Perhaps, Carrie thought, the sight of people pretending to be Bohemians hit him a little too close to home.

In truth, she wasn't completely sold on the story herself; Carrie preferred *Madama Butterfly*—a far sweeter work.[4] In both operas, the woman died, but in *La Bohème*, Puccini had asked her to believe that a Bohemian poet would be devoted to the love of his life. In *Butterfly*, the soprano is betrayed and kills herself. Much more realistic.

Carrie would have gladly stayed on in the Piedmont permanently, but George's stamina for real work again proved anemic. He calculated that if they vacated their Piedmont house and let it out, they would have sufficient income from the rent without his having to work at the Syndicate and they could move back to Carmel. After the publication of his "A Wine of Wizardry" in *Cosmopolitan* that August, he told her, the writing jobs would flow in.

Carrie tried to protest, but George complained that he was not going to be a slave to capitalism just to fund her evenings out. Having no income or prospects of her own to contribute, she was in no position to object. She was devastated. Her brief sojourn in society, surrounded by music and congenial friends, was now at an end. She wrote Blanche the news and urged her to visit their house in Oakland one last time before they left.[5] Then Carrie packed her dresses in trunks and put them in storage. She threw a bedsheet over the piano. She cleaned the house top to bottom so it would attract the best possible renter. She shuddered to think of what unscrupulous tenants would do to the place.

No sooner had they arrived in Carmel than Carrie was again chained to the kitchen. It was an unusually heavy summer for high-profile guests. James Phelan, past mayor of San Francisco, visited and told them tales of the immediate aftermath of the earthquake: Phelan had driven around with dynamite in his wagon to blow up unsteady buildings, while carrying $100,000 worth of his sister's jewels in his pocket (no bank vault after the quake could be trusted).[6] When Phelan left them, a reporter from *The New York Times* came to interview George, Jimmy Hopper, and Mary Austin for a story on the Carmel colony. And after he left, the parade of guests began in earnest. The trips down 17-Mile Drive. The hikes to Point Lobos. George swimming for mussels and abalone.

Mussels could be cooked in their shells and eaten immediately and so Carrie preferred them, but an abalone dinner gave George an opportunity to demonstrate how fun Carmel could be. All the guests were enlisted to help pound abalone, a mollusk so tough it had to be whacked with rocks for a full hour before it was ready for the grill.[7] George made a song to accompany the activity, which quickly became the Carmel literary circle's anthem:

> Oh! some folks boast of quail on toast,
> Because they think it's tony;
> But I'm content to owe my rent
> And live on abalone.[8]

Participants in the ceremonies were invited to make up their own lyrics. Soon, there were dozens of verses.

They could have just bought a can of abalone from the grocery store and saved themselves the trouble. The verses began to grate on Carrie's nerves. Midway through July, she had seen one rich person too many sing about poverty while walloping a shellfish. She had always thought that her marriage had allowed her to escape her mother's fate of running a boardinghouse, but now, making up the spare room for every new guest, she realized how wrong she had been. She was beginning to wonder if she couldn't kick them all out and take $50 for a decent, stable, nonartistic tenant.[9]

Crass as charging rent for boarders might be, it would at least bring in some money. Otherwise, what was she getting out of Carmel's success? She had abandoned the notion that Carmel would reform George. His halfhearted attempts at sobriety had all failed. At the age of forty, he was drinking as if he were still twenty years old. If anything, he was getting worse, while she scraped pots and pans till her knuckles were raw. Meanwhile, her sisters, Mrs. Havens and Mrs. Maxwell, were wearing furs on their backs and diamonds around their wrists.

In late July, George left for the Bohemian Club's annual camp-out. This year, in the absence of Jack London (still at sea), George shared a tent with Harry Lafler and Jimmy Hopper. They pitched a simple army-style A-frame and spent the next two weeks pickled every moment of the day. When George returned to Carmel, he brought a photo his friend photographer Gabriel Moulin had taken of their site: Harry Lafler, tipping his chair back in ease, leaned against the central tent pole, threatening its stability. Jimmy Hopper, his curly hair crowning his head, sat across at the camp table. Visiting the group, another writer in Ambrose Bierce's ambit that George knew well, Herman Scheffauer—overdressed for the occasion—sat in a camp chair to Lafler's right. George sat to Lafler's left, his cap low on his brow, gazing lizard-eyed at the photographer; he wore the same socks he'd worn for the photos Genthe had taken the previous fall. His Bohemian chic.

Their tent's billboard (all the Bohemian club members decorated their tents with billboards or Japanese lanterns) depicted George in a toga gazing at a bust of William Shakespeare, with the caption "Me and Bill." George was the Bohemian Club's honorary "Shakespeare" for the gathering, as his play *The Triumph of Bohemia* had been chosen for the club's Midsummer "Jinks." He had been working on it all year, turning down paid work to do so (when Carrie pointed this out, he argued that the appreciation from the club members would lead to more commissions). The drama pitted the Spirit of Bohemia against Mammon, the disguised Spirit of Care. The two spirits battle each other for the souls of mortal workers of the woods—all played by members of the Bohemian Club. In the end, the Spirit of Bohemia triumphs by promising the one thing Mammon's gold cannot procure: a happy heart in tune with Nature.[10] The night of the performance, hundreds of businessmen watched George's vision performed under calcium lights. As the Spirit of Bohemia triumphed at the close of the play, the audience rose and dragged the spirit of Mammon onto a bonfire to burn it in effigy, drinking and howling as it went up in smoke.

Carrie thought it ridiculous. All those businessmen pretending to cheer the death of Mammon while they secretly prayed for the stock market to rebound. That March, shipping, mining, and railway stocks had all experienced double-digit falls. U.S. Steel had reported a 25 percent decline in its value over the previous year. While the club members gathered at what they called "Bohemian Grove" in Sonoma County, a judge handed down a $29 million judgment against Standard Oil of Indiana for violations of the antitrust Elkins Act.[11]

George returned to Carmel fiercely hungover, very tanned, and reeking of coconut oil and whiskey. He'd managed to contract a blood infection from cutting his finger—how, he had no recollection. His finger required slicing to the bone in order to drain the pus. Usually, he took a break from drinking after the campout, but Carrie noticed that this time, he barely paused. A crop of male writers—Will Irwin, Mike Williams, and Jesse Lynch Williams—came down to Carmel, and they quickly monopolized his attention. One night at Jimmy Hopper's cabin, they ran out of liquor. Goaded on by his friends, George burglarized Dr. Beck's pharmacy, dry Carmel's only source of alcohol (the development company had long before adopted neighboring Pacific Grove's family-friendly policy of no saloons).[12]

The next morning, *Cosmopolitan* magazine came out with Sterling's "A Wine of Wizardry," prefaced by Ambrose Bierce's judgment that Sterling had no equal in poetry on this side of the Atlantic. "Wine" was this century's "Faerie Queene," Bierce decreed. "Whatever the length of days accorded to this magazine"—Bierce hated *Cosmopolitan*'s editor—"it is not likely to do anything more notable in literature than it accomplished in this issue by the publication of George Sterling's poem 'A Wine of Wizardry.'"[13] George's mother bought several copies of the magazine and mailed them to all her friends out east.[14]

In the buzz surrounding her husband, Carrie felt more lost than ever. Callers came to congratulate him, barely giving her so much as a hello. She had accepted in the past year that she would never be seen as anything more than the "poet's wife." She found herself craving stimulating female companionship beyond the other wives, like Mattie Hopper, who lived in town. Mattie was prone to lean on Carrie for help with the kids and had become obsessed with neighbors she suspected were sleeping with Jimmy. "Being a virtuous woman she assumes no one else is," Carrie quipped in a letter to Blanche.[15] Little Jimmy Hopper seemed the least likely man to secure a mistress.

Another neighbor, a Mrs. Schwilk, vulgar and ignorant of the basic rules of grammar, frequently dropped by unannounced with her children; she pretended to be bringing Carrie news but invariably asked for a favor before she left. Mrs. Josephine Foster, who ran everything from the Arts and Crafts Club to holiday festivities, was always happy to enlist Carrie's help in some time-wasting activity in the spirit of community uplift. As if Carrie hadn't been uplifting the community from her own home daily. And finally, to "cap the climax" as she put it to Blanche, Bessie London had invited herself to visit. Carrie knew she would be stuck with the primary responsibility of entertaining Bessie, who had few connections in Carmel and had never really forgiven George for supporting Jack's affairs.[16] In the meantime, Blanche and Charmian had made up and were now regularly trading letters on the difficulties of finding a competent Japanese cook.

Even Carrie's dear friend Kate Partington, bright and intelligent and as close as the cabin in the back, was no longer a comfort to her. That boyfriend of hers, Toddy, had become the sole focus of Kate's world. She fawned over him, urging him back to the cabin to make love to her, even when visitors were present. It was unseemly.

George, once close to Toddy, had tired of the pair as well. "Grafters," he called them—they existed simply by grafting on to other people.[17] They still owed the Sterlings money and had proposed to earn off their debt. But instead of taking good care of the bungalow when Carrie and George were up in the Piedmont, Kate and Toddy drank all the wine and whiskey in the house and raided the stash of pine nuts. Not a word of apology followed.[18] Instead, Toddy gave them a couple of books at Christmas as a present—for their "kindness," as Kate had put it. The Sterlings' "kindness" of feeding them and letting them live on their property free for a year didn't exactly square with the gift of two books. Neither Kate nor Toddy had ever had childhood experiences of poverty, Carrie observed to Blanche, and so they failed at being poor "gracefully."[19] And now, though unable to care for themselves, they were expecting a child.

She needed to find a way to evict them that wouldn't appear too cruel or she would spoil her relationship with all of the Partingtons. So when George proposed that Nora May French could replace Kate and Toddy in the cabin, Carrie readily agreed. In the Piedmont, Carrie had better gotten to know "the French girls," as they often called Nora and Helen. The girls had occasionally joined them for walks in the hills or over to Xavier Martínez's house.[20] Carrie felt a kind of kinship with Helen. She seemed the practical one, sadly tasked with reining in her flighty sister.

By the early summer of 1907, however, the French sisters were no longer living together. Helen had moved to Los Angeles to accept the marriage proposal of her former employer, making Nora's situation in San Francisco truly untenable. She had no work. The telephone company had just settled with the striking workers, who had secured a huge increase in pay, a shorter day, longer breaks, and the dismissal of some supervising chief operators. All the women Nora had fought through, the ones who jeered, threw eggs at her, and chased her in the street, would now be returning to work (somehow, Carrie had noticed, none of the socialist men of the Bohemian set had condemned Nora for scabbing). Making matters worse, bubonic plague was beginning to spread throughout the city. The papers had suppressed news of the extent of the outbreak, but George had heard that new cases were mounting, despite the campaign to eradicate rats along the docks.

Even if Nora had wanted to stay in the city, she had no place to live since her split with Harry Lafler had turned acrimonious.[21] For a few months after they had broken up, Harry seemed determined to win her back. *The San Francisco Call* reported he was even suing his wife, Alice, for desertion.[22] The very idea of Lafler—a man who could never keep his trousers buttoned up—suing a woman for desertion made Carrie laugh. To Nora's credit, she wouldn't take Harry back even if his divorce went through. Instead, she had renewed her relationship with her old flame Alan Hiley, the wealthy and reputable British war hero, who had secured his divorce. Nora and Hiley were soon to be engaged. A brilliant decision, Carrie thought.

George approached Carrie with the proposition that Nora needed a place to stay for only a couple of weeks, until Hiley sailed down on a yacht to pick her up. Armed with the excuse that Nora was in the greater need, Carrie sent Kate and Toddy back to the Piedmont. Nora moved out of the cottage on Telegraph Hill. In one final stunning act of cruelty, Lafler replaced her tenancy with his ex-lover Bertha Newberry and her husband, Perry.

. . .

On August 24, the afternoon Del Monte Express left on time. Nora took her seat in one of the steerage-class cars. The better-dressed men and women headed for the club car, where they would be served drinks and dinner as they lounged in upholstered chairs. The train was crowded with people escaping the city, if only for the weekend. She was leaving forever.

Nora gazed out the window as the train rolled through the inner part of the Mission District, which was still very much under reconstruction, and then the outer district, which had changed little from when she had come to town not quite a year before. But how much she had changed in such a short time. Then, her life had been brimming with possibility: a new love, new friendships, a place where she thought she could flourish on her own terms. What was the Russian proverb? "Bells from over the hills sound sweet"?[23]

Now she was scurrying for safety, like a rat down a drain. Twenty-six years old and with no other option but to rely on yet another married man. Exhausted from packing, she laid her head back and dozed, waking to see the garlic fields of Gilroy out her window. Rows of parallel lines fanned out toward the distance. The sight reminded her of the orchards of Glendale and her years of playing among the trees with her sister and brothers. As the train reached the Monterey Peninsula, it began to hug the coastline. She opened her window and leaned her head out so she could smell the ocean breeze.

George met her at the Monterey train station and lifted her few bags, clearly relishing his role as rescuer. His officiousness, reaching for small bags she could easily have carried herself only made her feel more pathetic. She was glad to see the renowned landscape painter Charles Rollo Peters also in the car; she would not be the only one with George on the trip. She talked with Peters at length about her experience at the Art Students League, and he told her about the École des Beaux-Arts in Paris. He had finally succeeded in goading the Pacific Improvement Company to open an art gallery in the Hotel Del Monte by telling them it would be devoted to exhibiting California artists whose paintings would extoll the scenery they were trying to sell.

As they made the final turn into Carmel, Nora noticed how much the town had grown since she'd last visited. More houses, more stores. They arrived at the bungalow, and George unloaded the car while Carrie extended her arms in greeting. After a welcome cup of tea and chat in the living room, Carrie showed her to the cabin. Nora hadn't been in it since she and Harry had stayed there on their first visit to Carmel. Left alone at last, she lay down and cried.

She awoke to see fog out the window, which made her feel comforted and sleepy. She stretched lazily before poking her head outside. Neither of the Sterlings seemed to be stirring, from what she could tell. She dressed and entered the yard, walking quietly around the side of the bungalow so as not to wake them. She would go into town for breakfast; lately she couldn't start her day on an empty stomach. When she returned, she found Carrie in the kitchen, picking through a box of corn. Nora asked what she could do to help. She was anxious to make a good impression with Carrie this time. It was the very least she could do.

That night the sky was clear and the air delightfully cool. The Sterlings hosted a barbecue in the backyard, which they seemed to do most nights in the summer. Mary Austin came by, and then Arnold Genthe, and the Hoppers with their adorable children. They all ate roasted corn together and talked about beauty and art. Genthe offered to take her portrait, which was very nice of him. Nora went to sleep with the sweet smell of corn smoke in her hair, buoyed by the evening of fellowship.

A bird woke her up early. This time she dressed quickly, grabbed breakfast in town, and then went down to the water. She walked along the shore in the direction of Pebble Beach and up the hill toward 17-Mile Drive. She stopped at Cypress Point, which featured one weather-beaten tree clinging to a rocky promontory. She climbed out to the tree and stayed there listening to the low rumble of the waves below, her face graced now and then by the spray. The sky off the peninsula was always in motion. You could see the fog roll in, or rather creep in. She could watch one pine tree for an hour as it went from shadow to pale whisper of itself and back to full form. Tiny ghosts passed before Nora's eyes, sometimes touching the ground near her feet, moving quickly and then slowly. Carrie had said she hated how often Carmel was shrouded in fog, but Nora loved it. Sunny days gave you so much less to write about. As she walked back toward Carmel, words were already coming to her.

> Because my love has wave and foam for speech,
> And never words, and yearns as water grieves . . . [24]

When she returned, Carrie was in the kitchen again (she was always in the kitchen, this poor woman). That evening they were joined by Mary Austin and the poet Ina Coolbrith, two of the West's most acclaimed women writers. They again roasted corn over an open fire pit and talked of the benefit being held for Ina in the fall—she had lost her house in the quake. Ina asked if Nora would read for it. Nora smiled widely and agreed. It was nice to be once again surrounded by intelligent women. Their conversation was interrupted by George, who gnawed at his cob so noisily they all stopped and stared at him.

Nora decided to give him the attention he clearly wanted: "Well, Greek, what do you think you're playing—a flute?"

Carrie perked up from her cob and said with a sly wink, "No, a cornet."[25]

Nora looked at Carrie and burst out laughing.

She could be funny, this poor, poor woman.

Chapter Ten

❧

Other Woman

ON THE LAST WEEKEND OF AUGUST, GEORGE RETURNED NEARLY breathless from the post office as if he had run the whole way. He announced to Carrie and Nora that he had stupendous news. Ambrose Bierce had just confirmed a visit to Carmel. Now in his mid-sixties, Bierce had grown weary of life in Baltimore and was considering retirement. If he could find a cottage he could afford without having to sell any of his favorite securities and if his asthma didn't react to any of Carmel's numerous trees, he would become their neighbor.

Carrie had never seen George so keen to make a deal. He immediately started on a letter to Bierce, explaining that the company was so hot to attract the literary elite, they would offer him half off the current price of $350 per lot. Not certain that would be tempting enough for his mentor, George set off to see the company manager to secure even better terms. He returned and added to the letter that the company would give Bierce a five-year option on his land and would buy back any improvements he made, in case he changed his mind and wanted to sell.[1]

Carrie feigned enthusiasm for Bierce's impending visit. The season was drawing to a close, and she had little energy left for guests. Currently, aside from Nora, she was down to just an excitable actress whose voice sounded like a bereaved hen. Even she would leave soon, and then it would be just her, Nora, and George.

Surprising herself, Carrie was beginning to like Nora. She seemed much changed in the past few months: More gracious than she had been in the past, quickly offering to help clear dinner plates and wash up. She didn't complain. She looked somehow . . . softer. In the past year, Carrie had often marveled at the gap between Nora's flighty affect and the gravity of her poetry. She no longer did. Now, knowing her better, she could well imagine Nora as the author of those painful lines.

The three walked together often. The day before, they had sat at the mouth of the Carmel River; it had just broken through after a dry spell and was again draining into the bay. From the banks of the river, they watched a seal diving in and out of the water, barking happily as it swerved and splashed and then, after a half hour of gymnastics, swam off.

The actress left. With the night air being unusually chilly, Nora came in from the cabin to warm herself by the hearth. Carrie, George, and Nora sat together in the living room that evening, sipping muscatel that had arrived in the mail as a gift.[2] George read them Jack London's story "The League of the Old Men"—a morbid Yukon tale—then moved on to Swinburne. He chose to read "Ave Atque Vale" as an homage to Charles Baudelaire, the original Bohemian, who had died exactly forty years before. The light from the fire illuminated their faces, and Skeet, the dog, curled up and snored softly on the rug before them. Carrie felt completely serene, listening to Swinburne's words in her husband's voice:

> Now all strange hours and all strange loves are over,
> Dreams and desires and sombre songs and sweet.

. . .

Nora heard the cadence of these lines and turned them around in her head. Long inspired by them, she had written her own "Ave Atque Vale," mixing Swinburne's meter with her own peculiar sorrow. Hers was also a farewell to love and innocence, but to a relationship ended by cruelty rather than through death:

> Now nothing is the same, old visions move me:
> I wander silent through the waning land,
> And find for youth and little leaves to love me
> The old, old lichen crumbling in my hand.[3]

George was reading steadily, trying not to look at her. She knew he feared his world might crash about him at any moment. He was quite the chameleon, she was finding. One minute he was flirtatious with her, another plaintive, and still another distant. Now he seemed jumpy. He had confided to her that one of his friends from the Coppa's set, a Captain Emerson, had just published an essay in the *Western World* calling George "the real estate poet of the Piedmont" and a practitioner of "free love." While the charge of being a "real estate poet" merely irked him, the mention of "free love" had him terrified.

Panicked, George had written to Blanche to find out who

owned the *Western World* so he could sue. He avowed to Blanche that he did not advocate nor practice free love and that if Emerson's mudslinging implicated any of his "woman friends," he'd have to murder the man.[4] Then, before even waiting for Blanche's reply, he sent letters to three of his friends, including Marty, telling them that if they chose to remain friends with Emerson, he would sever his acquaintance with all of them on the spot.

This was the stupidest thing he could have done. Protesting too much, George lent substance to what had previously only been whispers. Nobody read the *Western World*. Blanche wrote back, wisely counseling George to find out what he had done to anger Emerson, make amends, and move on. George agreed, but Nora could see he was still chewing on it. How odd it was that men couldn't see that their discomfort stemmed only from their own actions. How nice must it be to live in this airy world where consequences never found you.

. . .

Labor Day weekend arrived, the date of Ambrose Bierce's visit. As Carrie predicted, Bierce had proved a difficult guest even before he stepped foot in town. With only a day's notice, he announced that he was bringing a couple of friends with him. An elderly couple. George groaned. He would have to rethink the whole itinerary. No one would want to walk. George brought Nora and the Hoppers to Monterey as a welcoming committee to pick up Bierce and his companions. He didn't return to the bungalow until 10:00 p.m., exhausted and ranting about the day. A high wind made for a miserable drive back as they rushed through 17-Mile Drive. The restaurant he had taken them to for dinner fed them slop, vilely served.[5] All the region's deficits came into sharp relief when viewed through the eyes of the uncompromising Bierce.

The next morning, George and Carrie rose at 6:00 a.m. to make preparations. Carrie packed several picnic baskets, and George secured even more cars to convey the whole crowd to Point Lobos—Nora, Carrie, Bierce, his friends, the Hoppers—anybody but Mary Austin, who George was sure would start chanting in Navajo and confirm Bierce's worst fears about Carmel being a den of lunatics. George had to make two trips to get everyone there. Carrie and Nora carefully guided the guests down the path to the point. They set up picnic blankets on a flat spot where the cave beneath them boomed with surf. George and Jimmy would have to swim carefully to avoid getting smashed against the rocks. The men stripped (the women obligingly hooted) and then clambered down to where the tidal pool yielded the most mussels. Jimmy was the better swimmer by far, but George was more proficient with the mussel rake. Coordinating, they collected several sacks of mussels for the barbecue.

While the men tended the fire, Carrie unloaded the baskets of wine, tomatoes, butter, and bread. Everyone drank far too much, especially Ambrose, for whom the wines had been chosen with care. Jimmy, using his former Berkeley football player arm, lobbed a mussel shell at George from ten feet away and hit him square in the back. George turned around, picked up half a tomato, and threw it back. The gathering devolved into a food fight. Dodging a flying bread hunk, Nora slipped on a rock, hitting her head. She began to cry. George ran over to her and parted her blond hair to examine the cut.

Carrie had had about enough for the day, so she told George she felt sick and asked if he would take her home. Let them all clean up their own mess.[6]

To her great relief, everyone left the next morning—Bierce and his friends to San Francisco, and Nora to her sister's for a week. Carrie had a few days to breathe. She relaxed on the veranda in the sun while George cleaned his golf suit and stockings. They were due that night at Charles Rollo Peters's house in Monterey for a dinner in George's honor. Carrie loved eating food that she didn't have to cook herself.

In the meantime, the reviews came pouring in for George's "A Wine of Wizardry," and they were disastrous. Bierce's introduction deeming "Wine" the pinnacle of American poetry had not helped George, instead raising the literary world's ire. Coast to coast, the papers decried George as Bierce's lapdog. He was parodied, scoffed at, called morbid, and accused of superfluity for using abstruse words like "gyre" and phrases like "blue-eyed vampire." Even his friends piled on, either with light critiques or such effusive praise it was clearly parody. The novelist Gertrude Atherton suggested that maybe he should just quit writing.[7]

Carrie had never seen George so furious. He sent a sample of the abundant criticism to Jack London, who was just then sailing on the *Snark* toward Australia. George had come to the conclusion that the whole fiasco had been orchestrated by the editor of *Cosmopolitan* as a ploy to sell copies in a down market, while George himself had been paid only $100 for a work that had taken him years to perfect. He wrote Jack, "Of course, I realize that Hearst is doing all this merely to sell his damned 'Cosmopolitan' but it doesn't make the whole row any less absurd and offensive to me. It's as though he had launched a drove of swine into my big sitting room, or had dumped a can of sea-sick-vomit on my head." Even Bierce was no help. He was, George noted to Jack, "preserving a terrified silence."[8]

Dick Partington came down, as did Carrie and George's

brother-in-law Harry Maxwell, for a quick visit, which mollified George temporarily. Carrie joined them on a walk to gather russet mosses and shells. They returned to the bungalow to find Nora May French in the kitchen, gnawing the bones of the grilled rabbit George had stored in the icebox. Three cans of sardines were missing from the pantry.

For such a small girl, Nora did seem ravenous. Carrie had no idea how she stayed so thin, but George seemed genuinely worried Nora might starve. The next day he walked to Monterey to meet some Bohemian Club friends for lunch, returning with Nora's favorite things to eat: enchiladas and tamales.[9]

The following morning, Carrie and Nora joined George and Jimmy on a trip to Point Mission. George and Jimmy undressed and made for a twenty-five-foot channel on the southern portion of the point where George had located a broad low rock with mussels. They had a new system where Jimmy would cast a rope to George with the sack and mussel rake, and George would fill the sack and send it back via the rope, allowing him to collect more than he could swim with.[10] Carrie and Nora stretched out and enjoyed the sun on their faces until the men finished their work. They returned to the bungalow, covered in salt water, sand, and grime, and were greeted on the veranda by Arnold Genthe, accompanied by the Bruguières, who had driven over from Monterey.

Mrs. Bruguière sauntered into the bungalow wearing a gray suit, a black picture hat adorned with feathers, and long white kid gloves. Her husband, Dr. Bruguière, wore a white knickerbocker suit with stockings of gray. Carrie took one look at them and exchanged a knowing look with Nora. It was all a bit much for the peninsula. To be polite, Carrie invited them to stay for supper, humble though it might be, and to her horror, the Bruguières accepted. Carrie had nothing but mussels, and that was already supposed to feed her, George, Nora, and both Hoppers. How was she to make that stretch for two more? She and Nora quickly repaired to the kitchen to see what else could be done.

Mattie Hopper took one look at Mrs. Bruguière and decided she herself was underdressed. She ran home, returning decked in a massive brown pleated skirt that looked like a maternity gown. Mattie was hopeless. Every effort she made to fit in only made her plainness more obvious. Even Jimmy looked embarrassed on her behalf. Carrie swiftly called the group to the table and began serving. Mrs. Bruguière picked at two mussels, clearly disappointed with the meager offering. Both Bruguières soon made their excuses and left, no doubt to eat a real supper somewhere else. Once they were alone, Carrie, George, and Nora felt they would nearly die from laughing.[11]

Nora's fiancé, Alan Hiley, sailed into Monterey harbor the following Monday. Carrie found herself looking at him often. Slightly older than George, Hiley was very much older than Nora, which was probably a good thing. He had that gravitas soldiers carry with them throughout their lives. Carrie found this masculine specimen a refreshing change from the willowy, soft artists who surrounded her daily.

The next morning, she and George said goodbye to Nora and Hiley, who were sailing off on an enormous yacht—big enough for thirty souls—owned by one of Hiley's timbermen.[12] Nora hugged Carrie and thanked her, promising they would return for a short visit before their nuptials. Carrie and George watched them sail off until they disappeared around the point. They went back to the bungalow and George sat down at the writing desk and wrote letters all day. Carrie worked in the garden.

Nora returned in less than a week. Alone. She broke down in

tears the moment she entered the living room. The engagement to Hiley was off.

. . .

Reader, pardon this interruption. So far, I have tried to avoid jumping into the middle of a chapter, but here it feels unavoidable.

I have no way of knowing what happened between Nora and Hiley on that boat, which annoys me. It annoys me because the collapse of Nora's engagement to Hiley marks the final significant turning point in her life. She was twenty-six years old, already four years older than the median age for a woman's first marriage in the early 1900s.[13] Her window for matrimonial and thus financial security was closing. She had every incentive to marry Alan Hiley.

Did she choose not to? Did she get on that boat, take a good look at her future husband in the flesh, and decide this was not what she wanted? Did he do that thing where he pretended to listen to her? Did he mention his war exploits one time too many? Maybe the traumatic memory of their past together overwhelmed her.

Or did Hiley break it off? Nora had been through many affairs since they had last been together, and another abortion. Did she confess something to him that changed his view of her? Did she suddenly appear no longer young and exciting but rather damaged and messy? Did the reputational costs of attaching himself to her suddenly appear too high? Or, after a first flush of reunion, did he finally understand that she had fallen out of love with him years before?

Although I have no idea what actually happened, of this I'm pretty sure: Carrie would rather have been the woman who had sailed into the sunset with Hiley. Her admiration of Nora's fiancé spilled into a letter she wrote to Blanche about "Capt. Alan Ille

Hiley," in which she described him as "a dandy fellow—intelligent and modest—We all liked him immensely and are glad she is going to marry so fine a fellow." She added the detail that he had a guardian "Sir something Markham of England"—she couldn't remember the particulars.[14] Carrie even overlooked Hiley's status as divorced; ordinarily, she disapproved of second marriages. But Hiley seemed to be beyond her reproach. The truth is, as much as Carrie disdained Jack London, she had a similar attraction to battle-tested masculinity. Her letters were sprinkled with discussions of what made for a real man. She had an eye for men in uniform; they reminded her of her own father, the police captain.

Seeing the caliber of suitor Nora was able to attract also changed Carrie's attitude toward her younger companion. She reported to Blanche that Nora had been a perfect guest, no trouble at all to host, as she mostly kept to herself and ate breakfast in town. Nora, no longer "a freak," Carrie now described as "an odd little monkey but is awfully bright."[15] After Hiley took Nora away, Carrie seemed satisfied she had played her part in helping a young woman get her unsteady feet set on the right path. She did like to put things in order.

So when Nora returned with the engagement off, Carrie had a genuine problem on her hands. For one thing, Nora returned in a shocking state. She cried constantly. She stayed in her cabin all that day and then the next. She stopped bathing. She walked out with them only once in the next five days.[16]

But her return also put Carrie in a delicate position. From this point forward, Nora seemed committed to living with the Sterlings on a permanent basis, without any clear termination date—a socially perilous situation. A single woman living with a married couple who was neither a maid, nor a governess, nor a blood relation always provoked speculation. Such a trio served the writer

Edith Wharton as the scenario causing the most scandal to heroine Lily Bart in *The House of Mirth*. The Sterlings could hardly keep Nora a secret, either. They had visitors in and out of Carmel constantly—indeed, drawing press attention to their life was built into their income strategy. All kinds of well-connected people would be able to verify that an attractive, young, single woman with no clear attachment to family was living with them. Lacking a legitimate explanation for Nora's presence, people would assume the worst: that she was George's mistress.

I marvel at the possible motivations that provoked the Sterlings to accept such a risk. George's are obvious: He wanted his lover near him. Carrie's seem opaque until I consider her history. She had lived with Kate Partington after Kate was widowed, even despite George's evident delight at having a young woman in the house. Carrie also liked to have a younger woman in distress under her care. It allowed her to play the role of big sister, when all her life she had been the little sister. But mostly, she needed someone around her whose life was such a disaster, her own would look wonderful by comparison.

. . .

In October, while Nora made another visit to Los Angeles to cry on the shoulder of her sister, Carrie prepared the house for the arrival of Herman Scheffauer. George had spent much of the 1890s drinking with "Scheff" at the Bohemian Club, before he met Jack London. Scheffauer, the son of German immigrants, had spent the past few years touring Africa and Europe, writing and doing translation work, before settling in England. Carrie had gotten to know him mostly through his long, self-absorbed, and nearly illegible letters to George: a mixture of remarks on poetry, art, and architecture punctuated by accounts of bil-iousness, constipation, and depression.

In the flesh, he was even less appealing. After two weeks of Scheff's voice echoing in her living room, she was ready to pack his well-traveled bag for him. At her pleading, Blanche came down for a visit to help absorb some of the conversational load. As he drank, Scheffauer expounded on his search for an "affinity" who would end his loneliness. Seeing as Scheffauer lacked even a rudimentary understanding of how not to bore women, Carrie felt sure he would die alone.

George was showing him some lots for purchase, though as the days wore on, even he was less enthusiastic about recruiting his friend to Carmel. Carrie tried to emphasize Carmel's more provincial aspects to Scheffauer in the hopes of deterring him. Thankfully, he was a skinflint, and Carmel lots would prove more than he would want to spend.[17]

No sooner was he gone than Carrie opened the front door to see Jimmy Hopper, overnight bag in hand. He sat down in the living room and declared he and Mattie had separated. He and George talked long into the night. As she was preparing for bed, Carrie heard snippets: Jimmy felt smothered. He had married too young, had kids too soon, and never had time to commit fully to his career as a writer. Carrie knew all this was true—she could not disagree that life with Mattie would feel like a prison sentence to anyone—but she couldn't bring herself to pity Jimmy. He should have been more careful before getting the woman pregnant. Now he was stuck. Jimmy spent one night in their guest room before moving to a cabin down the street with his writing collaborator, the former gold prospector and novelist turned journalist Fred Bechdolt.

In late October, George went to San Francisco on the evening train with Jimmy and stayed through the weekend, returning with Nora, whom they met at the Oakland train station on the return from her sister's. Nora seemed much better for having spent a couple of weeks with Helen. She eagerly settled back into Carmel life. She went mushroom picking with Carrie and George (an errand made fruitless by low fog) and even cooked spaghetti for that evening's dinner.[18] She made pots and pots of it. They were hosting a literary salon in honor of Mary Austin that evening, as it was Mary's last night in town before one of her dreaded visits to her husband.

After spaghetti and everyone telling Nora it was marvelous, they gathered in the living room to hear Mary read from her new novel in progress. Set in the fictional California college town of "Santa Lucia"—named for the very real mountains that surrounded Carmel—it featured three intrepid women: the first was known to "talk like a man"; the second, named William, had an interest in science; the third was Julia, a brilliant yet oversexed girl from San Francisco.

Mary had written this book as revenge for having been overlooked as a significant writer on account of her sex. The women of Santa Lucia were continually underestimated by their intellectually inferior husbands; they rebelled against the dictate that they leave their financial lives to their husband's care (finances were a critical issue with Mary, as her husband had squandered their money in dubious schemes). Bored to death by housework, they were condemned to stale, purposeless lives. Mary had subtitled the novel "A Common Story."

Late in the book, the marriage of the tormented and impassioned Julia crumbles. Mary read from the part where Julia discovers a vial of poison in her closet under her stored wedding dress.

It appealed to her now as the thing she had always meant to do. She was to go out of her husband's house and life. Well, here was a way of going that provided her with the last word, that should dissolve whatever of blame was directed against her in poignant regret. . . . She did not know much about the nature of the poison except that death by it was said to be painless; she was glad of that, for she was very tired.[19]

Carrie listened as Mary read through to the heroine's end. After drinking the poison, Julia stumbled blindly to her husband's study calling his name—"Antrim, Antrim, Antrim"—until she reached him seated at his desk. She collapsed between his knees and died. It was melodramatic beyond belief. Mary set the manuscript in her lap and looked up, awaiting response. For a minute there was silence, unbroken except for a pop of sap exploding in the fireplace. Carrie hardly knew what to say and tried to think of something polite.

Then Nora asked a question: Did death by cyanide really look like that?

. . .

October had brought Nora two significant publications: a poem in *Sunset* magazine and her "Diary of a Telephone Girl" in *The Saturday Evening Post*. She had a copy of the *Post* in her cabin, and she looked at the cover warily. On it, her story title appeared with a sketch of a girl resembling her, but not her: wide eyes, red lips, and blond curls poking out from a flower-bedecked straw bonnet (she would never wear such a thing). It was someone's imagination of an empty-headed coquette with Bohemian pretensions. That was who the *Post* thought she was.

It seemed to her as if she had written the "Diary" piece a lifetime ago. "Between Two Rains," her poem in *Sunset*, was far more recent and far more like her. She had been inspired to write it on a hike back from Point Lobos. She had emerged at Monument Beach, which stretched between the point and Carmel, and had taken a moment to rest. From her spot on the sand, she watched a cormorant weave and dart through a wave, seemingly fearless, while the gulls circled above it. She could see gray clouds and streaked sky indicating rains to the north and south of her. Where she sat, however, was calm, and she could inhale the sweet scents of earth and sea.

> It is a silver space between two rains,
> The lulling storm has given to the day
> An hour of windless air and riven gray.[20]

The issue of *Sunset* where "Between Two Rains" appeared also held an essay by Mary Austin on "literary myths." A scathing critique of the typical magazine offerings for women, Austin's essay lampooned the ridiculous plots in which wives secured their husband's fidelity by being faithful themselves.[21]

Oh, the shapes that stories bent women into. They offered women fantasies of duty rewarded, while for men, they offered sexy Bohemian girls wearing bonnets. Nora's ex-boyfriend Gelett Burgess also had a piece in that month's *Sunset*—a short story entitled "A San Francisco Flirtship." A thinly disguised portrait of the Bohemian crowd, it told of a man who introduces his girlfriend, Fancy Gray, to his chums at the restaurant where they regularly gather. In the course of the tale, Fancy cozies up to several of the men, enraging her original boyfriend. As she canoodles with one of his friends in a corner of the restaurant, he storms out, yelling, "You'll be sorry you threw me down, Fancy Gray! You want too many men on the string at once!"[22]

Fancy Gray. Nora May. Very clever. What a mistake Burgess had been. She remembered the numerous times Burgess had made her laugh, but now that his wit was aimed at her, she felt its sharpest edges.

She didn't have much time to dwell on him. Jimmy Hopper arrived at the bungalow, riding a horse, leading another in tow for her. They had planned the night before to ride through the hills. Nora could see Carrie raise an eyebrow as she and Jimmy headed out without other company, but she didn't care. Though obviously attracted to her, Jimmy always maintained a gentlemanly distance, respectful and courteous, but not off-putting or formal. He was in his own liminal space—a man who realized that while he loved his children, he had fallen out of love with their mother.

As their horses ambled up the hill, Jimmy assured Nora that she shouldn't worry about the Burgess story. Everyone considered him a bitter fool. But she had stopped even thinking about it, distracted by the rhythmic thump of her horse's hooves through the tall grasses. They had arrived at the sea cliffs, where they could look out over the ocean. Jimmy allowed enough silence for her to hear the rolling of the surf. She began to write another poem in her head.

> I face the tranquil day with tranquil eyes
> On high sea hills, my cheeks are cold with mist
> In white foam-fingers quick desire dies.
>
> Dies as a strangled bird the wave has torn—

Ay, drowns and dies this winged desire of mine
In white sea fingers of the tidal morn.

But I would kill the restless silken night
And I would still the wings that beat the dark,
And grasp the little throat of heart-delight,

And drown the savage will that understands
How love would laugh to clasp your bending head,
How love would hold your face in her two hands,

How love would press your angry lips apart,
And leave the willful bruising of her kiss,
In the sweet satin flesh above your heart.[23]

She would call it "The Panther Woman." Let the world think she existed for men to consume. She knew who she was.

Nora returned to the house to find George in the backyard, building an outkitchen to help her get through the winter. The Sterlings had invited her to stay on in the cabin, and she had accepted. She had nowhere else to go. With storms to the left and right, she would rest in this one last space of relative calm.

· · ·

On November 10, Carrie opened the door to find Bohemian Club member and amateur playwright William Greer Harrison standing on her veranda. "Greer," as George called him, had risen to prominence in the wake of the earthquake when he represented the insurance industry on the famed Committee of Fifty, the group of citizens charged with overseeing San Francisco's restoration. Of all the villains emerging from the earthquake, none provoked more universal hatred than the insurance men. They showed up at a pile of rubble, offered dazed people a fraction of what their house had been worth, and moved on to the next street. Then they ran out of money and stopped paying claims entirely. George hated Greer. He said of the man that he left a trail of slime wherever he went.[24]

But Greer's main offense to George was that he had charged Ambrose Bierce with precipitating a poet's suicide. In 1895, David Lesser Lezinsky shot himself in the head shortly after Bierce published a caustic review of his work. Lezinksy had been thirty-one years of age and suffered from periodic attacks of mania.[25] Lezinsky's own father had killed himself. Nevertheless, Greer had decided that it had been Bierce's criticism of the young man's poetry that had pushed him over the edge.

Airing his views in *The San Francisco Call*, Greer dubbed Bierce a "literary eunuch" and "the most complete literary failure of the century." Greer continued. "It would be easy to say of Mr. Bierce that he is a stuttering ape, a shambling idiot, an ill-visaged 'maphrodite, a literary monstrosity. . . . But that would be merely following Mr. Bierce's later and most objectionable methods."[26] And so on, for a column and a half.

Carrie showed Greer into the living room and invited him to sit while she called George into the house. It was George's last night in town before he was due at the Realty Syndicate for at least a week. She found him in the yard chopping wood to make sure she and Nora would have enough until he returned. As soon as George and Greer were together, Carrie ran back outside to alert Nora that a scene was to unfold in the living room that should not be missed. Nora grinned, rubbed her hands together, and followed Carrie into the house.

George had brought out the muscatel bottle and was offering some to Greer, knowing full well that Greer was a teetotaler. He made a great show of filling glasses for Carrie, Nora, and of course himself while Greer drank water. Greer soon turned to the subject of his visit. He was considering retirement in Carmel. He had been alerted, however, that Ambrose Bierce had recently visited. He wanted to know if Bierce had made an offer on a house. Carrie asked for a refill of muscatel from George, and Nora, sensing things were about to get interesting, raised her glass as well. There was little Carrie enjoyed more than the spectacle of men revealing that they were just as petty as they accused women of being, especially when it came to their neighbors.

Greer started in on Bierce delicately but then opened the full throttle of his disdain, suggesting that Carmel would be a less attractive place should Bierce decide to move there. George raised his hand to stop him and cleared his throat. He told Greer that if he wanted to extend his already libelous smears of Bierce, he would have to do it in some other house than his. Then he got up, opened the door, and dramatically swept his arm to indicate the path for Greer to exit.

Greer for a moment looked stunned, his white mustache twitching. He rose from his chair, straightening his coat.

Carrie held out her hand. Greer took it in his and raised it to his lips. They were dry, not slimy. He moved on to Nora.

Nora couldn't withdraw her hand quickly enough.

Greer tapped on his hat, nodded curtly to George, and left.

George shut the door harder than necessary, and Nora howled in laugher.

Carrie tried to contain herself until Greer was out of earshot but couldn't.

They refilled their glasses and toasted George for ridding Carmel of the odious Greer.[27]

Nora began patting George on the back.

Carrie kissed her brave husband on the cheek.

Nora threw her arms around them both.

They laughed so hard they all almost fell over.[28]

Chapter Eleven

꘎

Cover Girl

The San Francisco Examiner, NOVEMBER 15, 1907

MIDNIGHT LURE OF DEATH LEADS POETESS TO GRAVE

Nora M. French Drinks Acid in Poet's Home

Dies in Few Minutes as Mrs. George Sterling Frantically Chaffs Colds Hands.

Had Beauty, Suitors, Fame and Many Friends.

But Brooded Constantly Over Ill-Health—Sister Is Prostrated.

Actors in the Tragedy of a Poetess:

Nora May French, writer of verse.

Mrs. George Sterling, wife of author of "A Wine of Wizardry."

James Hopper, author.

Fred Bechdolt, author.

Dr. Beck, who sold poetess cyanide of potassium.

Uncle of Poetess, minister with a suicide theory.

Scene—George Sterling's bungalow at Carmel-by-
the-Sea.

Time—Midnight.

At the final stroke of midnight Nora May French put poison to her beautiful lips—lips that in all reason should have had the happy seal of love and marriage placed upon them by some one chosen from her many admirers—and in a moment was herself "with yesterday's ten thousand years."

Cyanide of potassium was the means to this sad end. So passed her soul, winging its way from the wooded shore where seemingly the most lightsome of her hours had been spent.

Every blessing was hers, save the one priceless possession of perfect health. What impelled her to destroy herself, who can say with certainty? She left no message in that last hour. She made no sign. . . .

Some little time ago the stately young beauty felt that her health was failing and that she needed a change. Her sister went to Los Angeles and she found a congenial home with Mr. and Mrs. George Sterling at Carmel-by-the-Sea. There the Sterlings have a charming home just at the edge of the pines, with an outlook upon the wondrous valley of the Carmel mission.

In this atmosphere of balsamic aromas and sea breezes her health rapidly improved and her natural robustness seemed about to return. She found also a congenial literary atmosphere, as there is the nucleus of a fine literary and artistic colony at Carmel and across the hills at Monterey. Her constant associates were the Sterlings, Mary Austin, Mr. and Mrs. James Hopper and the others of their brilliant coterie.

. . .

My son stops typing and turns to me: "This reads like an advertisement for the Sterlings, and it's supposed to be about this woman who died?"

My son has been on winter break from high school and bored, so I gave him a job: type the very long *San Francisco Examiner* story reporting Nora May French's death. Yes, I resorted to child labor. This is a story about the life of women writers, so you might as well have the truth: We are opportunists.

The *Examiner* story on Nora's death does read like an advertisement for the Sterlings, for their friends, for their publications, and for all of Carmel. On November 15, 1907, California readers picked up their paper to find a tableau of Nora's death dominating the front page. "Sketched from a recent portrait by Arnold Genthe," Nora's luminous eyes and gently cascading curls take up the top of the illustration. George Sterling appears just below, in Dante-esque profile, his eyes cast downward. Another inset shows Mary Austin with Nora discussing her novel featuring a suicide. Below that, Nora wearing a flowing robe and holding a glass of water stares at a grandfather clock, awaiting the stroke of midnight.

Such illustrations were typical of newspapers one hundred years ago. The line between "news" and "tabloid" was very thin. The trial of the multimillionaire Harry Thaw, shooter of the famed architect Stanford White, had set the standard for reporting high-profile dramatic deaths in exotic locations. Thaw had felled White at the rooftop theater of Madison Square Garden, allegedly over White's rape of Thaw's wife, Mrs. Evelyn Nesbit Thaw, when she had been a teen. The daughter of an uneducated seamstress who became a chorus girl at New York's Floradora Club, Evelyn Nesbit achieved national fame when Charles Dana Gibson used her as the model for his 1903 portrait *Woman, the Eternal Question*. In it, Gibson drew her hair draped over her shoulder fancifully, in the shape of a question mark. Women. Who can figure them out?

At the trial of her husband, Mrs. Thaw testified that Stanford White drugged and then raped her when she was only sixteen. She spared no detail: How she went to a luncheon with a friend to meet White. How her skirt was short and her hair was long. How she and her friend were taken to a room that featured a swing suspended on velvet cords with a screen with a Japanese print hanging from the ceiling. How she swung on it with her friend till their feet broke through the print. How White sent a car to get her at a later date for a party, but when she arrived, no other guests were there. How the glass of champagne White gave her made her head spin and everything go dark. How she woke up naked next to White, also naked. How the room had mirrors on the walls, floor, and ceiling. How she screamed and White made her promise never to tell a soul. How he told her, "Women in society were clever," and she should be like them and keep her mouth shut. She should also not get fat.[1]

It was dubbed "The Trial of the Century." The transcript was so lurid that the Women's Christian Temperance Union and the National League of Catholic Women called for an embargo on the publication of verbatim transcripts. They feared naive girls would take Mrs. Thaw's experience as advice on how to get a rich patron, rather than read it as a cautionary tale of a ruined girl. The newspapers worked around these restrictions as much as possible. If newspapers had learned anything in 1907, it was that while the New Women's accomplishments sold some papers, their scandals sold many, many more.

In April 1907, a deadlocked jury in the Thaw trial left journalists scrambling for the next beautiful face. *The San Francisco Examiner* in November 1907 was doing its utmost to convince the nation that that girl was Nora May French. If Nora May French and the Sterlings were not quite as high-profile as Stanford White and the Thaws, they would work with what they had. The West Coast needed its own girl to die for.

There was no trial over Nora May French's death, but there was an inquest later in the day at which witnesses gave their testimony to a jury hastily convened by the Monterey County coroner. Dr. Beck affirmed that Nora May French had bought the cyanide from the Carmel Pharmacy the morning of her death. Jimmy Hopper and his roommate, Fred Bechdolt, both of whom had been awakened by Carrie in the middle of the night to come to Nora's aid, testified that Nora was already dead when they arrived.

But Carrie Sterling had been the only person home with Nora the night she died. Carrie and Nora had been alone in the bungalow since November 11, when George returned to Oakland for work. Just as newspapers across the globe had printed "Mrs. Thaw's Story" in full (before the embargo, that is), Carrie's testimony was given several column inches under the headline "Mrs. Sterling's Story"—supposedly a verbatim transcript of what she told the jury in the hours after Nora died. Let me prepare you. It is, in my considered opinion, one bananas account:

Nora May and I retired early last night, about 10
o'clock, and Nora May seemed to be in most cheerful
mood. We slept in the same room in separate beds.
Between the beds was a small table. I was awakened by
the creaking of the bathroom door just as the clock was
striking midnight. I called out, "Is that you, Nora May?"
She answered, "Yes, I want a drink of water." I heard
her pour a glass of water and then return to the room
and lie down on the bed. A few seconds after I heard
a strange catching noise in her throat. I lit a match.
Nora May lay back on the bed stiff. There was foam at
her lips. I thought she had hysterics. I said, "Now you
be good, Nora May." The foam went away, the catching
noise stopped, her face became normal and then pale. I
thought she was getting better. I put wet towels around
her head. I sat on the edge of the bed until I became
chilled. Then, finding her cold, I got into the bed beside
her, to warm her. While lying there trying to warm her
I saw on the table a glass at the bottom of which was
a white powder sediment. I ran out of the room and
looked up a medical book in the library. Mary Austin,
the author, is writing a book in which the heroine kills
herself with cyanide of potassium, and I remembered
that Nora May asked all about the effects of cyanide of
potassium, and I looked for an antidote. Then I became
frightened and ran across the stretch of woods and the
sand dunes to the home of James Hopper and Fred
Bechdolt, the writers.

I first read Carrie's account on microfilm, the predigital
world's solution to preserving degrading documents like old

newspapers. Microfilm is the bane of archival research. You have to load spools of low-grade film stock onto glitchy viewing machines, then fiddle with the focus, then scan through sometimes hundreds of pages to find the one you want. After reading Carrie's account, I rolled my chair back from the machine and stared into space for a minute. Then I rolled forward and read it again. And again.

Carrie's description of the physical stages Nora went through as she died seem plausible enough. Death by ingestion of potassium salt of hydrocyanic acid, or "potassium cyanide," is quick but not pretty. Once ingested, it releases hydrogen cyanide gas, which asphyxiates the victim by cutting off major organ systems from oxygen, resulting in respiratory arrest. Fluid can gather in the lungs and, mixed with carbon dioxide, produce foam at the mouth. Cyanide also attacks the central nervous system, causing muscle stiffness and rigidity just as Carrie described.

So far so good in terms of matching Carrie's account. What I struggle with are Carrie's reported reactions to Nora's distress. I try to imagine the scene as Carrie paints it: Nora's stiffness, the foam at her mouth, the "catching sound," which would have been her choking. At the point at which Nora became pale, she was either already dead or near to it. But Carrie looks at an unresponsive Nora and concludes that she is getting better. Why, then, go for wet towels? Why would she sit on the edge of the bed after placing the towels around Nora's head? How would Carrie sit at such a moment? Facing her friend, who is lying stiff? Facing away? A blanket around the shoulders to ward off the chill? At what point did Carrie conclude that it was time to warm (the still wet, presumably) Nora by joining her in bed?

Is it even possible to hold someone for an entire hour before you realize that they're dead?

Whenever I'm puzzled by an account that seems, for lack of a better word, inconsistent, my next step is to scour my other sources for corroboration. I find nothing in the Sterlings' diary. November 13 begins in Carrie's hand: "Another perfect day. Nora May and I had coffee and toast on the front porch at ten AM." George's hand finished out the entry, simply remarking "Phyllis killed herself with cyanide of potassium at midnight."[2] These two entries back to back are jarring in their spareness, though George does use the nickname Nora most preferred.

I look next at the Sterlings' correspondence. The day after the death, Carrie wrote Blanche an account of Nora's final moments similar to what the *Examiner* reported, but she added the detail that Nora had experienced some convulsions: "The poison caused the blood to rush to her face & after a few spasmodic movements of her arms she lay so quiet with flushed face & her lips apart like scarlet threads & her heavy white eyelids drooping half way over her queer luminous eyes—She died in less than a minute but I didn't know she was dead & lay by her side an hour trying to *warm* her. God."[3]

Convulsions are certainly in keeping with death by cyanide. But reading this account only makes me doubt Carrie even more. If Carrie's story is to be believed, she watched Nora flush, convulse, and then lay still with her eyes half-open. Then Carrie got into bed with her and tried to warm her up for an hour. And then she realized her mistake and ran to Hopper and Bechdolt's cabin for help.

The *Enquirer*'s play-by-play of Nora's death throes is not even the most sensational, nor the most dubious, element of "Mrs. Sterling's Story." Carrie revealed that Nora had attempted suicide on Monday, two days before that fateful night. According to Carrie, Nora had taken George's revolver to the woods and tried to shoot herself. Nora explained that she had once been told by a morbid and depressive uncle that if she ever felt suicidal, the best way to do it would be to sit down in a pasture near an approaching shadow, like that of a tree located not too far off, and imagine that shadow as Death. Then, at the moment the shadow touched her, she was to fire a shot at her head.

The *Examiner* described Nora's failed attempt as if it had been eyewitnessed: "She shot away just one golden curl from her fair head, and the breeze played pranks with the bit of hair that lovers would have fought over. She picked up the hair and returned to the house. . . . Nora May French came tripping in, bearing the curl in triumph. That night she told Mrs. Sterling how she had intended death and made all her preparations, and then how she couldn't bear the shock of the rude bullet in her brain."[4] Carrie testified that Nora appeared as though she had been cured of the impulse and would not make another attempt. This incident was illustrated in the *Examiner*'s report: Nora sitting under a tree branch, her head tilted upward, her eyes closed, a revolver held at an oblique angle next to her head, poised to pull the trigger.

Again, I'm looking for any material in the archives that would corroborate this event. Nora did have minister uncles on both sides of her family, including a brother of her father's who spent much time living with the French family after they moved to California. I can well imagine Nora's relatives were worried that her periodic depressions would result in a suicide attempt. This conversation about suicide may have occurred and may even have been relayed in some form to Carrie.

But I struggle to reconcile the physics involved with shooting off a lock of hair near to your head, particularly without causing noticeable hearing loss, or leaving visible gunpowder residue, or producing some other remarkable change. And I can find no other source in the archives that mentions the event. Carrie didn't note it in the diary on the date Nora allegedly almost blew her brains out, which is not surprising. But the day after the attempt, Carrie records that she and Nora had dinner with Jimmy Hopper, Fred Bechdolt, and Mrs. Hale. Afterward, the group went to take dance class at the Arts and Crafts Club. A normal Carmel evening, in other words.

I look at the correspondence. No letters between members of the Carmel set refer to Nora's suicide attempt, either at the time or afterward. George had written to Blanche shortly after Nora's split with Hiley that Nora had asked him for some morphine, which worried him. He also remarked that she had stopped bathing and was not very "appetizing."[5] She was at that point notably depressed. But following her second visit with her sister, the correspondence suggests that Nora was back to her merry self.

Like most of the other details of Nora's death, the story of suicide attempt by gun has one source only: Carrie Sterling.

．．．

George, in Oakland, received a wire from Carmel early on the morning of November 14 telling him of Nora's death. He quickly relayed the news to Lafler, who left San Francisco for Monterey immediately on the 8:00 a.m. train. George followed on the afternoon train, arriving in Carmel at 3:00 p.m. Alan Hiley came in from Santa Cruz that evening.

The coroner's men had taken Nora's body to Monterey. Hiley and Lafler went there to sit with her corpse all night, each to one side, glaring at each other lest either man presume to be the more bereaved. George stayed at the bungalow and recorded that he slept in his own bed, but not soundly.[6] The next day on a walk he found

Nora's whistle—the one that she always wore around her neck on hikes—hanging from the limb of a pine tree near the house; nobody could account for what it was doing there.

Helen French had just returned from an afternoon of holly gathering in the Los Angeles hills when she got the news. Jimmy Hopper met her at the Monterey train station and drove her to Carmel, where Carrie settled her into the guest room. That evening in the bungalow, Carrie, Helen, and Fred Bechdolt gathered up Nora's belongings. Someone had said Nora's wish was that her earthly possessions be burned upon her death. Into the fire went her favorite khaki suit, her velvet cloak, and her leather gaiters. Then the trio walked to the Carmel Mission in the moonlight. On the way back, they sat at the mouth of the Carmel River and stared wordlessly out to sea.[7]

George and Jimmy had already left for San Francisco, George to pick up Nora's ashes at the crematorium, while Jimmy made straight for the *Examiner* desk to turn in his notes from the inquest. The hand he had in shaping the story of Nora's death must have been considerable, if he didn't write it completely himself (there is no byline). Notably, the report was phrased to avoid any hint of romance between Nora and George. The stakes could not have been higher. Even the merest suggestion would have provoked the average reader to wonder why Nora wound up dead and if Carrie had a hand in it. George and Jimmy would have had the entire trip up to San Francisco to discuss how to quash any speculation that the Sterlings were in a ménage with Nora. In the end, the report only gently alluded to Nora's long history of involvements with men of the Bohemian set; it divulged only that one writer was disappointed at not winning her affection, but that she had been engaged to a respectable Englishman at the time of her death. George Sterling was simply a friend who had supported Nora's poetry. He was quoted as saying she wrote the best sonnets of any young poet he knew.[8]

The *Enquirer*'s report goes on for an astonishing several pages. I kept reading through it to see if there were any questions from the jury, if the coroner proposed an autopsy, if the police were alerted, or if any other investigation had been undertaken to reconcile the bizarre circumstances under which Nora died. But if the jury assembled for the inquest had any questions of Carrie's testimony, they were unrecorded in history.

Could there be any more definitive sign that Caroline Rand Sterling had made it in society? Whereas Evelyn Nesbit Thaw was treated in her husband's trial as a tramp who had married up, few knew that Carrie's early life had also been shaped by a father who died too young, leaving a mother to take in boarders to pay the rent. Carrie's marriage to George Sterling (and more so her sister Lila's to Frank Havens) had erased her humble beginnings from the record. Carrie moved in the highest social circles. Her Carmel neighbors (who undoubtedly made up the jury) had seen even former mayor James Phelan come to call. They had witnessed journalists from East Coast newspapers travel thousands of miles to interview George. They knew of the Sterlings' generosity after the earthquake. So of course Carrie sailed through the inquest. The *Enquirer* asserted that although she had been "forthright" and undramatic in giving her testimony, the jury was nevertheless moved to tears by her words: "As Mrs. Sterling testified, the jury wept. No sadder tale had ever been told in the pretty village in the pines by the sea."[9]

While Jimmy was working his connections at the *Examiner* desk, Blanche had contacted her former employer *The San Francisco*

Call, using her influence to redirect any taint of scandal away from the Sterlings. The *Call*'s coverage of Nora's death was particularly dishonest. It asserted that Miss French had been staying with the Sterlings in Carmel for only two weeks, when in fact she had used them as her home base for several months and was intending to stay on for the foreseeable future. But the *Call* also reported that a close friend of Nora's in San Francisco "whose veracity cannot be questioned" received a telepathic message from Nora at the moment she drank the cyanide. This friend (unnamed—but obviously Blanche) "saw the act in a dream—saw the poison lifted to the girl's lips, and saw her writhing in the death agony."[10] No longer could a reader claim that Carrie was the only witness to Nora's last breath. Her testimony had been psychically corroborated.

I can only imagine that the readers of the *Call* raised an eyebrow but quickly moved on to worrying about the tanking economy. Nora May French's death was not the only high-profile suicide reported in the nation's papers that week. On the morning of November 14, 1907, the banker Charles T. Barney pointed a .32 at his abdomen and fired while his wife entertained a guest downstairs. Barney had recently resigned his position as president of the Knickerbocker Trust Company after his careless speculations sparked that year's massive financial panic. The Knickerbocker had been one of the bigger New York banks, operating from its headquarters in a stately building designed by McKim, Mead, and White at Thirty-Fourth Street and Fifth Avenue. (Yes, *that* White. Charles Barney partied with Stanford White regularly and financed his activities with young women.) Barney, a key investor in New York's subway system because he had invested heavily in Upper West Side properties, had unwisely associated himself with a dubious attempt to corner the market in copper. When the market collapsed, hundreds of Knickerbocker's depositors rushed to the bank to withdraw their funds.[11]

Bankers of the Gilded Age being a close-knit group, there was an oblique connection between Nora and Charles T. Barney. Barney's father, Ashbel, had been a president of Wells Fargo and Company. Ashbel's brother Danford had served as president of Wells Fargo before him, remaining on the board of directors until Henry Wells stepped down. Danford had been responsible for negotiating the complex mergers that established Henry Wells's monopoly over the express industry while keeping it from the public eye.

By 1907, the public had lost enough money that they were beginning to view bankers as threats rather than as saviors. They wanted bankers to suffer for their misdeeds. The press obliged by dragging Barney's immediate and extended family through the mud with accusations of infidelity with Parisian mistresses and impending divorce. But all bankers were up for reappraisal in the public eye. Below the fold from the illustration of Nora holding a gun to her temple, the *Examiner* reported, "Morgan Can't Get French Bank Gold," referring to J. P. Morgan's failed attempt to secure $20 million worth of bullion from France to bail out American banks.[12] Next to it, "Gould Grilled as Beneath Contempt" revealed the embarrassing details emerging from the divorce proceedings of the banker Jay Gould's son Howard (including Howard's charge that his wife had cuckolded him with Buffalo Bill).

Helen French would have known that had the Wells name been attached to Nora's, the salivating public would have cheered one more confirmation of the moral turpitude of banker families. Remarkably, for all the name-dropping the newspapers did to raise the profile of Carmel's writers, they remained silent on the subject of Nora May French's illustrious family connections. Not one of the many newspapers coast to coast covering Nora May French's death mentioned her connection to the family of Henry Wells. None mentioned she was the granddaughter of former Illinois governor Augustus French. Her father was identified only as a man employed in an old soldiers' home. Of the two sisters, Helen seemed to be prouder of her extended family connections; her notes contributed to the Bancroft Library on the subject of her life with her sister dwell for the most part on their relationship to Henry Wells, a man neither of them had ever met and the head of a family they had been cut off from entirely. Helen would not want to smear the legacy of the Wells name with any connection to her sister's scandalous life and death. As a result, Nora May French died without her pedigree—the stain of suicide hers alone to bear.

"Every blessing was hers, save the one priceless possession of perfect health," the *Examiner* concluded. If only this had been true. To me, this lie—that Nora squandered everything she had been blessed with—is the big lie that encompasses all the little ones. For if ever there was a life cursed by the actions of neglectful and malignant men—from her father's embezzlement right through to George Sterling's predation—it was that of Nora May French. She died covered in shame so that they could be remembered in glory.

. . .

On November 21, George returned to Carmel with Nora's ashes. Walking under a bright moon from the Carmel stagecoach stop in the center of town, he met Jimmy Hopper and Alan Hiley on the path. Lafler arrived in Carmel around 9:00 p.m. It was a quiet evening as they reflected on the task before them.

The next morning, everyone arose and dressed somberly. George got the car to drive himself, Carrie, and Nora's ashes to Nora's favorite spot on Point Lobos. Helen, Jimmy, Bechdolt, and Hiley traveled to the point on horseback. Lafler had decided to walk there earlier and was waiting for them all when they arrived.

They had given the *San Francisco Chronicle* an advance scoop on their memorial service for Nora, except they told the papers they would throw Nora's ashes from Cypress Point, just off 17-Mile Drive. They lied deliberately to foil journalists and nosy neighbors. The Sterling diary reveals that they instead made for Point Lobos.[13]

This exclusive ceremony suggests that their authority over Nora's body had become absolute. The *Chronicle* reported that Nora's friends, the only ones who had cared for her, "well known in the field of letters," would send her to her rest. No one, the *Chronicle* admonished, should inquire further into the circumstances of her passing: "Those who knew Miss French well, who understood her life, need no explanation of her leave-taking." But as a partial explanation, they printed Nora's poem "The Outer Gate," as if to say Nora had suicide in her very soul:

> Life said: "My house is thine with all its store;
> Behold, I open shining ways to thee—
> Of every inner portal make thee free:
> O child, I may not bar the outer door.
> Go from me if thou wilt, to come no more;
> But all thy pain is mine, thy flesh of me;
> And I must hear thee, faint and woefully,
> Call on me from the darkness and implore?"

Nay, mother, for I follow at thy will.
But oftentimes thy voice is sharp to hear,
The trailing fragrance heavy on the breath;
Always the outer hall is very still,
And on my face a pleasant wind and clear,
Blows straitly from the narrow gate of Death.[14]

The *Chronicle* reported that no speeches, no verses, no music, would accompany the casting of Nora's ashes. Only silence, "broken, if Nature so wills it, only by the swish of the waters or of the wind filtering through the pines."[15] On the day itself, however, the silence was shattered when the men got into a heated argument about which of them would have the honor of doing the actual casting. The argument ended when George grabbed the urn and threw Nora's remains past the rocks and into the sea.[16]

The group stayed at Point Lobos all afternoon. The surf was high, the water colder than usual. George and Jimmy swam for mussels, their skin freezing the moment they stepped into the rock pool. On the way home, the sunset left a rosy afterglow on the hills, tentacles of pink clouds radiating from the spot where the sun dipped below the horizon.[17]

. . .

That was supposed to be the end of it. Case closed. But despite the *Chronicle*'s quick foreclosure on speculation over the reasons for Nora's suicide, her possible motivations were dissected in the national press. Newspapers offered their own theories about why she had killed herself. Boston readers were told she had been depressed over a failed love affair.[18] In Albuquerque, the news reported she had been brooding over a story she'd been unable to finish.[19] Hardened Chicagoans were told she had tired of life,[20] whereas in Oregon, the story would be that she had been in excellent health, her life running smoothly.[21] Citizens of Plymouth, Indiana, heard that she had learned of suicide by cyanide of potassium from a book written by Miss Mary Austin, an Illinois native, who, they were told, also lived with the Sterlings.[22]

In Australia, Jack London read of Nora's death in a copy of the *Los Angeles Times*. After an arduous journey from Hawaii to Sydney on the *Snark*, he and Charmian were barely more than wraiths. In the Solomon Islands they had been greeted by residents with bows and arrows, rifles, spears, and war clubs. They escaped, but then the whole crew succumbed to one tropical virus after another. The *Snark*, Jack wrote, had become "a hospital ship," with no man well enough or trustworthy enough to aid him in navigating the waters.[23] Some of the crew had even gone crazy from fever. Jack arrived in Australia close to insanity himself, with painful, itching psoriasis and a fistula in his bowels that required surgery. He was in the hospital when he learned of Nora's suicide. He read in the *Times*, "Mrs. Sterling is prostrated by the affair."[24]

"Carrie didn't mind the suicide, and was not rattled a bit, much less 'prostrated,'"[25] George wrote in response to Jack's letter, when it finally reached him. They weren't surprised by the suicide, he explained. Nora had been swearing to do it for months. "She had no particular reason, just no taste for the poor compensations of living." But George also confessed to Jack that unlike Carrie, he was more than rattled: "Gee I wish I could stop thinking about that poor girl!"[26]

In a letter to Bierce, George was more circumspect with his feelings. He wrote, "Her death has made Carmel, and our home, more beautiful than ever to us, because she did us the honor of dying in my house. And it has brought Carrie and me very near together."[27] Carrie had written almost identical sentiments to

Blanche the evening the *Examiner* article appeared: "I feel she is happier so why be selfish & wish it undone—If she chose this place to die in I am sure I do not mind & the atmosphere will be sweeter with her parting breath. It was hard to go thro' but it's past and I am so old, oh so old & wise."[28]

This similarity between these sentiments is uncanny. And suspicious. George and Carrie must have agreed upon an account of Nora's death to pass on to their friends.

After reading this correspondence, I am more unsure than ever what really happened the night Nora died. I look back to the Sterling diary to reconstruct the days before the death to see if there are any clues I missed. On the morning of Monday, November 11, George awoke early and departed in the Carmel fog to catch the first train from Monterey to Oakland. Frank Havens needed his help urgently. He knew the coming economic downturn would be worse even than the recession of 1893 to 1897, only this time, Frank Havens would not have the capital to take advantage of the misery of others.[29] J. P. Morgan had gathered the heads of the trusts to create a money pool, which provided some relief to New York, while President Roosevelt assured the nation that the crisis was over. But the price of American securities was still tumbling abroad, and the runs on the banks continued. Banks were forced to suspend withdrawals, causing another blow to confidence.[30] Under the circumstances, George would be gone for at least a week.

Carrie's entry for November 11 reads simply: "Sun came out forenoon & beautiful day followed. George left for Oakland on early train. Nora May & I alone." Not very revealing. Carrie only ever wrote in the diary when George was out of town, though sometimes she editorialized. Early in their life there, when George had recorded that he had caught and prepared snails for them to eat, Carrie had added, "Rotten—CS." George had replied "No, not so bad—GS."

But as Carrie was tasked with recording the events while George was gone, she would have had ample opportunity to read his most recent entries. George had captured the dizziness of the previous weeks, the onslaught of guests as well as the odd mishaps, which included wrestling an octopus and nearly being swept off the rocks of Point Lobos by high surf. He had noted that Jimmy and Nora had gone out riding together in the hills.

Paging further, Carrie would have seen George's entry for November 5: "Had a poker game from 4 to 6 with Jimmy, Bechdolt, Carrie, NORA MAY FRENCH and I. C and I won $1.00."

NORA MAY FRENCH.

George had written Nora's name in all capital letters, taking up nearly a whole line. He had done it again on October 30, marking his return from Oakland when he brought "NORA MAY FRENCH" with him. As all poets do, George thought carefully about every word. He used all caps rarely, reserving them for things he truly loved, like MUSSELS. And sometimes his own name.

Carrie would have noticed.

She wrote to Blanche that on the night of Nora's death, she and Nora had been up late talking about love and disappointment. It had been their most intimate conversation to date. "I loved Nora May & she told me the night she died that I & her sister were the only two women who had loved & been kind to her."[31]

We will never know what words passed between Nora and Carrie that night. Carrie's letter to Blanche doesn't reveal any more details. She only says of Nora, "She played the game—She died looking so beautiful."[32]

These words haunt me. When Carrie referred to "the game," she only ever meant one thing: the game of doing what you needed to do to advance yourself in the world. Which leaves me with this last question, unanswerable given the available documents:

At exactly what point did Carrie learn Nora was pregnant? Because certainly by the time she stood on the black rocks and watched her husband pour the ashes into the ocean, she knew he was throwing away the remains of two.

Chapter Twelve

၆၈၈၉

Femme Fatale

ON APRIL 22, 1908, THE POLICEMAN JOSEPH F. LYMAN WAS WALKING his usual beat in Prospect Park, Brooklyn, when he saw a dead body on a bench. A brand-new .22-caliber revolver lay on the ground nearby. The victim, a slim but well-dressed youth with fair skin, dark brown hair, and blue eyes, had taken one shot to the heart, his body shrouded in a black coat and vest, striped trousers, buttoned shoes, and a striped shirt secured with a brown cravat. His underwear was spun from camel's hair. His black derby hat, embossed with the initials "R. P.," gave a clue to his identity.

Russell Peck—he would eventually be identified by his optician, whose name was on his spectacles case—was a seventeen-year-old clerk at the five-story colonnaded central offices of the American Express Co. at 65 Broadway, a grim stretch of street in 1908. Six months before, the area had been mobbed with depositors crushing against one another, desperate to withdraw their money from the banks before it vanished. Although it was again possible to walk Wall Street's narrow, shadowed alleys, now that the initial run on the banks had faded, the effects of the crash lingered as unemployment had more than doubled and bankruptcies had reached their second-highest peak in American history.

At first blush, this well-dressed young man appeared to be yet another casualty of the financial crisis, one more disappointed would-be millionaire added to the spike in suicides at the time. Lyman searched the pockets of the young man's jacket for a suicide note but couldn't find one. Instead, he discovered a newspaper clipping referencing the death of a young woman in New York who had poisoned herself five months before, imitating the widely reported suicide of the poet Nora May French in November 1907 at the arts colony in Carmel-by-the-Sea, California. A poem of French's had been reprinted by the newspaper:

SUICIDE

I tilt my hallowed life and look within:
The wine it held has left a purple trace—
Behold, a stain where happiness had been.
If I should shatter down this empty vase.
Through what abyss would my soul be tossed
To meet its Judge in undiscovered lands?
What sentence meted me, alone and lost,
Before him with the fragments in my hands?
Better the patient earth, that loves me still,
Should drip her clearness on this purple stain;
Better my life, upheld to her, should fill
With limpid dew and gradual gift of rain.

"NORA FRENCH"

Without a suicide note to clarify his intentions, the press attributed Peck's death to French's poem, not the desperate times of financial panic, not his recent losses at the pool halls (revealed in hushed tones by his coworkers), nor any other misfortunes of his own life. He simply had been lured to death by lyric—"fatal literature," New York's *Evening World* called it. Peck was the third victim of French's "Suicide" poem, the paper reported, which the poetess had written at the home of "Mr. Stirling" of Monterey. The girl mentioned in the article who had killed herself (she was said to have kept a scrapbook of French's "Suicide Verses") was the second casualty. The poem's first victim, the poet herself. Who would be next?[1]

• • •

Carrie read to the end of the article. At least they had spelled "Sterling" wrong—thank goodness for small mercies. Next to the article on Peck, *The Evening World* had a profile on her neighbor, the writer Grace MacGowan Cooke, who had just been sued by her husband for divorce. Against his charge that she had chosen to write rather than devote herself to childcare, Grace maintained that she wasn't doing anything different than what men did. She worked to support her children. Women, she affirmed, shouldn't have children unless they were prepared for the eventuality that they might have to support them. "I can see no objection even to her supporting her own husband," she proclaimed.

Two articles on the women of Carmel on one page. Had the papers nobody else to write about? Soon none of them would be able to breathe without a journalist covering it.

Carrie and George had spent most of the winter away from Carmel in the Piedmont. Frank Havens had made George an irresistible offer to lure him back to work: $300 a week, plus free room and board. George could pull in another $80 a month renting their Piedmont house, because they wouldn't need to live there.[2] Instead, they would be put up in the Havenses' mansion, Wildwood, a $1.5 million, twenty-eight-room palace designed by the famed architect Bernard Maybeck.[3] In keeping with Mrs. Havens's fascination with the exotic, the house exterior looked like a Cambodian temple, the interior done up in abundant gold leaf and Burmese teak. Antique Ming rugs lined the floors. An opium-smoking bed graced Frank's billiard room. A Chinese temple within the house featured a two-thousand-year-old drum brought from the ruins of Angkor Wat. Mrs. Havens practiced her yoga in front of it, her thick ankles wobbling. Consistent with her recently acquired understanding of Asian design principles, no portraits or other paintings were allowed on the walls. Instead, Mrs. Havens imported artisans and their families and paid them to carve doors and cornices. They had been put up in temporary housing around the property, which was being landscaped with ornate gardens.[4]

Carrie took full advantage of the respite from cooking and cleaning, but all George could do was mope. His job had become more taxing than ever, he complained. Havens had been sloppy and even malfeasant with the books, using one deal to finance another before anything had really closed. Complicating matters, key financial documents had burned (or so Havens said—George had his doubts) in the fire of 1906. When pressed to remember even the broad outlines of his deals, Frank was less than forthcoming. George was following a vanishing—and in some cases, wholly imaginary—trail to bring the records into alignment.[5]

The effort seemed to have deranged him. On a grim, rainy

Sunday in early February, George had gone to the Oakland Public Library to look a word up in the dictionary and gotten into a fight with the janitor. In the janitor's account, he met Mr. Sterling in the reference room and informed him that it was Sunday, and being Sunday, the reference room was closed. He also pointed out that Mr. Sterling had tracked mud onto floors that had just been mopped.

Insulted, flabbergasted, George wrote a letter to the board of the Oakland Library detailing how poorly he had been treated. The "sub janitor," as he called him, a menace to citizens, an irresponsible hoodlum, etc., etc., had verbally assaulted him for the crime of consulting a dictionary. The name of Sterling, Havens, or at least the Realty Syndicate should mean something to the board, he declared. He expected quick action in the dismissal of his assailant.

The board asked the janitor to apologize to George to settle the matter, but the janitor refused to back down. He told the board that Mr. Sterling had responded to the request to leave a closed area with the threat: "If you think you can put me out, try it." Not only did the janitor refuse to apologize, he stated that on reflection, he should have taken Mr. Sterling up on his offer and busted his jaw to show him who the better man was.

The board kept the janitor on, having no real cause to fire him.

"Poet Sterling Demands Scalp of a Janitor" was *The San Francisco Call*'s headline of choice to report the incident, just days before George and Carrie's twelfth wedding anniversary.[6] The *Call* included Sterling's photo (in profile), identifying him as the author of "A Wine of Wizardry," which had been pronounced the greatest poem of all time by Ambrose Bierce. Perhaps, the article jested, Sterling had mistaken the janitor for the "blue-eyed vampire" of his poem.

George had managed to take a minor misunderstanding and make it a public embarrassment, duplicating, possibly even outdoing, Jack London's fight with the Piedmont grocer. Carrie dropped the paper in George's lap and kept walking.

Meanwhile, the public mourning of Nora May French continued. *Sunset*'s February issue included a memorial page to Nora (as well as yet another Klondike story by Jack—he really could crank them out by the yard). Several newspapers announced that *Sunset* had published the last photo taken of Miss French by Genthe. Carrie looked at the photo. More than any other, it captured Nora's sadness. Instead of her khaki suit, she was wearing a flowing white gown that bared her beautiful collarbones in the half-light. Eyes cast downward, hair framing her face, she looked like a woman for once, not a girl.[7]

Below Genthe's photo, *Sunset* had printed Nora's poem "Ave Atque Vale," which she had submitted the week before she died, though she had composed it years earlier.

> Now nothing is the same, old visions move me,
> I wander silent through the waning land,
> And find, for youth and little leaves to love me,
> The old, old lichen crumbling in my hand.
>
> What shifting films of distance fold you, blind you,
> This windy eve of dreams, I can not tell;
> I know through some strange mist they grope to
>   find you—
> These hands that give you Greeting and Farewell.[8]

In February, the Havenses announced they wanted to go down to the Monterey Peninsula. Carrie didn't miss Carmel at all,

Nora as a child.

*The Bancroft Library,
University of California, Berkeley*

Nora May French; her mother,
Mary; sister, Helen; brother,
Henry; father, Edward; and two
guests in Aurora, NY.

*The Bancroft Library, University of
California, Berkeley*

George and Carrie Sterling
in the Piedmont.

*Jack London Papers, The Huntington
Library, San Marino, CA*

Carrie, right, in men's clothes.

*Jack London Papers, The Huntington
Library, San Marino, CA*

Nora in the redwoods.

*Photograph by Alan Hiley,
The Bancroft Library,
University of California, Berkeley*

Nora by a river. | *The Bancroft Library, University of California, Berkeley*

From left to right: James Hopper, George Sterling, Carrie Sterling, Carlton Bierce, and Unidentified. Elsie Martínez depicted in painting.

James L. Henry Collection of Herbert Heron Papers, Harrison Memorial Library, Carmel, CA

Sacramento Street, San Francisco, during the fire on April 18, 1906.

Photograph by Arnold Genthe

Harry Lafler in Portsmouth Square, San Francisco, April 20, 1906.

California History Room, California State Library

Arnold Genthe taking a photo of George Sterling, Mary Austin, Jack London, and Jimmy Hopper. Carmel, 1906.

Jack London Papers, The Huntington Library, San Marino, CA

George Sterling, Jimmy Hopper,
Charmian Kittredge London,
Jack London, Carrie Sterling,
and friends.

Photograph by Arnold Genthe,
Jack London Papers,
The Huntington Library, San Marino, CA

Charmian Kittredge London,
Jack London, Carrie, and George
at the Sterling bungalow, Carmel.

Photograph by Arnold Genthe,
Jack London Papers,
The Huntington Library, San Marino, CA

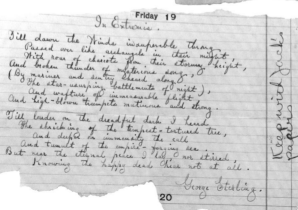

Nora writes to Harry Lafler
of her abortion, 1907.

*Henry Anderson Lafler Papers,
The Bancroft Library, University
of California, Berkeley*

Nora May French, 1907.

*Photograph by Arnold Genthe,
The Bancroft Library, University of California, Berkeley*

Nora May French's
"Rose" poem on George
Sterling's ledger paper, 1907.

*George Sterling Papers,
The Huntington Library,
San Marino, CA*

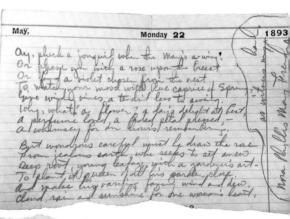

George Sterling's
"In Extremis" poem,
1906.

*Jack London Papers,
The Huntington Library,
San Marino, CA*

From left to right: Jimmy Hopper,
Herman Scheffauer, Harry Lafler,
and George Sterling at Bohemian
Grove, 1907.

Photograph by Gabriel Moulin,
Copyright © Moulin Studios,
San Francisco, CA

Nora May French's death
reported in *The San Francisco*
Examiner, November 15, 1907.

The Bancroft Library,
University of California, Berkeley

From left to right: Josephine Foster, Carrie Sterling, and Mrs. Connolly at the "Dutch Market" fundraiser for Arts and Crafts Club, Carmel, 1909.

Photograph by Louis Slevin, Harrison Memorial Library, Carmel, CA

Herbert Heron plays a knight.

James L. Henry Collection of Herbert Heron Papers, Harrison Memorial Library, Carmel, CA

Vera Connolly as a young woman.

Vera L. Connolly Papers, Rare Book and Manuscript Library, Columbia University Libraries

but after months of living off her sister's hospitality, she could not decline. They went by motor instead of by train and stayed at the Hotel Del Monte for a couple of nights.

Carrie lowered her body into the heated saltwater pool of the Del Monte's baths and felt the chill of San Francisco leaving her bones. Her muscles relaxing, she tipped her head back and looked at the vines hanging from the ceiling. How odd, Carrie thought, to have lived for years so near to this splendid resort, but to have never before been a guest in one of its five hundred sumptuous rooms. Earlier that day, she and George had strolled through the hotel's 125 acres of roses, cacti, and palms, through the hedgerow maze—a replica of the original at Hampton Court Palace in England—past the charming lake graced with swans and pedal boats. They had lunched in Del Monte's massive chandeliered dining room, which could accommodate as many as 750 diners. All this just three miles from where she spent her days skinning rabbits for dinner.[9]

With no house to clean, no meals to cook, Carrie finally had enough time to reflect on the past few months.

The weeks following Nora's death had been a blur. Helen and Alan Hiley had stayed another week in Carmel, Hiley gallantly helping George cut wagonloads of wood to prepare for winter before he departed. Then, a week later, Carrie and George received shocking news: Their beloved friend Kate Partington had died in pregnancy. To save money, Kate hadn't been going to the doctor as regularly as she should have and had been struck with uremia. After falling into convulsions and then into unconsciousness, she was taken to a hospital. Not in time. Kate and her baby died together on the operating table in a pool of blood.[10]

While all the world was mourning Nora May French, Carrie was mourning Kate. Grief brought clarity and she now regretted having judged her friend so harshly. Carrie knew her own greatest flaw was that she was overcritical. She was trying to work on it, but it had been so hard to change behavior that seemed second nature; she had been raised in a home with a mother who endlessly criticized but never praised her. She could now see that Kate had never recovered from the death of her daughter. Kate's ingratitude had simply been desperation born of poverty and misfortune.

Carrie feared poverty again herself—not just as an abstract concept but as a memory that roared back from childhood. Despite the past weeks of living in luxury at Wildwood, the reality was that the Sterlings' financial situation had never been more precarious. George had still not been able to sell the Piedmont house—they had dropped the price to $11,000, but so far they had had few inquiries. Nobody had money to buy. "We thought we'd be floating in the Lap of Prosperity about this time but the hard times have biffed us too," she wrote to Blanche.[11]

Looking for advice to guide her through these rocky times, Carrie picked up Prentice Mulford's *Your Forces and How to Use Them*.[12] Mulford emphasized that in the middle stage of life, it was crucial to be forward-looking. Do not indulge in sad memories of the past. Lose yourself in pleasant diversions. Do not visit graveyards![13] Very sage advice, Carrie decided. If she could focus her energies on what she could improve rather than waste time on regrets, she would be better off.

It was time to get the Carmel bungalow ready for the hectic summer season. George had sent her back down on March 15, telling her that he had just a few things to settle up in Oakland and then he would join her on April 1. But the first of April came and went and still no George. He wrote that she could now expect him April 14. He didn't come then, either. Carrie knew she was being punished, but she didn't know for what. What had she ever done except everything he had asked of her? And what was he doing up there without her?

She banished these thoughts and threw herself into gardening around the bungalow. She would make peace in her mind and in her immediate surroundings her priority. She would not be blown off her center by small things. She would lose herself in pleasant diversions. She dug in the dirt with fury, tossing weeds and roots aside.

When George finally arrived, he brought with him the news of the "gloomy morose youth" who shot himself with Nora's poem in his pocket. Jimmy Hopper in New York wrote to George that Nora's "death poem" was the talk of a party thrown by Edward Markham, a writer in the Bierce ambit. Jimmy had been sipping his drink when he heard Herman Scheffauer off in one corner holding forth about meeting Nora in Carmel (in fact he never met her). Scheffauer announced salaciously, Nora was "living with Sterling!"

The crowd went deathly silent, and all looked Scheffauer's way. Jimmy watched with amusement as Scheff stuttered through adding an "s" onto "Sterling" to make "Sterlings."[14]

Carrie felt her carefully cultivated sense of peace crumble. She had entertained that insufferable German for two weeks, and this is how he paid her back. To hell with him. To hell with them all.

. . .

How weird is it that the suicide of a young man who worked on Wall Street was attributed to a poem instead of to his evident financial distress? Pretty weird. After all, following the economic crash of 1907, people were killing themselves at a rate unmatched in the previous decade. But approached through the lens of cultural rather than economic history, it's perhaps not that far-fetched at all.

In 1774, Johann Wolfgang von Goethe published the fictional *Sorrows of Young Werther*, perhaps the first book to earn a reputation as "fatal literature." The story was semiautobiographical, and Goethe had written it feverishly, capturing his despair over a love triangle that had ended with his beloved marrying a close friend. In the book, young Werther ends his misery by shooting himself with his friend's pistol. The story was a commercial success and captivated Europe, propelling Goethe to fame; after its publication he was comfortably set up by a duke in Weimar.

But the character of Werther soon took on a dangerous life of its own. It became the fashion to dress in a blue coat and yellow vest like Werther and moan inconsolably about disappointed love. Goethe would soon be stalked by his own creation, as would-be Werthers began writing him of their distress, hoping he could solve their problems. Sometimes they even showed up at the author's door, begging for help.

Authorities became concerned that "Werther fever" would result in an explosion of youth suicides throughout Europe. Four years after the book's publication, a Fräulein Christel von Lassberg was dredged out of the River Ilm with a drenched copy of *Sorrows* in her pocket. Several decades later, a twenty-year-old German immigrant to America shot himself next to his copy of *Sorrows*, open to the page where Werther writes his beloved that his pistols are fully loaded.[15] The phrase "Werther effect" is used to this day to convey the contagious nature of suicide.

The bodies chalked up to Nora's poem kept coming. On October 14, 1908, Francis Cahill, formerly a San Francisco journalist, locked the door to the flat of his Denver rooming house, turned on two gas jets, and breathed deeply. Among his effects were a packet of love letters, a lengthy self-authored poem, and a newspaper clipping on Nora May French's death.[16]

On the one hand, it was irritating to the Sterlings that Nora kept reappearing in the press. But on the other hand, the more Nora was presented as some kind of siren of suicide, the less likely that people would inquire into the Sterlings. So Carrie and George repeated as often as necessary that Nora had always been suicidal, therefore her death at her own hand should come as no surprise to anyone. They did little to combat even the wildest rumors of her mental fragility, including the unlikely tale that she tried to poison Jimmy Hopper by sprinkling cyanide on his sandwich, but failed as the sandwich fell off the table and was eaten by Skeet the dog.[17]

There was one rumor, however, that they were frantic to put an end to because it happened to be true: that Nora was pregnant when she died.

Even Ambrose Bierce had heard it. George had not told Bierce much about Nora since their correspondence over her "Rose" poem years before. Then he had admitted to Bierce that he harbored tender feelings for her. In hindsight, that might not have been wise, as he had lent credence to the rumors that followed. So when Bierce wrote George asking if it was true that Nora had been pregnant at her death, George responded with a lie. He wrote that Nora had not been "enceinte" (he used the French term for "pregnant"), although she had had many lovers.[18]

Herman Scheffauer, perhaps jealous that Bierce liked George better than he liked him, kept George's name linked to Nora's throughout the spring. Bierce wrote again in June that Scheffauer had suggested Nora killed herself over Bierce's criticism of her "Rose" poem. Panicked that he was being charged with another emotionally frail poet's death, Bierce wrote to George to make sure he had not shown Nora his quip about someone seducing her to make her poetry stronger.

Bierce's letter as I found it in the archives had been edited, probably by George. One sentence began, "Well, I know that Scheff told *me* that she was . . ." and I couldn't make out the rest of it. At least two, maybe three, words had been vigorously crossed out with pen. The sentence continues after the redaction, "which I doubt not is a lie. He slanders every woman that he knows."[19]

The problem the Sterlings faced in their campaign to suppress the truth was that shortly after Nora's death, Helen French had all but confirmed her sister's pregnancy to the Los Angeles correspondent of the *St. Louis Post-Dispatch*. Her words as reported: "Nora had undergone three operations and she felt that she was compelled to face another," and, "She was despondent because of her condition, and rather than suffer another operation she determined to die."[20]

What could these operations have been? As I look through the archives, I find no references to Nora's medical procedures, other than her surgical and self-managed abortions; no letters testify to any lingering illness aside from the respiratory distress she experienced when she first moved to San Francisco, which did not require an operation. In Helen French's undated notes on her sister's life in the Bancroft Library, she had termed Nora's first abortion "an illegal operation." Euphemisms such as "condition" for pregnancy and "operation" for abortion circulated so widely that it's impossible for me to believe Helen was unaware of them. She must have known that she was telling the readership of a major city's newspaper not only that Nora was pregnant when she died and struggling with the decision of whether to have the child, but also that Nora had had several abortions before.

The more I learn about Helen, the less I am able to see her as the benevolent sister Nora took her for. Was Helen still bitter about their expulsion from Uncle Cash's and New York? Did she blame her sister for dragging her to San Francisco? Somehow, Helen seemed to want to punish Nora. At the very least, her notes left to the Bancroft Library demonstrate that she wanted posterity to know that Nora was "over-sexed" and had brought about her own ruination by being indiscreet.[21]

Significantly, even as Helen alluded to Nora's pregnancy to the papers, she gave no hint as to who the father might have been. Perhaps she didn't know. Perhaps Nora never told her. But the timing suggests George was the likely father. In late August, George wrote Bierce that he was shaken by a matter so delicate he couldn't even confide in his closest friends: "Something happened a couple of weeks ago (I can't very well say *what*) that has so worried me that as yet I have found no will to write."[22] In the first week of September, as he waited on Hiley to arrive, he wrote to Blanche Partington, apologizing for having been so inflamed by Emerson's accusation that he was a practitioner of free love: "I was in a nervous condition from worrying about another matter, now allright, and I struck out almost unconsciously."[23]

Whatever the "matter" was, George didn't elaborate either to Bierce or to Blanche. But in his despair after Nora's death, when he was drinking heavily, he might have revealed more than he meant to Scheffauer, who visited George at Oakland's Key Route Inn in January 1908. Scheff, an incorrigible gossip who felt he had missed his own chance to seduce Nora, made a partial report of that meeting to Bierce, including the detail that George, despite rolling in wealth from his uncle, was despondent "according to certain things he confided in me."[24] Sometime in the next six months, Scheffauer likely relayed more of the substance of that conversation to Bierce, while suggesting that Nora had been hurt by Bierce's criticism.

George tried to put Bierce off the scent by assaulting Scheffauer's reliability ("Scheff must be bug house!"). As for Bierce's assertion that Nora's poetry would be improved by her seduction, George assured him she would have laughed it off. "She played with men as with pebbles."[25]

George had just emerged from his fight with the janitor when he wrote the "pebbles" comment. Emotionally, he had been ricocheting between bitterness, guilt, and frustrated lust for months. Maybe he remembered what he told Scheffauer back in January. More likely, he remembered nothing until Bierce wrote him; he frequently blacked out when drinking. Yet contrary to what Carrie believed, George had actually been productively writing that spring. He worked in secret, often in his uncle's white limousine, going back and forth between engagements.[26] His trip to the reference room of the Oakland library to look up a word was doubtless in service of finishing the sonnet he sent to Bierce in late February, titled in draft form, "Nora May French":

> I saw the shaken stars of midnight stir,
> And winds that sought the morning bore to me
> The thunder where the legions of the sea
> Are shattered on her stormy sepulcher;
> And pondering on bitter things that were.[27]

If Bierce was on to him, George couldn't blame Scheff entirely. He had made his obsession with Nora apparent enough. By July, George had thirty-two love sonnets inspired by her stashed away and was petitioning Bierce to read all of them, even though Bierce despised love poetry. He cautioned Bierce that these sonnets could not be circulated—to anyone: "I'd like to have you see them all; and I'd like to have *no one* else do so—least of all Carrie!"[28]

Meanwhile, Nora's own poetry was becoming more visible than ever. The poem found in Russell Peck's pocket was described by Mississippi's *Vicksburg Evening Post*, Wisconsin's *La Crosse Tribune*, *The Palladium-Item* of Richmond, Indiana, and the *Reno Gazette-Journal* as "the final struggle of her genius for expression."[29] All told, an astonishing thirty-three papers nationwide printed the story of the victims of Nora May French's "Suicide" poem.

Which is fascinating when you consider that Nora never wrote a poem entitled "Suicide." She never authored a collection of "Suicide Verses." The constructed story of Nora's death had become the lens through which all her words were to be read. In fact, the verses that the newspapers printed under the title "Suicide" had been written by Nora, but they had been taken from her long poem "The Spanish Girl." In it, she had written of a "hollowed" life, not a "hallowed" one, as the paper misreported. The "stain where happiness had been," the "fragments in my hands," referred to her first abortion, the doctor-assisted one Hiley had arranged for her when he decided not to leave his wife. The "Judge" she meets when "alone and lost" might be a reference to God, or perhaps to Hiley. It was not an act of self-murder Nora had described, but one of self-preservation.

Chapter Thirteen

☙

Fool Sex

ELEVEN. TWELVE. THIRTEEN. FOURTEEN. FIFTEEN. CARRIE COUNTED the number of times the illustrious Upton Sinclair moved his jaw up and down to chew the sliced apple she had served him. After the twentieth chew precisely, he swallowed it. Then he took the tiniest bite of the next slice and did it again.

Cows masticated their cud more quickly, she was tempted to say, but she managed to hold her tongue. She and George needed to make a good impression on Sinclair so he would buy in Carmel. Frank Havens wasn't employing George at the Syndicate over the winter, so they would need to stay in the Carmel Development Company's good graces. Upton Sinclair was now perhaps the most famous author in America, having channeled his fear of food usefully into an exposé on the conditions of the meatpacking factories in Chicago. Jack London had helped *The Jungle* find a publisher, after numerous presses turned it down, balking at its graphic detail of rats and fingers pulverized into sausage meat. But Jack vouched that *The Jungle* would be the *Uncle Tom's Cabin* of wage slavery, and he had been right. *The Jungle* was an overnight sensation and even spurred Congress to approve the Meat Inspection Act.

The book hadn't moved George much. He found it well-meaning politically, but more tract than literature.[1] It wasn't exactly Carrie's cup of tea, either. But there was no question that Carmel would benefit from a writer of Upton Sinclair's stature taking up residence there. As the financial panic wore on, fewer people seemed interested in buying lots even though the town offered residents more services than ever. The Carmel Development Company had circulated new brochures that boasted of recent improvements: a barbershop, a clothing store, and a Sunset Telephone Company office. Residents could amuse themselves on first-class tennis courts or at a new bowling alley. Or they could take advantage of the naturally healing properties of sea ozone and pine balsam at a sanitarium run by the eminent San Francisco physician Dr. Himmelsbach. Havens was even laying out a 13-Mile Drive to pull people away from Monterey's 17-Mile Drive. Lots on this stretch of road, which would follow the curve of the beach and the river, would be "sold under restrictions as to character of buildings" to preserve an image of luxury.[2]

Such improvements had come at great cost, met only through the company's neglect of the town's basic infrastructure. Sanitation and water supply failed to keep pace with Carmel's growth.[3] Those living farther up the hill were served only periodically with water from a barrel that arrived on the back of a horse. This getup was lampooned in the Fourth of July parade with a float featuring a barrel with a sign on it reading "Carmel Reservoir." The pile of rubbish that had been ceremoniously swept into the middle of

Ocean Avenue and set alight each week had become so huge it threatened to burn down the town.[4]

The Sterlings were actively contributing to the town's over-crowding, as George had invited virtually every writer that he knew to visit that summer. Carrie had to host guests nonstop: changing bedclothes, cleaning, and arranging picnics, lunches, suppers, and parlor games of charades long into the night. She and George rarely got to bed before midnight.

Although she remained as busy as ever, Carrie noticed that the caliber of writer she entertained had dropped off. Her guests had either anemic reputations or horrible habits. Bert Heron, a Los Angeles–area playwright and actor, had come on Jack's recommendation.[5] Heron was young—only twenty-four years old—but he looked even younger. Incredibly scrawny, he told Carrie he suffered from chronic appendicitis and had at one point dropped to 113 pounds from it. His infant daughter suffered occasional convulsions, possibly due to an old fracture of the head. Heron had had to borrow $100 just to make the trip to Carmel, so Carrie was unsure how he would ever put the money together for a down payment on a lot, much less support his wife and child while paying a mortgage.

On his visit, Heron shared the cabin out back with Charles Warren Stoddard, the corpulent writer of Polynesian sea tales. An openly gay man whose passes had unnerved George and completely alienated Bierce, Stoddard became so inebriated one night that he tumbled ass over teakettle down the bungalow's front steps. It took six of them to carry his massive bulk back to the cabin, where they dropped him into the cot. Carrie hardly expected to see much of him the rest of the visit—she would have hidden in shame after such a performance—but the next morning, Stoddard, with a freshly combed beard, walked into the bungalow inquiring after breakfast as if nothing had ever happened.[6] Hours later, Heron crawled in, clutching his back and complaining of a night of sleep ruined by Stoddard's thunderous snores.

The one bright spot of the summer had been the town's "Hobo Party." On a balmy July night, Carrie dressed in rags, tied a tomato can to her belt with a string, and strolled down to the water to join her similarly attired neighbors. She dipped her can into one of the kegs of beer set up at intervals along the beach and took her place near a driftwood bonfire. The smell of beer always ignited dim memories of her father. It was also the one drink George couldn't stand—he considered it a poor man's thrill. He would choke it down for the sake of appearances, but he would far rather be drinking mint juleps.[7] Sitting around the bonfire, Carrie looked up at the sparks from the fire flying up to the moon. Maybe tonight she would get drunker than usual. Maybe she'd even get drunker than George. Maybe if their luck didn't turn around, they would be dressing like this every day.

By September, when George told her that Upton Sinclair would visit, Carrie was in no mood to clean up after another writer. But then George told her the most wonderful thing: Upton didn't drink liquor. Not a drop. Nor could he tolerate the presence of heavy drinking, as it reminded him of his alcoholic father. Sober people generally terrified George, but he was so eager to impress Upton, he vowed to Carrie he was getting on the water wagon and this time for good.

On Halloween 1908, George drove to Monterey to greet Upton at the train station. Never having met the man before, George didn't know what to expect. He found Upton genial if a bit nervous in person and tried to put him at ease by taking him to the Hotel Del Monte for lunch. That had been a mistake. Upton seemed uncomfortable with the lavish dining room. He preferred the trip down 17-Mile Drive past the beaches, through the redwoods, and under the druid oaks dripping with Spanish moss.

That night, Carrie encountered Upton's eating habits and quickly adjusted. Aside from his lunatic notions of nutrition—and talking about them incessantly—she found she liked him. He would make a lovely neighbor. He was so industrious. He was already at work on his next book—another exposé, this time on the recent Wall Street crash. He would paint J. P. Morgan not as the savior of the recent crisis but as its cause. He talked a good deal about the ills of capitalism, but Upton did not strike Carrie as the typical socialist. His was a respectable lineage, including a long line of Virginia naval officers going back to the Revolutionary War. Like her, Upton had seen poverty and been forced to live in boardinghouses after his father's drinking ruined the family. But as an adult, he had earned the respectable sum of $30,000 from his writing, more than enough to support his family and buy him anything he wanted in Carmel.

As a guest, Upton was undemanding and even chivalrous. Carrie had a girlfriend visiting, so he suggested he would be delighted take the cabin out back. The next day, Arnold Genthe called to offer Upton his entire house for the duration of his stay. Built to blend artistically into its surroundings, with a sloping roof that exactly followed the lines of the hills behind it, Genthe's house overlooked the beach and featured a thirty-by-sixty-foot living room and studio, built of redwood, accentuated by skylights.

The very first night Upton slept at Genthe's, George fell off the water wagon, getting drunk at Mrs. Josephine Foster's house down the street.[8] Upton thankfully didn't notice George's hangover the next morning as the pair took a brisk walk to the mission, followed by horseback riding through the shallow surf in Carmel Bay. Upton was delighted with the place. He felt the sea air was restoring him to full health. He wrote to his wife of the salubrious effects of the climate on his body and mind. "Poetry just rolled over me," he declared.[9] After one week, Upton felt sure enough of Carmel that he and George began investigating possible building sites near the Sterling bungalow. He planned to put a down payment on two full acres.[10]

Before he could write the check, however, Upton was called up to Oakland to deliver a lecture at the Ruskin Club. George went along as the featured poet on the program. He was mainly excited, however, to make a stop at the Bohemian Club so he could show off Upton Sinclair to his business colleagues. Some had doubted the soundness of George's move to Carmel. He could now rub their faces in it.

Carrie spent November 13, the anniversary of Nora May French's death, alone in the house for the first time in ages. The weather was just as it had been the year before—beautiful, clear, and warm. She lingered over her morning coffee. Sinclair would soon be her close neighbor, cramping George's drinking for years if not decades to come. Although she had not yet met Upton's wife, Meta, Carrie considered it promising that she was a musician. She imagined long afternoons in Mrs. Sinclair's company, discussing opera over tea.

She was stunned, then, when just a week later Upton Sinclair came by to thank her for her hospitality and explain that he could not move to Carmel. His wife didn't care to live so far away from Los Angeles after all.[11] But Carrie couldn't help wondering what had happened to make him change his mind so quickly.

. . .

Upton Sinclair had lied to Carrie. His decision not to buy in Carmel had nothing to do with his wife and everything to do with George. He wrote about why in his memoirs. He had indeed been serious about moving to Carmel—until that trip up to San Francisco.

As planned, George had first taken him to the Bohemian Club before they ferried to Oakland. Amid the bankers and businessmen, Upton kept a wary eye on George, who drank one cocktail and immediately downed another. Still traumatized by the memory of his alcoholic father, Upton hated watching any man drink. He was relieved when George appeared to stop at two drinks.

The pair was about to depart for Oakland when a man entered the Bohemian Club with shocking news. Assistant District Attorney Francis J. Heney, who was prosecuting Mayor Schmitz for corruption and graft, had been shot in the courtroom in front of his bodyguard, four uniformed policemen, and five hundred stunned onlookers. The shooter, Morris Haas, an ex-convict who would be portrayed in the newspapers later as a neatly dressed man "having a decidedly Jewish cast of countenance," had been swiftly arrested.[12] Everyone suspected that behind the scenes, Schmitz's political boss, Abe Ruef, had arranged the assassination attempt.

The mood of the Bohemian Club altered immediately after the announcement. San Francisco had been struggling to wrench itself from the mire of corruption that followed the earthquake, and with Heney's life hanging in the balance, it seemed that it never would. As it would happen, Heney's luck was uncanny—the bullet lodged under his jaw and missed his brain. The next day, people would be informed that Heney would pull through, but on the night of the shooting, no one could have expected he would survive.

Leaving the Bohemian Club still buzzing with the news, George and Upton made their way to the Embarcadero to catch the Key Route ferry to Oakland. On the trip over the bay, George became unsteady. He leaned over the rail as if he might tip into the water, and extemporaneously composed a poem aloud to the circling waves beneath. Upton listened to him, entranced by an impromptu poet at work, until he noticed George was slurring—and on his way to a speaking engagement!

Once they reached the Ruskin Club, George became violently ill and couldn't read at all. He ruined the evening. After their return to Carmel, Upton dropped a note to George, informing him that his behavior in San Francisco had been unacceptable. He told George that although he admired him as a poet and considered him a generous spirit with more friends than any other man he knew, he could not help but think that all the time George spent drinking would have been better spent writing verse.[13] Upton likely intuited how much it meant to George to have him move to Carmel, because he declared flatly that he would leave the next time he saw George take a drink.

George ran straight to the Genthe bungalow and tearfully vowed abstinence for as long as Upton chose to stay in Carmel. He claimed he had been sober several weeks prior to their trip. That night he hadn't eaten, and the two cocktails overwhelmed him.

After leaving Upton, George returned home and wrote a letter of apology to Ruskin Club president Frederick Bamford.

Dear Comrade:

I trust that you'll excuse the regrettable incident of
Friday evening when I tell you that the small amount of
wine that I had taken had never before, even in larger
quantities, had any untoward influence. But for the first
time in years I'd not had a drink for a month and the effect
of what I drank at the Bohemian Club . . .[14]

Etc., etc. George had grown accustomed to writing these apologies. Adding a socialist flourish, he blamed his drinking on his grief upon hearing the news about "brother" Heney's shooting.

George thought his promise of sobriety would satisfy Upton, but he was wrong. Upton had realized—accurately—that he would be surrounded by heavy drinkers at Carmel and decided to leave. This was not his idea of utopia. George could not bring himself to be too disappointed. Upton would have hindered his drinking more than even Carrie.

George, of course, had lied when he blamed his state on two drinks on an empty stomach. I marvel that anyone could believe that Jack London's closest drinking buddy could get sick on so little. In fact, George Sterling had been drinking on the sly throughout Upton's stay in Carmel. Although he had managed to maintain a presentable facade for most of the time Upton was in Carmel, by November 13, when they went to San Francisco together, George had been aiming for obliteration. It was the first anniversary of Nora May French's death.

What a year it had been, one in which George had morphed from a self-aggrandizing blowhard into a self-pitying wretch. Instead of the expected demand for his writing that he had anticipated after the publication of "A Wine of Wizardry," he could wallpaper his spacious living room with the rejections he had received from magazines. The Realty Syndicate needed him less and less, so he was quickly running out of money. His most recent tenants at the Piedmont house had fled without paying their last two months of rent, leaving him and Carrie without that small cushion of income they now relied upon.[15] His attempts to grow vegetables on his pine-shaded lot predictably failed. A neighbor's cows had trampled his crop of peas and ate the tops from over one hundred of his potato hills.[16] "What's the use," he wrote in the Carmel diary.

He wrote Bierce of his woes: "Now that I look back, I do not seem to have 'been myself' for a year. . . . The worst of it is, I don't care. And I do not know how it's going to end. I'd rather be semi-demented than not in love."[17]

In a perfect example of what the philosopher Kate Manne has termed "himpathy," George's friends all came to his rescue.[18] Bierce tried to persuade George to meet him in New York for a men's getaway. He told George that after two weeks in the company of men, "you'd not be mooning and moping about the fool sex, alive or dead. (I don't know if any of your Dulcineas ever die, but I wish they'd all take theirselves off you somehow, and let you write big poetry about big things.)"[19] Dulcinea is the young woman that the much older Don Quixote unwisely fell in love with. In Bierce's formulation, all of George's problems were to be blamed on Nora's active haunting: *She* wouldn't let *him* go and was ruining his poetry besides. No longer the writer of poisonous verses, Nora had become the poison herself: Bierce wrote, "I promise to work the woman poison out of your blood and bones—the smell of woman out of your clothing, and off your breath."[20]

Jack London was returning to America on a steamer (he and Charmian had abandoned the *Snark* in Australia) and would join the crusade to cheer up George. The Londons brought presents for the Sterlings: Carrie would get some Samoan tapa cloth. George was to receive Fijian war clubs and an ear ornament from the Solomon Islands made from a human clitoris "dried with appurtenances attached," as Jack described it.[21]

Ah, the dried clitoris. If you flinched, know that it's not a surprise to London scholars. Alex Kershaw's *Jack London: A Life* quotes from Jack's letter where it is presented as just a passing reference, no different than the tapa cloth or the war spears. Just a gift. Unremarkable.

But from Jack to George, from "Wolf" to "Greek," it was much more than a gift. Jack continually lionized George's prowess with women. The dried clitoris was a trophy, a celebration of their masculine bond. When you consider that Charmian likely typed the letter in which it was mentioned, and that the letter was also addressed to Carrie, it takes on an even more disturbing connotation. What is a dried clitoris but the result of genital mutilation, a practice conducted usually upon young women so they can never experience sexual desire or liberation? The woman to whom this clitoris once belonged would have experienced unimaginable pain while being butchered and could well have suffered infection and shock in the days afterward. If she survived the procedure, she faced a lifetime of compromised sexual, physical, and reproductive health. The "appurtenances" likely referred to the crura and bulbs, if we are getting specific, perhaps with labia minora as well. I've often wondered how Carrie received the news that such a "gift" was coming to her husband.

When Jack returned to the States, his plan to boost George's spirits included a sailing trip. Photos from this excursion, which Carrie joined (but not Charmian—the Londons were having a fight), show George looking gaunt and miserable. It probably didn't help that the boat was named *Phyllis*: Nora's nickname.

Jimmy Hopper was the one friend who departed from the prevailing view of George as the real victim of Nora's death. Well, not initially. At first, Jimmy, who had also fallen in love with Nora, was as bitter as George.

For a moment, let's imagine the weeks leading up to Nora's death from Jimmy's point of view. After his separation from Mattie, Jimmy felt happier than he had at any time in his life. His time was his own. He could write as long as he wanted without interruption. Then, unexpectedly, Nora May French of all people turned her luminous eyes his way. I'm sure he could not believe his luck. Jimmy had always been the shy guy at Coppa's, watching Lafler and George pick up women night after night. He had watched from the sidelines as Burgess and Irwin took their turns with Nora. Then she became engaged to the wealthy Captain Hiley, a man so tall Jimmy had to crane his neck to talk to him.

But all these men had failed Nora. Now Jimmy had his chance to woo this talented and beautiful woman, who, perhaps for the first time in her life, had learned that looks weren't everything.

On the evening of November 13, Jimmy had been dancing with Nora at the Arts and Crafts Club and likely went to sleep that night with thoughts of her whirling through his mind. He was awakened by a loud banging on his cabin door. Carrie Sterling stood outside, her overcoat thrown over her nightdress, shaking and crying so violently he could barely make out her words. Once he understood that Nora's life was in danger, he grabbed his shoes and ran to their bungalow as fast as his athletic legs would carry him. Flying through the living room, he made for the bedroom. Nora lay on the sheets, as still as a marble statue, though not white. Her freckled cheeks, which he had been gazing at over dinner only hours before, flushed as vividly as a painting—the telltale sign of cyanide in the blood. When he reached for her hand, it was cold. Remember, Jimmy had dug mangled women out of piles of rubble during the earthquake. As he left the bungalow and ran for the doctor, he would have already known Nora was gone.

In early 1908, Jimmy left Carmel for New York to write for the newspapers. He had reconciled with Mattie but had never stopped thinking about Nora and what could have been. That following September, he wrote to George about a museum visit where he had seen the marble tomb for Ilaria del Carretto by fifteenth-century sculptor Jacopo della Quercia. He had found himself unable to remove his gaze from the stone-white face of the young woman, with her gently closed eyes and "riddle of a smile." She looked so much like Nora. "And George, suddenly the old passion of regrets went through me, with an abruptness that threw me almost to the floor. I thought I had forgotten better," he wrote. "She certainly 'did' us, George, the swift-souled one. She was playing toy with us tangle-footed blunderers and suddenly with a dodge and dart eluded us—forever."[22]

In the weeks after his experience in the museum, Jimmy seemed to develop a conscience. He next wrote George that Nora had not toyed with men so much as they had toyed with her, all the while pretending to help her: "We thought we had the lifeboat out, but we were only hitting her on the head with our oars."[23] Jimmy knew that George blamed Nora's death on Dr. Beck, the man who sold Nora the cyanide. George had sent Jimmy a poem he wrote, "The Apothecary's," which used a clever play on words to implicate Beck.

> There beck the traitor joys to him who buys,
> And Death sits panoplied in gorgeous guise.[24]

But Jimmy felt strongly that Nora's friends had failed her most, including Carrie. He blamed Carrie for scuttling his nascent relationship with Nora. Carrie could accept only a single path for love, one that followed the strict line of courtship, marriage, fidelity, and death—even though she herself was trapped in a marriage to a man who humiliated her at every turn. Unable to end her own misery, she sat in judgment of others, like Jimmy, who had been trying to free himself from Mattie. "Carrie must cease to judge; if she does not, she will cause only unhappiness—and sometimes catastrophes," he wrote to George. "The morality with which we judge other people's lives is a deception. It isn't morality. It's only that subtle jealousy of the happiness of others which we all carry, a drop of bitter poison at the bottom of our hearts."[25] This vivid description of jealousy as a poison strikes me as bold, given how Nora died. Jimmy seems to imply that Carrie played some role—if only an oblique one—in Nora's death.

After Jimmy wrote this letter, George must have told him that Nora had been pregnant before she died and that Carrie knew of the pregnancy. Carrie had only been trying to protect Jimmy by discouraging his involvement with Nora, who had become desperate to ensnare a man—any man—as a way out of her troubles.

Jimmy was infuriated by this revelation and responded: "I can't help thinking that if you people, instead of trying to spare me, or distrusting what I might do, had told me what *was* during the two weeks before Nora-May's death, had told me the truth, instead of leaving me blind, and hence cruel as all blind things are, I can't help thinking that then I would have been able to solve *that* problem for her."[26]

It's not clear what Jimmy meant by solving "*that* problem for her." Did he mean that he would marry Nora? Did he mean he would help her secure an abortion? Either route would have been more complicated than his cavalier assessment of her situation suggests. In the weeks before Nora's death, Jimmy was separated from but still married to Mattie. A divorce would take time and would leave him with two kids to support and alimony to pay on no savings. He was already regularly borrowing money from George to stay afloat, who was himself borrowing from Jack London.

If, on the other hand, he meant solving "*that* problem" by procuring Nora a surgical abortion, he would also be in difficulty. Surgical abortions were getting more difficult to obtain. America was in the midst of a rising anti-abortion movement. The American Medical Association had begun cracking down on physicians who performed abortions, and newspapers were rejecting advertisements for abortion services.[27]

But Jimmy, like the other Bohemian men, never thought to consider what it was Nora might have wanted. They presumed they had the answer for her anyway.

Jimmy continued, in this latest letter to George, to rail against all the men who "kicked that radiant being about like a football, and in the mud all the time."[28] He blamed Harry Lafler the most, convinced that Lafler had never truly loved Nora, nor appreciated her poetic genius. It bothered him that Lafler planned to edit Nora's poems for publication as a book. He complained to George, "He'll probably try to 'fix up' some of her lyrics—a book-worm repairing a moon-beam. His insistence in the matter is simply a result of his monstrous vanity. He wants to keep up his odious pose of the tragic lover."[29]

Jimmy's fear that Lafler would use his editorial position to craft a distorted portrait of Nora would prove well-founded. The

1910 volume of her work he published left out some of Nora's more joyful poems, like "Happiness":

> Deep in the sunny grass I lie,
> And breathe the garden-scents, wind-driven—
> So happy, that if I should die
> They could not comfort me with Heaven.[30]

Instead, Lafler included the poem Nora never intended the world to see: "Vivisection," which contained her graphic depiction of her first abortion.

> We saw unpitying skill
> In curious hands put living flesh apart,
> Till, bare and terrible, the tiny heart
> Pulsed, and was still.[31]

Another poem of Nora's that never made it into the volume was one Jimmy Hopper kept in his possession: "The Panther Woman." It's not clear that Jimmy ever even revealed to George that this poem existed. I imagine him stashing it away to pull out and read when Mattie wasn't near, when he could meditate over what Nora might have meant by its final lines:

> How love would press your angry lips apart,
> And leave the willful bruising of her kiss
> In the sweet satin flesh above your heart.[32]

"The Panther Woman" has never been published. The original copy, written in Nora's hand, rests in the James Hopper Papers at the Bancroft Library. Also in these papers is a partial draft of an unsigned story, "The Suicide," in Nora May French's unmistakable handwriting. It describes a man's sleepless night during which "his body had fought for its life against his brain."[33] It surprises me as I read her careful excavation of a suicidal man's thoughts that no news reports of Nora's death mention this story. Even though unfinished, it would certainly have bolstered the Sterlings' portrayal of Nora as destined to kill herself. Perhaps Jimmy no longer felt the Sterlings deserved his help in this matter.

By 1909, a rift had opened between Jimmy and the Sterlings. Jimmy had considered returning to California but decided to go to France for the summer instead. He explained to George why: "The very thought of ever seeing Lafler again gives me gastritis and puerperal fever," he wrote. "And I am afraid as to our friendship too." Jimmy seemed to be getting angrier as he composed this letter. He mistyped. He crossed out words and rephrased, perhaps worried about burning his bridges with George completely. He tried to end on a gentler note but couldn't quite manage it: "This is all past and gone, and I may be wrong; but about the whole matter I feel even still a haze of evasion."[34]

As I review the letters Jimmy wrote to George in the years after Nora died, I find it remarkable that they made it to the archives. George burned many letters, but he didn't burn these, even though they indicted not only Carmel's Bohemian brotherhood but also Carrie. They show that Nora had lodged herself deeply in the psyche of her survivors. Her memory haunted them, a gentle but insistent ghost, raising questions and awaiting answers.

Chapter Fourteen

❦

Mother

"Hotbed of Soulful Culture." "Vortex of Erotic Erudition." "The Most Amazing Colony on Earth." Such were the phrases the journalist Willard Huntington Wright reached for to describe Carmel to readers of the *Los Angeles Times*.[1] Wright and his illustrator had become the latest guests Carrie had to paste on a smile for. George put them in Nora's old cabin and took them on the usual tour: the motor down 17-Mile Drive, the pilgrimage to Point Lobos, and the obligatory abalone thumping on the beach. Carrie made sure their beds were made and their breakfasts prepared and tried not to look as tired as she felt.

The Sterlings' efforts resulted in a several-page feature on Carmel's writing colony. The illustrator had depicted the town's literary elite sitting together under a tree, looking out toward the sea. There was Jack London, puffing smoke, near Mary Austin with her long braids, George Sterling with his Bohemian socks and cap, and Upton Sinclair reclining against the tree trunk. Wright described all the writers, portraying Harry Lafler as a "shagpated troglodyte" and Jimmy Hopper as "only temperamental occasionally."

Carrie couldn't believe the *Times* had printed it. It was a complete fabrication from top to bottom. To boost the star power of Carmel, Wright had to place writers at the scene who weren't there at all on his visit, some of whom had spent only a mere few weeks in Carmel in their lives. Sinclair was two years gone, having never bought property. Jimmy and Mary were abroad in France and England, respectively. Mary's wiki-up received special mention even though she hardly ever went there even when she was in town, much less wrote and slept there as she led everyone to believe.[2] Wright wrote of the Sterling bungalow: "It is here that Jack London creates his red-blooded yarns"—a blatant lie, as Jack hadn't visited since the previous February, when he made a quick trip with then-pregnant Charmian and their two Japanese servants. Nevertheless, Wright had described the athletic figure of Jack London coming out of the glade as if he'd seen it with his own eyes.

George got a special inset illustration that depicted him chopping wood for the hearth, sweat popping from his brow. Carrie had been rendered only as a disembodied voice calling from the bungalow, "George, come in and help wash the dishes!" The illustrated "George" responds, "All right 'Mother.'" Carrie realized with horror that she had been the source of this. She had mentioned offhand to Wright that George hated when Carrie called him "Father"; anytime she wrote it in the Carmel diary, he crossed it out and wrote "GEORGE" in capital letters over it. And now Wright had used this detail against her.

Even though in the article Wright had described the Sterlings as "happily married," the message from the illustration was clear: She was the shrew of Carmel. A know-nothing woman ruining everyone's good time. In the illustration, the head of the enormous ax George held pointed menacingly in the direction of Carrie's voice. That could not have been a mistake.

Carrie finished the article, fuming. She had spent the weekend entertaining these men only to have her marriage mocked for the amusement of tens of thousands of California readers.

Again, she wondered why she was doing any of this. George had not managed to recruit any notable writer to Carmel in a year. Instead, they faced a parade of nobodies moving to town. The Newberrys came, which surprised Carrie, as she thought of them as devoted to city life. The husband, Perry, struck her as human enough, but the wife, Bertha, was odd. All smile, but with a dead look in her eyes. They were building a house near the ocean.[3]

Bert Heron had found money somehow and bought in, bringing his wife and baby. Bert was an intelligent boy, but a goody-goody who was always sick with a cold or a stomachache or a migraine. "No guts," as Jack used to say of such measly men.[4]

These people took the place of the famous, congenial neighbors she was supposed to have. Now, instead of the Sinclairs, Carrie had the young, clueless Opal Heron next door, who would likely be depending on her night and day for help with her child.

In the meantime, Carrie and George's financial situation had gone from inauspicious to dire. George hadn't sold as many poems as he had hoped. They were forced to economize. It had been a while since she had prepared a meal that wasn't dependent upon George's kills—pheasant, rabbit, even snipe—whatever he could get in a day. If he shot nothing, Carrie would make her mother's bean stew, now her bean stew. She had eaten far too much bean stew that year.

Carrie decided to try her own hand at writing. Maybe she could earn a little money—and possibly her neighbors' respect—by getting some small articles published in one of the many new women's magazines. She had read enough of them to know what they wanted—simple stories about flowers or animals. Carrie could watch the wildlife in Carmel for hours on end and draw inspiration from even the smallest creature's movements. With a little work, she was sure she could write something passable about the nature surrounding her house.

She hired her new neighbor, Vera Connolly, to help her prepare her manuscripts. Vera had come to them through Elsie Martínez, Marty's wife. Similar in age, Elsie and Vera had met in the Bay Area and become fast friends. Carrie had hosted them over the Christmas holidays for a week and had written to Blanche of the visit, "I like them all so much, quite my ideals of what girls should be at their ages."[5] Since then, Vera had taken a leave of absence from college to care for her newly widowed mother and now lived in Carmel full-time.

Vera was one of those young women who seemed to move through the world with confidence. She had grown up on military bases and Indian reservations where her father had been posted, and as a result she seemed more worldly than her contemporaries. She wrote prodigiously, landing a short story in print even before she started college. Twenty-two years old, almond-eyed, thick-haired, and very, very serious (she and her mother were devout Christian Scientists), Vera professed to be indifferent to men. She told Carrie multiple times that she believed women could make their own decisions, even after marriage. Carrie laughed. Perhaps Vera, for all her experience, still had much to learn.

Vera's job, aside from typing, was to give Carrie light critiques of her works in progress and scout magazines for where the work would best fit. Carrie wrote an article about the native plants of Carmel and sent it off to *Sunset*, hoping the Carmel Development Company would be pleased. She had another flower poem that had already been rejected by two places, but she planned to send it to *Suburban Life*. A children's story had been rejected by *St. Nicholas*; Vera was looking for a new magazine to send it to. And Carrie had another story in development about a plucky squirrel.[6]

It was refreshing to have a bright young woman around her home. Vera was so much more interesting than Carrie's gossipy old neighbors. But as Vera became a fixture in the bungalow, Carrie noticed George turning on his familiar charms to monopolize her attention. Carrie had expected this. Social dictates would require Vera to reject George's advances. She watched Vera carefully to see how she would manage the situation, expecting a display of tact and finesse. But Vera didn't push George away. Instead, to Carrie's horror, the girl encouraged him.

Then George started peppering the Carmel diaries with entries about Vera, just as he had with Nora May French. On May 29: "Vera helped me hang cow-skulls in the backyard. A dark, starry night, with Halley's comet very conspicuous. Stayed up late."[7] The next day he described a hike to the river mouth for a swim, and a fire on the beach afterward with Carrie, the Newberrys, Lafler, and Vera, adding, "Vera had cramps and I miraculously discovered a flask ¼ full of whiskey on the beach."[8]

"Miraculously." Carrie scoffed reading it. George had been stashing liquor around Carmel for years, just as he had on the paths through the hills above the Piedmont when they lived there.

Carrie was outraged, but she wouldn't satisfy George by showing it. She would wait for the right moment to confront him. She continued to associate with Vera and her mother even when George left for a couple of days to put their Piedmont house on the market again (it still hadn't sold). When George returned, the Connollys invited them for dinner. As Carrie sat at the table next to Mrs. Connolly, she caught a glimpse of George and Vera giggling and touching each other's arms.

Carrie cut the evening short. She and George fought all the way home and then for hours into the night. George's excuses were variations of the same tune he had sung whenever they argued about his philandering. He claimed that his interest in Vera was not serious, that he only needed to flirt with beautiful women as an invocation to the muse. Should Carrie not understand the needs of a poet, well, that was her own failing. And then he went to bed.

Why didn't he just say: "You don't inspire me"? That was the message behind his words, over and over. You, wife, do not inspire me. You, wife, are not beautiful. You, Carrie, will never be truly loved. Not by me. Not by anyone.

You must be humiliated, again and again, so that I may feel free.

Carrie whipped open the diary, grabbed a pencil, and pressed hard as she wrote: "G. S.' sentiments per impudence of V. C. 'Blessed sunshine.'!!! . . . Went to the Connolly's (— 'em!) for supper. Bored to death."[9]

. . .

After this fight, George seemed to come unglued. His drinking intensified, but instead of producing his usual stupor, it only seemed to make him agitated. The Sterlings passed their fifth anniversary of moving to Carmel in a similar blanket of fog to the one that greeted them every June. But Carrie was determined she would not be dragged down by the gloom or by George. She spent the month painting her kitchen a lovely cream color and putting down linoleum. July brought the usual visitors, bridge games, and trips to Point Lobos, but George was barely sleeping. Even when they sold their Piedmont house, temporarily resolving their financial difficulties, he did not relax. At the end of July, he threw a huge mint-julep party in the backyard and drank so much that she became convinced he was trying to do himself in.

The morning after the party, she pleaded with him to get help, and for once he agreed. They left Carmel to see George's friend Albert Abrams, the celebrity doctor in San Francisco who treated all bodily disease through oscillations surrounding the spine; he had even cured dilated heart arteries by tapping the seventh cervical vertebra. George stayed at Abrams's clinic at 246 Powell Street for a few days before being discharged with the mundane prescription to quit drinking for a year.[10]

They then traveled to Yosemite to hike with Ambrose Bierce. Carrie hoped that time in the fresh air with old friends unconnected to the Carmel crowd would help restore George and their marriage. She had given herself a project on the trip: get to know this man, Bierce, who had such a profound effect on her husband. He seemed like a gentleman. Even while camping in the middle of deep wilderness, he took several hours to wash himself and dress, emerging from his tent with his splendid white hair combed, mustache waxed, eyebrows pressed into line. Carrie hardly spent that much time on her own toilet every morning.

Around the campfire at night, Bierce entertained the company with clever quips, but Carrie observed he would mock his friends as easily as he would his enemies. Maybe they weren't so different, she and Bierce: Carrie the Cad and Bierce the cynic. Both had grown up poor in overly large families with too much religion and too little love. Both had been burdened by a weird mating of pessimism and Puritanism. Happily, Ambrose hated the same people she did—the pretenders, like Jack London—and he was pragmatic about money; he had always counseled George to keep his job at the Realty Syndicate when George whined about it.

After a few days together, Bierce seemed to let his guard down with her. She got him to talk about women. Bierce admitted that he had wanted to marry Blanche Partington once upon a time. Carrie asked him why he didn't make a proposal. It seemed to her that Blanche and Bierce would have made an excellent couple, an alignment that could have spared them both grief and loneliness. He looked at her and said matter-of-factly, "I had a wife." They took a few more steps. George within earshot, Carrie said, "A wife never seemed too much of an obstacle when a man desired another woman."[11]

To this, Bierce said nothing. Carrie let him plod ahead. He was, in the end, not that much different from Jack or any of George's friends. They would never betray each other, no matter how many women they had wronged.

Was this marriage? Was this all it offered? It seemed to her men could forever find a woman other than their wives to attach themselves to. When she and George returned to Carmel, Carrie got a letter from Blanche that revealed that even Kate Partington's husband, Fred, had cheated on her, and that this, more than his illness and death, had broken her. Carrie sighed and wrote back ruefully, "Yes, it is funny to find out things that are happening under our noses. It so often solves many problems for us too, for we are blind bats who see only that which hits us in the face."[12]

She considered telling Blanche about her trials with Vera Connolly but decided in the end not to. She didn't trust Blanche with the admission that she herself had been buffeted with evidence of George's adultery.

She couldn't stop George's affair with Vera, she was coming to understand. But she shouldn't have to live with it shoved in her face every day. She decided to accept the invitation of Mr. and Mrs. Havens to join them in New York over the winter holidays. Once away from daily reminders of George's infidelity, she had a divine time. In ten days, she saw fourteen plays or operas and then returned to the Piedmont to celebrate New Year's Eve with her sisters at Wildwood.[13] George stayed in Carmel, throwing a huge party in the bungalow, to which he invited Vera and her mother. Four gallons of rum eggnog were consumed. He recorded the event in the diary, calling January 1, "A day of recuperation and remorse."[14] At least, Carrie thought when she returned and read the entry, he'd had the sense not to write remorse for what.

She would carry on in spite of him. In February, she invited Vera and Mrs. Connolly and other neighbors for a "bean and gab" fest. The women sat in her kitchen, the air thick with gossip and the smell of beans from the stove.[15] To Carrie's delight, Vera seemed uncomfortable, talking less than usual, nearly hiding in her mother's skirts. The more Carrie directed the conversation her way, the more Vera stammered and fidgeted. The more Vera stammered and fidgeted, the more victorious Carrie felt. It was like having a bug under a magnifying glass in the sun.

The next morning, George woke as if shot from a cannon and declared it was time to visit the Londons at Beauty Ranch. She and George spent much of March there and part of April visiting friends in the Bay Area. Scarcely had they returned to Carmel in May when he announced he had accepted Frank Havens's invitation to spend the entire summer in Sag Harbor.

Carrie was stunned. She had been prodding George to bring

her to his hometown for years, but George had always concocted some excuse to stay in Carmel. George hated Sag Harbor and swore he would never return. When he left at age twenty-one for San Francisco, he chalked a poem on the train platform:

> Sag Harbor, now I leave you;
> I'll bid you fond farewell.
> And when I hear you spoken of
> I'll surely think of Hell.[16]

Carrie wrote gleefully to Blanche about the upcoming trip: "Yes, sir it's true—I never thought George would do it."[17]

• • •

Here's what I imagine happened the evening of the bean soup dinner to send George scurrying out of Carmel. He must have been white-knuckling it: he had reached his fortieth day of sobriety, his longest stretch on the wagon in twenty-one years.[18] When George couldn't drink, he craved sex even more. I can see him offering to walk the Connolly women home, hoping for an opportunity to pull Vera away to make love to her in the woods. But when he got her alone, instead of wrapping her arms around him in a warm embrace, she burst into tears. She looked up at him and said she was pregnant. And that wasn't all. She wanted him to divorce Carrie, marry her, and become a family.

What I wouldn't give to have seen the look on George's face. He would not have expected this. He thought Vera, with all her maturity and experience, all her beliefs about independent young women declining family to pursue a career, would be the type to do the modern thing and get rid of it quietly. But he had miscalculated badly. Vera was independent, but she also firmly believed in justice. And justice dictated that George take responsibility for what he had done.

Whatever conversation they might have had that night resulted in George waking the next morning with singleness of purpose. He and Carrie needed to get out of Carmel. As soon as possible. He wrote a hasty letter to Jack. "Where are you? And when do you want us to go a-visiting you? I'd like to down six straight cocktails! Martinis—with you sitting, or standing, opposite." He didn't reveal to Jack why he needed to leave, just implied that he did, and the sooner the better.

George was well aware that Charmian opened all Jack's mail, so he didn't share anything that he wouldn't have wanted her also to know. But his guilty conscience revealed itself in a casual aside: Of a story Jack had just sold to a magazine about a former drunkard who had rescued a woman from harm, George offered that Jack should quit writing the "reformed tramp" narrative: "If you'd been true to life you'd have had to make him rape her."[19] It was one of the coarsest sentiments George ever committed to print that remains extant.

Jack responded that he couldn't receive the Sterlings until March at the earliest. That was in a month. George immediately wrote that he and Carrie would go somewhere else first. With only a slight indication of his predicament, he explained, "I only wanted your invitation as an excuse to leave town as soon as possible. But Carrie sent for some fruit trees and refuses to leave till they've come and been planted. We expect them any day now, and I'm hoping to leave here by Wednesday or Thursday."[20] Any further mail, he wrote, should be sent to the Bohemian Club.

Carrie, unaware of the recent developments, waited for her trees. She may have noticed that George was declining all social invitations. She went alone to the masked Mardi Gras Ball at the

Arts and Crafts Club and had a grand time—better than if George had accompanied her. She got to lead the Grand March with another gentleman. At last, the trees arrived and they could depart. She and George spent the next two months out of town.

The Connollys were long gone from Carmel by the time the Sterlings returned from the Londons' Beauty Ranch, but Vera had been indiscreet and the town buzzed dangerously with gossip of the affair. George realized he had to find another way to get himself and Carrie out of town—and for longer. Notably, during this time he seemed to feel little concern for Carrie. To George, Carrie was simply an impediment to his freedom. He wrote to Bierce in early May, referring to his "billion-ton wife-anchor."[21]

George wouldn't marry Vera, but he was assiduously working to provide her with what he believed was the next best thing: the imprimatur of Ambrose Bierce. Throughout the spring of 1911, George tried to secure a meeting between Vera and Bierce in Washington, DC. Finally, pressed by Bierce as to why he should meet this young writer and offer his assistance, George confessed the affair.[22]

Bierce was not pleased with this revelation. Maybe he had grown to like Carrie on their hike together, or maybe he was tired of having to meet every girl his apprentice had slept with. Or maybe he felt that a steady marriage was best for men of public stature to maintain. Whatever the reason, Bierce took the side of matrimony and urged George to sever his relationship to this woman and recommit himself to Carrie. In response, George proclaimed he could not. He was in love with Vera. It was unusual for him to fall for someone so young, he acknowledged (he usually chose married women to avoid entanglements), and Vera, who had been a true virgin—even her friends verified it—loved him equally.

This is the letter in which George confessed to Bierce that his marriage to Carrie had long been sexless: "As to Carrie, I feel and must always feel affection towards her. I intend to stick by her, since she needs me. But she never cared for the physical side of love, and we gave that up years ago." He quickly segued into selling Bierce on meeting Vera: "She's good company when at her ease; but she got such a mauling in Carmel that it's made her shy and sensitive." Note: George attributed Vera's vulnerable state to the gossip in Carmel rather than, say, his having impregnated and then abandoned her. The rest of George's description of Vera reads as if it were clipped from a recommendation letter in support of tepid applicant for a job. "I'm sure she'll be an unusually fine short-story writer, one of these days. 'McClure's' is taking a story from her now though that doesn't mean much to *you*. I'm not saying she's to become a *classic*."[23]

He had been willing to stake his reputation with Bierce on Nora, introducing her as the "Tennysonian crystal." Vera would get no such favors.

. . .

I find the originals of the correspondence between George Sterling and Ambrose Bierce in the Berg Collection in the New York Public Library. The Berg fits the most classical image of what one thinks of as archives: walls of dark carved wood and full bookshelves supporting the busts of famous writers. It is the home of cherished literary realia, including Charles Dickens's chair, Charlotte Brontë's travel writing desk (tinier than you can even imagine), and Mark Twain's spectacles. Visitors to the Berg must be prescreened. Random tourists to the New York Public Library may walk under the chandeliers of the famous Rose Reading Room and gaze up at the frescoes in the main halls, but they may only peer through the glass windows of the Berg's doors to glimpse the relics, unless they have made a prior appointment.

For the practicing scholar of the digital age, however, the Berg for all its wonderful collections poses some difficulties. The holdings haven't been completely digitized, so when the need arises, you have to pull out an actual drawer from the actual card catalog and flip through actual pieces of paper to find out what's there. The Berg is dimly lit—not ideal for photographing records. And worst of all (this may have changed, though it was true at the time I was there), researchers are limited to twenty photographs of documents. For their entire visit.

That restriction meant I entered the Berg knowing I had to transcribe hundreds upon hundreds of sheets of handwritten correspondence, impossible to do in the weeklong visit to New York that I had been able to afford. As I worked, I quietly thanked my mother for allowing me to take typing in high school with the proviso that I never reveal this skill to any future employer. For her, the typing pool was the end of female professional ambition, a pit where women were consigned to vital but repetitive drudgery while men rose through the ranks. My year spent tapping keys on an electric typewriter that had nail polish over the letters turned out to be one of the best investments I could have made in my career. What do writers do all day but type?

But even my eighty-nine words per minute proved no match for the stack of correspondence in front of me. I was forced to make some painful decisions. I would save my precious photographs for any letters that appeared ripped or altered so I could examine them later. As I typed, occasionally flashing passive-aggressive glances back at the tourists peering at me through the windows (I felt like a zoo animal), an email from the head of my department at my university with the subject line "In Memoriam" popped into my notifications.

Usually such messages mark the death of an emeritus faculty member—someone who roamed the halls of the department so long ago I never met them. However sad, such notices don't touch me personally. I clicked. I read.

"It is with great sadness that I write to inform you that our colleague, Professor Everywoman, passed away Friday morning. . . ."

I found myself screaming before I even finished reading the sentence. In the Berg. In the silence. In full view of the tourists. Professor Everywoman (an alias—obviously—and a clumsy one, but I can't bear to give her someone else's name) was my dear colleague of almost twenty years and one of the few people I've known in my life who was not simply smart, but a genius. She walked the hall, her head cocked at a downward angle, her long hair—rarely cut—tucked behind her ears. I often didn't want to stop her with a hello, knowing that whatever was going on in that mind deserved to continue undisturbed. Beloved by her students, she rejected the spotlight even as it often found her. She was a finalist for a Pulitzer, a recognition few professors will ever see. Had I been a finalist for a Pulitzer, I would have had that tattooed on my forehead, but she never mentioned it. She counseled me once that prizes were mixed blessings. They put a target on your back.

In those years, the department had become grim with women stalled in the middle ranks while men zipped up the promotion ladder. The head of the department was a man who exhibited what are now called "anger issues"; it was well-known he had punched a hole in his office wall. I and the other five women who had succeeded in reaching the top rank met several times in a nearby bar to share horror stories and write petitions for redress. We dubbed these gatherings "Unhappy Hour." In fact, they were sustaining and full of the jokes that smart women tell only in the company of other smart women. Professor Everywoman had us all laughing when she observed that academia had become a rat race where the only thing that mattered to people was landing a cushy administrative post, no matter how many colleagues you had to burn in the process: "The motto seems to be 'Every Man for Himself,'" she observed wryly. "I don't know why they don't carve it over the door."

In retaliation for our complaints, the head enacted petty vendettas. One by one we were to feel his wrath. Research money withheld. Administrative hurdles multiplied. Professor Everywoman called me after a meeting with him that had become particularly rancorous and humiliating; she had told the head that he had lied to her, and he responded by becoming apoplectic, yelling and jabbing his fingers just inches from her face. There was nothing she could do or say given such vehemence. She told me she could see no other way forward than to take early retirement.

With a galvanizing sense of mission I always get when I'm about to make a huge mistake, I drove out to her house twenty minutes outside of town. I had to convince her to stay. I wasn't sure how I would. We all knew there was no ombudsperson, and the office that was supposed to ensure equity seemed content to simply ensure that the university was never sued.

Her house sat on a bare patch of land surrounded by cornfields, no neighbors for a mile, the kind of terrain where, as they say, you can watch your dog run away for three days. I got out of my Subaru and the wind blew the car door shut for me.

She apologized that she had little more than jam and butter and toast to offer. I saw inside the fridge as she opened it. She wasn't kidding. I thought perhaps this ethereal creature really did live on words and air.

"Would you like some tea?" she asked. She got up to fill the kettle. As she turned on the tap, she looked out the window over the sink. Sunlight illuminated the lines of her face, but also its softness.

She stared out the window as the water streamed into the kettle and said quietly, "This place kills women."

At the time, I thought by "this place" she meant our university. But that wasn't the direction she was looking when she said it. She was looking at everywhere.

Chapter Fifteen

ᏁᏁᏁᎧ

New Woman

On June 3, they boarded the train for the Overland Route to Chicago. Carrie was ecstatic that she would escape another foggy June in Carmel. She was looking forward to all the time she'd have to read undisturbed. She had brought a couple of books recommended by Mary Austin: Olive Schreiner's *Woman and Labour* and Sylvia Pankhurst's *The Suffragette: The History of the Women's Militant Suffrage Movement*, which had just come out that May.[1] The Havenses had paid for their entire trip, so she could relax and sleep and eat as much as she wanted. Dick Partington and his wife, Ida, also came along, which made it much more fun.

The train passed through Echo Canyon in Utah, her favorite spot, and then chugged on through the spectacular Rockies. Engine trouble stalled them outside Omaha, so they arrived in Chicago too late to make their connection. Mr. Havens put them all up at the Auditorium Hotel, where Carrie tried the signature cocktail, the Golden Dream. It was creamy and orangey and delicious. They followed Dick around the Art Institute for a while (very nice, Carrie thought, but nowhere near as good as New York museums) and then made their connection. Traveling east, she saw the first violent thunderstorm of her life—it terrified her, but nobody else seemed worried. George remained pleasant and jocular the entire trip, even when the train was held up and even though he slept very little between Chicago and New York. Ordinarily, he would have been kicking and complaining—he hated travel—but he was an angel the entire time.[2]

They pulled into New York around 9:00 a.m. on June 7 and got breakfast, Mr. Havens of course paying for everything. Carrie went shopping with Mrs. Havens and Ida along Fifth Avenue and then stopped by an employment bureau to hire another girl for summer help. They made sure to get someone ancient so the men wouldn't have anyone to flirt with. That night they all went to dinner at the Waldorf Hotel, every bit as spectacular as the Fairmont. Carrie ordered a Pink Lady—a frothy, rose-colored gin drink. It was even better than the Golden Dream. It came in a fancy glass and went straight to her head. There were some whirlwind visits with a few New York friends of George's and then they boarded the train bound for Sag Harbor.

Cormaria, as the Havenses called their summer mansion, was situated on eighteen acres atop a gently sloping private beach, a short way past the Sag Harbor yacht club. After the servants took her luggage, Carrie walked through the front door and looked up to see an exquisite Tiffany lamp. She spent a moment admiring the foyer. She had never seen so much solid wood in her life: hardwood floors, hardwood paneling, and in front of her, two majestic spiraling staircases whose railings were supported by more woodwork carved in interlocking circles. Frank Havens had wisely made sure all the main rooms faced north, taking advantage of the cooling breeze off the sound. Carrie and George were given their own room over the parlor. Dick and Ida had rooms down the hall. The servants' quarters seemed to go on forever, housing six maids, the cook, and additional help for Havens's yacht and the grounds. Carrie spent most of the first day unpacking. Then she drew a bath in the enormous tub. She felt she had thousands of miles of grime to scrub off her skin.

At 5:00 p.m., they were all invited to go sailing on Frank's eighty-seven-foot yacht. Shelter Island Sound was not the azure blue of Carmel Bay, but it seemed much calmer. Carrie sat up toward the bow and let the wind gently toss her hair. Upon their return, scotch and soda was waiting for them on the columned veranda; after cocktails they moved to the dining hall for a chicken dinner.[3] That night, she fell asleep to the gentle ticking of the grandfather clock down the hall.

Next day, swimming and sunbathing. Frank Havens had gotten permission from the town to construct his own breakwater so his beach wouldn't be destroyed by erosion. By July, they'd settled into a routine of water sports during the day, early-evening cocktails on the veranda, and then dinner.[4] At night, they played bridge under stained-glass windows. One evening she and George even managed to take $14 off the president of the National Bank of Oakland, who was visiting.[5]

George seemed surprisingly content to be back in his hometown. He had never had a good thing to say about it, always portraying it as a stifling clutch of small-minded yet self-important people. But perhaps he was finally maturing. They had one of Frank's cars at their disposal, so George took Carrie around and showed her the house where he had grown up. Once a tiny cottage, it had been expanded to hold the swelling Sterling clan. Then he took her to Shelter Island, the Havens ancestral stronghold. His grandfather, the whaling captain Wickham Sayre Havens, famously harpooned 985 adult whales with his own arm—more than anyone on the eastern seaboard. His house had been the center of town, acting as post office, general store, and tavern.[6]

As a youth, George had been wayward. After he failed out of St. Charles College and moved home, he joined a gang of like-minded pranksters who dubbed themselves the Night Hawks. One night, the gang removed Sag Harbor's street lanterns, attached them to the bathhouses on the beach, and then rolled the assemblages into the sea. They watched the bathhouses float off, bobbing away on the water as panicked townspeople ran after them. Not content with this small victory, George planned ever more ambitious pranks. He and his friend Roosevelt Johnson scaled the 168-foot steeple of the Presbyterian church in the center of town—known as the Old Whaler's Church—and attached a pirate flag to the top. Carrie could see that it hadn't been an easy ascent. The steeple was constructed in the Egyptian Revival style, with cylindrical sections providing little to cling to. His mother was furious. Everyone knew who had done it, but no one could prove it.[7]

So this was her husband, she thought. A man accustomed to "owning" the town, whatever the town was, while pretending to rebel against it. And he saw no contradiction in that.

Mary Austin visited in July. She had been in New York since the winter, overseeing the production of her off-Broadway play *The Arrow Maker*. About an Indian medicine woman, the play exposed, as Mary put it, "the enormous and stupid waste of the gifts of women."[8] Mary was now a radical suffragette. She had joined the National American Woman Suffrage Association, then agitating in advance of California's ballot measure in October to give women the vote. When the question of women's enfranchisement had first arisen in California in 1896, Carrie could only count two avowed suffragists in her acquaintance: Ina Coolbrith and Anna Strunsky. As the question reemerged in 1911, it seemed that every other friend was one. Even Jack London claimed to be one. It was all the rage. Five states had already passed measures extending the franchise: Wyoming, Colorado, Utah, Idaho, and Washington. It seemed more than likely that California would join them.

Gamely, George invited Mary to convince him of the merits of letting women vote.[9] He was adamantly opposed. For George, a woman's vote meant a vote against liquor.

Carrie did not have strong thoughts on the matter. Whether women voted or not on one day of the year wouldn't change how they lived every day, toiling in their homes while being ignored by their philandering husbands. She liked the book Mary had recommended, Olive Schreiner's *Woman and Labour*, because it put the focus exactly where she felt it most belonged: on the gap between the work women did and the credit they received for it. Schreiner asked why women should labor simply so that others could hold positions of acclaim. Why couldn't women do the jobs men did? From the judge's chair to the doctor's office and everywhere in between, women deserved to be put in front rather than working behind the scenes to advance their husbands.

Although advocating for women in the workforce, Schreiner rejected the moniker "New Woman": "It is often said of those who lead in this attempt at the re-adaption of woman's relation to life, that they are 'New Women.' . . . But, the truth is, we are not new."[10] Women have for time immemorial worked and labored beside men, Schreiner argued. The women of today have their ancestors in their blood, but they have been taught that they are helpless and need to depend on others.

Carrie thought Schreiner was absolutely correct in defining a state of female "parasitism," where women made wealthy from inheritance completely lost the ability to cook, clean, or do anything useful for themselves. Carrie suddenly realized the benefit of her humble upbringing: She had learned how to take care of herself. But she had allowed it to become a curse in Carmel, where numerous people lived off her sweat. Now she understood: Those people were parasites, absolutely.

Most promising from Schreiner was the vision of a changed man who must emerge as women altered their expectations. Carrie thought about how different George had been that summer, away from Carmel. Pleasant, attentive, and focused. He seemed poised to find gainful employment, making frequent trips into Manhattan to get advice from his connections on Wall Street. Maybe the man she had married would come back to her at last.

. . .

While Carrie was enjoying her well-deserved respite in Cormaria, George was not turning himself into any kind of changed man. The meetings with stockbrokers in Manhattan were just alibis. He had launched himself into yet another affair, this one with Mary Craig Kimbrough. It would place him in a romantic rivalry with Upton Sinclair.

"Craig," as she was called, had grown up on a sprawling cotton plantation in Greenwood, Mississippi, with Jefferson Davis's widow as a neighbor. The daughter of a judge and a traditional Southern woman who threw a lot of parties, Craig embraced the culture of New Womanhood and white women's liberation. Rather than get married immediately after she left her finishing school in New York, she decided to stay in the city and become a writer.

Upton Sinclair had met Craig at a lecture he had given in Michigan. Subsequently, with his marriage to Meta breaking apart, Upton had gotten back in touch. He encouraged George to look up Craig when he was in Manhattan and help her with her writing. He should have known better.[11]

According to Craig's memoirs, she had not been expecting George Sterling when he knocked on her door. Her attire and hair were well below her standards for receiving a gentleman caller. Nevertheless, when she opened the door, George immediately dropped to one knee and proclaimed, "Goddess!"

Even without her best clothes on, Craig was a knockout. She had an aristocrat's straight nose and firm jaw, softened by come-hither eyes. When she spoke, her words came out coated in a honeyed drawl. Startled by this strange man kneeling before her, she invited George to stand. He explained to her that he was a friend of Upton Sinclair and that although he was spending the summer with his uncle in Sag Harbor, he would stay in town if she asked him to so as to be more readily at her service. Ever demure, she declined to put him through any trouble.

The next day, George sent her two of his poetry books, *The House of Orchids* and *A Wine of Wizardry*, as well as a sonnet he'd written to her beauty.

The following day, George wrote to tell her that he had promised to help crew his uncle's yacht for a regatta—a great bore—but that he would be in Manhattan the day after and would call on her for a walk.

They met on Riverside Drive at the appointed hour. George, Craig found, walked quite briskly and she struggled to keep up. He talked the whole way, mostly about his poems. He called her "Beatrice," but with the Italian pronunciation: "Beh-yah-tri-chay." He explained that Beatrice was Dante's muse and therefore she was destined to be his companion.

Midway through this seduction, Upton Sinclair happened upon them. The three talked briefly about Craig's progress on her stories. Upton suggested that Craig looked terrible and should eat more, as she was beginning to look like a skull. Then he abruptly walked off.

George saw an opportunity to thwart a potential rival. He told Craig that he would have killed Upton for that comment if he hadn't felt so sorry for him. He took pains to remind Craig that Upton was currently embroiled in a messy and public divorce and that by entertaining his advances, she risked her reputation.

Craig replied, "But I do look like a skull. . . . I know it, and if he were not a married man I'd want to marry him. He's the first one who ever told me the real truth."[12] No, no, you mustn't, George cautioned immediately. Upton really had nothing to offer a woman. The man had no warmth. He was "an ethical machine" and would turn Craig into one as well.[13] George recommended that she leave New York before rumors connecting her to Upton began to circulate. Craig had an aunt in California, did she not? She could move there and then visit him in Carmel. He could help her with her short stories once she arrived.

He went on and on. She belonged with him and him alone. He would quit drinking for her, he would suffer for her, he would even die for her, "only let me worship you."[14]

George continued visiting Craig in Manhattan throughout the summer. When back in Sag Harbor, he wrote Craig poems. He sent her a photo of himself (in profile) so she could keep him ever present in her mind when he wasn't there. As mid-September approached and his days on the East Coast became few in number, George made one last attempt to convince Craig to follow him back to Carmel. Craig, well aware that George Sterling was married, declined.

George still could not take no for an answer. En route to California, he wrote Craig a sonnet nearly every day. He persisted even after arriving in Carmel, sending her love letters of four, five, or six pages, along with new sonnets composed for her eyes only.

Finally, he begged her to end his torment with a visit to California. In what has got to be one of the least savory invitations a woman has ever received, he explained that they would have to work around the gossips of Carmel, but that they would surely be able to conduct their trysts in secret:

> *I'll have to take lots of care about you, to keep any of the "old cats of Carmel" from sinking their claws in you. It can all be managed most easily, if only one shows rudimentary caution. Of course this is for you. As for me, I'd be only too proud to have them think I was loved by so glorious a creature as you. . . . But there will be days when we cannot meet, or meet only in public, or but for a few stolen moments. For you must take no risks, and for us to be always together would lead to gossip.*[15]

This letter gives me some idea of what George probably said to Nora to encourage her to move to Carmel years before. The effect of such sentiments upon Mary Craig Kimbrough, however, was nil. She collected George's letters in a tin breadbox, which they soon overflowed, and married Upton Sinclair.

. . .

You might be wondering what happened to Vera. There is no letter that mentions exactly what she did about her pregnancy after she and her mother left Carmel. Vera was another letter burner, so what survives of her ordeal can only be accessed through the accounts of others. George's letters to Bierce suggest that he was vacillating between fear and resentment with regard to her. He told Bierce that Vera had been threatening to kill herself if he didn't continue the affair. At first, he believed she was serious, but when she continued living, he decided she had threatened suicide just to manipulate him. "Killers are not such liars," he wrote.[16] He then imagined that Vera had deliberately gotten pregnant simply to extort money from him. "Heaven help me!" he complained to Bierce. "I'll never get thro' paying for that business! Damn virgins and their schemes!"[17]

I had imagined that Vera, being a strict Christian Scientist, would have carried the baby to term. I looked at her genealogical records. No children. My next guess was that she gave up her child for adoption. George had mentioned to Bierce that Vera's first stop after leaving Carmel was Leavenworth, Kansas. Kansas at the time was a hot spot for unwed women having children. But there are no indications from Vera's records at Columbia University that she stayed in Kansas long enough to bear a child. Perhaps she gave the child up for adoption in New York, where she landed next. I called the state office for records, but records for old adoptions are sealed.

I stepped back from the problem and thought about it from a different angle. Vera Connolly, though devout, was also a woman not ready to give up her life. Having spent years on Indian reservations watching the government take children from their families only to force them into workhouses, she would have had no confidence in adoption. I looked again at the timing. For a pregnant woman, Vera traveled a lot. The most likely explanation was that she wasn't pregnant anymore. And then I found Elsie

Martínez's oral history, in which she said Vera had a miscarriage on a brief trip to San Francisco.

Women don't travel to a city just to have a miscarriage. She had been forced into a decision that would determine the trajectory of the rest of her life.

Chapter Sixteen

ʕᙏᙏᙐ

Woman of Genius

EVERYWHERE CARRIE WALKED IN CARMEL, WOMEN LOOKED AT her—sometimes with pity, sometimes with scorn. A few neighbors greeted her a little too warmly, hand on her elbow, a look of dripping concern in their eyes. The entire town knew of George's affair with Vera and her humiliation, and even simple greetings of "How are you?" reeked of prurience. Old Mrs. Josephine Foster, the Arts and Crafts Club president, seemed the most prying. She dropped by on the barest excuse, always directing any conversation topic back toward the Connollys' swift departure, watching Carrie's face closely for signs of distress. Carrie wouldn't give her the satisfaction. And when Mrs. Foster walked off, Carrie smirked as she watched her adjust her stockings through her skirt—a habit the woman couldn't seem to break.

Carrie began to think she should have stayed in Sag Harbor. She had found out the full truth about Vera in August, and it had ruined what was left of her summer vacation. The train trip home had been miserable, she and George barely speaking. George spent the whole time writing and drinking. He seemed to be under the misconception that now that he had officially ended his affair with Vera, Carrie should be grateful. He accused Carrie of being "moody."[1] How could she not be? He had destroyed their marriage.

Back in Carmel, Carrie felt like a caged bird. She spent her days hiding in the house or working in the yard as surreptitiously as possible. George was hiding, too. If anyone seemed likely to call, he fled to the woods, leaving her to face whoever was at the door.

For temporary relief, they took frequent trips out of town.[2] Just before Christmas, they went to visit the Londons. George got more drunk than usual, and his usual drunk was impressive enough. Even Charmian stopped smiling for once and got fed up with him. They left the ranch without saying goodbye, slinking out the door before the Londons arose one morning. On the way home, Carrie told George he had made a fool of himself. George wrote a letter of apology for his behavior to the Londons at Carrie's urging, though he hardly thought it necessary.[3] She guilted him back onto the wagon, but he fell off again on New Year's Eve, when she was up in Oakland. Fifteen friends came down to Carmel from San Francisco for a huge party George threw at the bungalow. His hangover lasted for days.[4]

When she thought she could bear it no longer, Carrie was saved by a cataclysm. Just after the first of the year, her sister Mrs. Maxwell's husband died suddenly. Harry Maxwell had suffered an abrupt businessman's death hastened by a life of hard work and even harder play. He collapsed in his garage not ten minutes after he had been talking to friends. Mrs. Havens offered to put Carrie and Mrs. Maxwell up at the Key Route Inn during the funeral.[5] As Carrie packed, she found herself throwing in more clothes than she needed. Even if she wasn't conscious of it, some part of her knew: She should leave Carmel and never come back.

She spent the first several days in Oakland crying into the inn's comfortable sheets. She took coffee in her room while looking out at the bay, ferries coming and going under clouds that lifted and lowered and then lifted again. She made up her mind: She would not return to Carmel. Of that she was certain. What to do about George remained an open question.

George seemed finally to notice his marriage was in peril. He visited Carrie periodically to perform sobriety, looking jittery and contrite. But when she asked if he could find some steady work in San Francisco—all those business contacts had to be worth something—he argued that if she just gave him another chance, he could provide for her in Carmel. It was still the only place he wanted to live. It was their only home, he told her.

So she stayed away. In the spring, she heard that one of Carmel's schoolteachers, Helen Vestal, only twenty-two years old, had gone missing. Miss Vestal had been last seen leaving her house at 2:00 a.m., lightly dressed and without her eyeglasses. The whole town spent the day searching the hills around the mission. They combed the riverbed and the dunes. Finally, her drenched and broken body was found by three of her students on the north end of the beach.[6]

It was presumed that she had drowned herself. She had given no indication of planning suicide, yet whispers circulated that there had been insanity in the family—her sister had been committed to an asylum the previous year. Carrie read all about it in

The San Francisco Call, where Miss Vestal was described as "dissatisfied with life at Carmel."[7]

Imagine that.

The next month, the *Titanic* sank. For days after, every time Carrie picked up a newspaper, she was assaulted with the names of people who had drowned. It made her feel unsteady. The next time George came up to visit, she offered to type up his sonnets for him, but with the caveat that she would do it only when she had the time.[8]

Over the next few months, as she kept her distance from George, her spirits began to lift. She started shopping for clothes again and putting her hair into better order. She allowed herself to socialize more. In August, Jack London came for a visit with his two daughters—but without Charmian. Charmian came for lunch herself the next day, clearly angling to see what Jack had talked about with her not present. She was pregnant again and delighted. Charmian's first labor had nearly killed her, and the baby had lived for only hours. To Carrie, it was unfathomable. She wasn't sure if Charmian really wanted a child or only wanted to outdo Bessie by giving Jack a son. The things women risked to stay in their husband's heart.

Charmian's pregnancy lasted only one month. Carrie ran into her in the street just a week later, and Charmian, still pale, told her she had miscarried. She blamed the doctor who had butchered her uterus during the first delivery.[9]

Carrie continued typing George's work through the fall and into the winter, but she often made him wait for it. She realized she needed to demonstrate that her labor was valuable and should not be taken for granted. George kept visiting. He was trying to show her that he was now a productive writer.

That he was sober. He pleaded with her to come back. Gradually, he wore her down.

When Carrie returned to Carmel on April 1, 1913, she had been away for almost a year and a half. George had stopped drinking, as promised, but the bungalow was filthy. She rolled up her shirtsleeves and flew into cleaning.[10] Grateful, George located several plots of wild strawberries and brought a basket of them back to her. They were red, fresh, and perfect. He thanked her for cleaning. He thanked her for cooking. He thanked her for everything she did—and had been doing—every day.

Once she had restored a modicum of order to the house, she attacked the yard. She got down on her hands and knees in front of the veranda, pulling up the weeds so she could plant spring flowers in pinks, purples, and bright yellow. She had missed the flowers that were everywhere in the Piedmont. Her flowerbed would be so colorful, it would announce to Carmel that she was her own woman no matter what they thought. She was unbowed and unashamed.

· · ·

Happily, since she had been away, her neighbors had found other things besides her to gossip about. There was trouble among the theater troupes of the town, and that skinny pot-stirrer Bert Heron was trying to drag George into the center of it.

Back in 1910, Bert Heron had pitched the idea of an outdoor theater to the Carmel Development Company. He envisioned the Carmel equivalent of Stratford-Upon-Avon, with a two-week festival every summer, showcasing plays written by California writers. Heron had gotten the idea for it when he had accompanied George to the Bohemian Club's summer encampment. He had been dazzled by the sight of theater performed against the natural backdrop of the woods. Carmel didn't have Sonoma County's spectacular redwoods, but it did have plenty of pine.

Frank Powers readily agreed to fund the theater, having become acutely aware of growing competition to attract the art-conscious wealthy. Art colonies were popping up from Monhegan, Maine, to Santa Fe, New Mexico. Florence Griswold's home in Old Lyme, Connecticut, had housed the famed painter Willard Metcalf and even hosted First Lady Ellen Axson Wilson. The art colony in Provincetown, Massachusetts, taught rich ladies from New York how to paint "en plein air." With water on two sides, Provincetown afforded light for landscape painting that was said to be the best that could be found without leaving America. And, unlike Carmel, it had a train station.

Frank Powers hoped live theater would showcase Carmel's strengths in the literary arts, differentiating it from other colonies. He astounded Heron by granting him fifteen acres for the theater when he had only asked for five. Not only that, the company would create a turnaround drive for carriages and cars.[11] In no time, a stage was built into a nook of trees up against the hill, and benches were brought in for a seating capacity of a thousand. It would be called the Forest Theater, and Heron would be its founding director.

Hardly had the first performance concluded, however, when the trouble began. Heron and Bertha Newberry both submitted plays for selection to the Forest Theater Drama Society. Heron read Bertha's manuscript and was aghast. She had lifted most of her play, *The Toad*, from an earlier work of his. Raging, he prepared a document detailing thirty-nine instances where Buttsky had taken language from his work. He would not leave George in peace until he had also signed on to his cause.

They took their case to the next meeting of the drama society, hoping to drive a vote to censor Buttsky. Perry Newberry, however, had just become the troupe's president, and he had locked down support for his wife. When the motion to censor was voted down, Heron and George stood, read their resignations, and left, declaring that they would form their own troupe. Half the group followed them.[12]

Frank Powers saw that his writers weren't getting along, and he wasn't happy about it. He decreed there would be a play produced in the next year, even if he had to take control of the enterprise himself.[13] Then Mrs. Josephine Foster, who never failed to make any bad situation worse, told Heron she had seen Powers indicating George to some ladies he was taking for a tour, "There goes my poet, George Sterling." Minutes later, Powers had pointed out the new 13-Mile Drive behind the beach, calling it "my new road."[14]

Heron received this news and smirked. *My* road, *my* poet; it was all the same to the Carmel Development Company—commodities to be harnessed for profit. Heron, who voted socialist up and down the ballot every year without fail, determined it was time for a revolt against Carmel's management class. This was no longer only a question of art but one of gross oppression. If Frank Powers was going to treat the artists of Carmel like mere employees, then the writers should do what workers were doing all over the country: go on strike. He and George began meeting with a representative of the Pacific Improvement Company about starting a new theater in nearby Pacific Grove.

Back in November, Carrie had read all about the crisis in *The San Francisco Call*. "Literary Ranks Split as Art Is Commercialized" was the headline. "Leading Members of Carmel Colony Do Not Take Kindly to Offer of Realty Firm to Utilize Great Artistic Project for an 'Ad' to Sell Land Sites," the lede continued.

Has satan invaded Carmel-by-the-Sea and tempted half the literary colony there to depart to a newer land, and will Geo. Sterling and Herbert Herron and the rest of his clique accept the bait of the tempter and go to Pacific Grove to occupy a new "Forest theater," the gift of the Pacific Improvement company to high art?[15]

Front page, left column, the story appeared below the international news: "Sultan Startles World by Resuming Balkan War."

Frank Powers acted quickly to crush the revolt. He told the Pacific Improvement Company that if they poached his writers, Carmel would no longer grant them an easement to the river for water. And that was that. The theater stayed in Carmel, but now there were two troupes forever at war with each other, in a town of a few hundred inhabitants.

Carrie found it farcical. There wasn't a teapot small enough for this tempest. The Herons were pathetic, and Carrie wished they would stop enlisting George in this juvenile rebellion. What did Heron think they were all there for, if not to create ads for Carmel? That was the job. With two children now and mountains of debt, Heron should accept the patronage and thank Powers on his hands and knees. Instead, he had half the town ready to kill the other half.

Into this keg of dynamite, Mary Austin was dropped like a match. Mary returned to serve as "artist in residence," invited officially by Jimmy Hopper on behalf of Heron's Western Drama Society.[16] She arrived brimming with stories of the victorious New York run of *The Arrow Maker*. The use of genuine Indian dress and artifacts borrowed from the American Museum of Natural History had won it a special notice from *The New York Times*.[17] Unlike any of the other playwrights in town, she had put on a production in a major city, securing a reputation that extended beyond California.

Carrie noticed that Mary's success only seemed to infuriate the men. The truth was that although they needed Mary to boost their sagging drama troupe, none of them could stand the fact that she had surpassed them. They called her horrible names behind her back: "Mary the Impossible" and "Mary the Festive Cow"—the latter being Jimmy's creation.[18] They snickered to one another about her claim to have clairvoyant powers. They whispered about the flea bites on her décolletage. In every way they could, they marked her as ridiculous, unwomanly, and too ugly to deserve notice.

Carrie knew Mary could be ridiculous. One night while walking home with Genthe, Mary insisted she had the powers of a cat and could see in the dark and would lead the way. Genthe watched her trip over roots and struggle through brush and was powerless to intervene, which taxed his German training in chivalry.[19] But instead of mocking Mary's independence, the men could try admiring it. How independent were they, really?

It seemed Mary had committed the sin of being unattractive *and* talented, a combination that baffled the men completely. Unlike Nora, she did not present as a potential sexual conquest. She neither sought nor wanted their protection. When their work was bad, she told them. And as the audience for her work grew, it magnified their inadequacies.

Years before, Mary had sent a letter to George expressing her true feelings about how she was treated in Carmel. She concluded, "Common people would do very well if only they would not so thrust their commonness upon me."[20] George thought this unmatched in arrogance. But then he had also choked down his pride and asked her to shop some of his poems around British journals. Mary said she had tried her very hardest to place them, but George's poems just wouldn't sell across the water. She told him that he should write less like Bierce and more like Browning. He should try just being human for a change.

Carrie thought Mary's advice was on the whole very sound, but George ignored it. Instead, he wrote back: "Of course I might be suffering from incurable immaturity, and I cheerfully confess I'm leagues less human than you—and Wells, and Browning."[21] George then denied he had ever asked her to shop the poems, and if he had asked for her assistance in that matter, he must have been drunk at the time, and she should have ignored the request.

George next turned to Jack London for help, sending him "The First Poet," a work of bitter resentment masquerading so poorly as verse that not even the ordinarily sycophantic Heron could spare a kind word for it. "The First Poet" told the tale of the world's first poet, a martyr. Despised by his tribe for being too noisy, he declares:

> I will make thee no songs, neither of thy club, nor thy
> cave, nor thy doe's-liver. Yea! though thou give me no
> more flesh, yet will I live alone in the forest, and eat the
> seed of grasses, and likewise rabbits, that are easily
> snared. And I will sleep in a tree-top, and I will sing
> nightly:
> The bright day is gone.
> The night maketh me sad, sad, sad,
> sad, sad, sad—

In the end, the first poet is clubbed into silence by his exasperated tribe.[22]

In dire need of money, George asked Jack to sell the poem

under his own name and give George $25 from the proceeds as his take. Jack could even edit a few lines so he wouldn't feel that he'd be cheating an editor.[23] Jack wrote back that he considered "The First Poet" a delicious satire and thought it a shame that George couldn't claim it as his own. But he was hesitant to accept the proposal. What if they were found out? Hadn't Heron and the writer Mike Williams (neither known to be discreet) already read a draft of it? Why was George lining him up to be exposed as a fraud? "Your showing THE FIRST POET to Heron and Williams, and then coming on and asking me to father it, is equivalent to exposing your penis to a couple of 90 cent alarm clocks, and then trying to rape a quail. I'm the quail. And if I let you rape me, both alarm clocks would immediately go off and tell the news to the world," Jack wrote.[24]

George quickly sent a sack of mussels packed in seaweed to the Londons as an apology. He reassured Jack that he'd take care of Heron and Williams. He again suggested Jack add a few lines to the poem to bolster a claim of collaboration, just to be on the safe side.[25] With minor edits, no one could argue who had written what. Just a few lines would do.

Then George Sterling flipped the pages backward in the Carmel diary one month. His entry for October 17, 1910, read, "Wrote 'The First Poet,' a satire." He squeezed in two words after it, "London collaborates."[26] Barely enough room left on the page, but he compressed the words to make them fit. "The First Poet" was published in the June 1911 issue of *The Century Illustrated Monthly Magazine* under Jack London's name. And George got the money.

In the meantime, Mary Austin had been writing her fourth book. Her 1912 semiautobiographical novel, *A Woman of Genius*, eviscerated marriage by depicting how women actually experienced it. Its call for sexual freedom for women was considered so radical, her publisher stopped printing it after four months.[27]

Carrie thought the book, a reflection of Mary's own unsatisfying marriage, contained lines that could also have been written about George and herself. She was struck by Mary's contention that a woman is hypnotized into believing that she is no longer her own person when she gets married to a man, "and becomes somehow mysteriously and inevitably his."[28]

Had Carrie been hypnotized? She had always supposed she entered into marriage of her own free will and with her eyes wide open. But George's weaknesses toward drink and women had led both of them to devolve from who they were when they first met. Their marriage was no longer on an equal footing. Instead of husband and wife, they had become like child and mother, she satisfying all his needs while he shirked his responsibilities to provide for her. To cherish her.

Mary Austin could be egotistical, maniacal, and outrageous, and she thought she was immortal. She was impulsive, following her feelings, inclinations, or visions wherever they wandered. But when it came to seeing the truth of relations between the sexes, Mary Austin was the sanest person Carrie knew.

In May, George and Carrie escaped Carmel and the daily skirmishes of the drama troupes and went to the Londons' ranch. George was still sober, somehow. Their visit was a total reversal of that disastrous trip a year and a half before—almost like the honeymoon they had never really had. They spent their days walking in the woods together, hand in hand. Even Charmian noticed, remarking that George looked rejuvenated.[29]

It helped that for once, Jack wasn't pushing liquor on George. Jack had shocked everyone by coming out in favor of Prohibition. He had begun publishing his next autobiographical work, *John*

Barleycorn, as a serial in *The Saturday Evening Post*, proclaiming that alcohol, or "John Barleycorn," as he called it, made a monkey out of a man by making him think he was a genius. It offered to the drinker a delusion Jack called "white logic." As men drank, they became convinced that the world was only a sordid sham, and all the people in it were mere puppets of fate—all but the drinker himself, of course. The man with the bottle believes that he alone sees the whole sorry mess for what it is. "And he knows his one freedom: he may anticipate the day of his death. All of which is not good for a man who is made to live and love and be loved. Yet suicide, quick or slow, a sudden spill or a gradual oozing away through the years, is the price John Barleycorn exacts. No friend of his ever escapes making the just, due payment."[30]

George read the whole book in manuscript form twice through in one day. He loved it. He thought it was a hundred times better than Jack's previous book (the one featuring Carmel), *The Valley of the Moon*.[31] Carrie found it appalling. Jack had laid it all bare—from his first swig at his father's bucket of beer when he was five years old, to his multiple failed attempts at sobriety. Why couldn't Jack have just quietly quit drinking? Carrie wondered. Why announce to the world your weakness and then crow that you had overcome it, knowing the press would lie in wait for your next slip? If George had published such a thing, she would have been mortified.

Carrie was relieved that at least Jack had done his best to shield George from any mention in the book. For once there wasn't even a character who in every way but name resembled George. George had been Brissenden in *Martin Eden*, a poet and the main character's best friend; Brissenden is generous, dissolute, and finally shoots himself in a fleabag hotel. In *The Valley of the Moon*, George had been the wayward scion of a wealthy family,

Mark Hall. At last, Jack had left George out of a book completely, even though he identified other friends by name, including Cloudesley Johns and Toddy (so nicknamed because he drank so much whiskey).

She hoped that Jack's conversion to temperance might extend George's streak of sobriety. But when they returned to Carmel and the season began, George again picked up the bottle. The war between the drama troupes gave George the excuse he needed to drink. He hosted, and drank through, frequent meetings of the Western Drama Society, which was choosing a play to rival the Forest Theater Society's production of William Greer Harrison's *Runnymede* (Greer had, despite the Sterlings' best efforts, moved to Carmel).

Mary Austin had offered her play, *Fire*, to the drama society, an adaptation of an Indian legend about the bringer of fire to humanity. Heron, egomaniacally, proposed instead his play *Montezuma*—the one he claimed Bertha had plagiarized. At a meeting hosted at the Sterling bungalow, an earnest debate ensued about the merits of both. Carrie observed the proceedings, no one paying her any attention. She watched her neighbors take exquisite pains to put Bert Heron, the author of locally produced plays, on the same footing as Mary Austin, who had written multiple books and whose reputation had become international. It was galling.

Mary's play won in a ludicrously close vote. Aware that she was surrounded by bruised egos, Mary mollified the men by giving them good parts. Heron would play the lead, the bringer of fire. He seemed happy with that. George got the part of Atla, the hunter. It fit him. George was now hunting daily, shooting rabbits by the dozen. For the play, he would get to strut around for hours of rehearsal in a primitive fur skirt that would show off his toned legs while he carried a club and tried to look menacing.

Carrie was entirely weary of hosting salons in her living room under any circumstances, but watching her neighbors pretend to be serious actors made her exhausted. After their business meeting, the troupe stayed for a game of charades. George sat and drank and drank. Carrie couldn't stand to look at him. Instead, she surveyed the room. There was the preening but talentless Bert Heron. Next to him, his wife, Opal, who constantly flirted with George. Across the room, the illiterate druggist Dr. Beck. Next to him, the busybody Mrs. Josephine Foster, a woman who poured George copious drinks whenever they went to dinner at her house, just so he would flatter her. She never had to deal with the aftermath. She never had to endure George's hangovers or mop up his vomit. She was the ultimate parasite.

Carrie began to see that she would never be rid of these people if she continued to play nice. So when it was her turn to do an imitation of a person, she did Mrs. Foster. It felt like the old days, imitating the boarders for her sisters. She stuck her nose into everyone's faces, clucked her tongue, and when they still didn't get it, she performed Mrs. Foster's subtle adjustment of her stockings through her skirt.[32]

She knew she had hit it spot on when Mrs. Foster got up and abruptly left the room. The next day, her neighbors let her know how offended Mrs. Foster was. Carrie pretended to be surprised and apologetic but felt secretly victorious.

To usher in a period of peace after the year of turmoil, George decided to throw a barbecue at the bungalow and invite the members of both drama troupes. He had fashioned a new grill that could accommodate far more meat than their last one. He drove over to Monterey and came back with a load of seltzer water to make mint juleps, his favorite drink. He snipped mint from the garden in bundles to add to the whiskey in a big vat.

Carrie greeted the guests as they came in. The Herons, the Phelpses, the Hardys, the Kelloggs, the Rogerses, the Hankses, the Turners, and Mary Austin (but not Mrs. Foster, who was still furious with her) all came. Bertha Newberry and Bert Heron had stopped hissing at each other for the sake of appearances. The floorboards started to shake from the dancing, or "ragging," as they now called it; Jimmy had returned from New York with new cocktail recipes and new dance moves. Carrie could hardly locate George amid the elbows and knees. Then she heard his voice from across the living room. Even at that distance, she could perceive he was slurring. She saw him, leaning against the hearth, his glass so overfull it was spilling onto the floor. He didn't seem to notice at all.

Her first impulse was to intervene. But then she stopped herself. He was not her child. If he wanted to behave like a fool, it was no reflection on her. Any confrontation at this gathering and they would be talking about what a scold she was for weeks. Instead, she kept her distance but couldn't stop herself from watching him. He was following Bertha Newberry from room to room like a puppy. When Bertha stubbed out a cigarette and announced she was going to the toilet, George raised his arms and cried after her, "Buttsky!"

At first Carrie thought George was mocking Bertha, but then later, from the living room, Carrie spied them sitting on the ledge surrounding the veranda and saw her husband's hands stray around Bertha's waist, his face drawing close to Bertha's ear. Heron, stricken by the sight of his best friend canoodling with his sworn enemy, quickly made excuses to Carrie and left.

Minutes afterward, George and Buttsky lost their balance and toppled together off the veranda into Carrie's colorful flowerbed.[33]

Chapter Seventeen

❧

Divorcée

She stayed with George. She couldn't say why. The marriage was over in every way that mattered, and yet she felt frozen in place, unable to make a decision. She began looking for some kind of sign to give her direction—any omen, good or bad. She didn't expect to see so many.

In July 1913, news of Harry Lafler's second divorce (the first one hadn't been finalized till 1911) was covered by *The San Francisco Call*. His new wife, Gladys, a socialite who raised Russian wolfhounds, alleged Lafler had twisted her arm while insisting "in an imperious tone" that he was "lord of the house." On another occasion, he shook her violently.[1]

Then, Jack London's alcohol-ridden appendix arrived in a jar as a gift.

Shortly after, a friend of George's brought a dancing girl, a

Miss Estelle Tuttle, to visit, and George and the girl disappeared for a walk and didn't come back until dark.[2]

In August, they found a dead hummingbird trapped in a spiderweb outside the kitchen window.[3]

In early September, she went up to Oakland for her mother's seventieth birthday.[4] Her mother, in tandem with her sisters, Mrs. Maxwell and Mrs. Havens, stepped up their campaign to get her to leave George. She was making a fool of herself, they maintained. She felt as though she were twelve again, the object of her family's scorching derision. She fled back to Carmel.

The October issue of *Young's Magazine* came out with a new story by Vera Connolly. It featured the scion of a sugar industry magnate, clearly modeled on George. In the tale, this scion pays a young woman he has impregnated to have his child out of town so he can keep his own prospects for a respectable marriage alive. The George Sterling stand-in reveals his error to an old friend in a law office in San Francisco, giving all too George-like excuses for his behavior:

> "I was drunk, Dean. I didn't know—I didn't mean—I've done all under Heaven I could for her, ever since—"
>
> "You're supporting her?" The words were sharp cut.
>
> "Supporting her!" Gunter faced him squarely in his petty indignation. "Why, man—a quarter of my income goes to that woman every month."
>
> "She's here?"
>
> "No. She's gone over to England. She's never coming back here. It's an agreement. I'm to pay her that for life— and she's never to come back."
>
> Dean leaned forward.
>
> "And you believe that?"

"I know it. She'll never come back."

"Why?"

"Because I told her I'd kill her if she did."

After this exchange the scion glances up to see a motto hanging on his friend's wall. "'Vengeance is mine,' sayeth the Lord. 'I shall repay.'"[5]

Eight pages later, the fictional George Sterling is found in a sleazy hotel in the slums of Paris—starving, disease-ridden, penniless (his father having lost his entire fortune overnight in one convulsion of the stock market), but finally penitent. He dies soon after.

Vera probably got $100 for killing George off in print.

In late October, Ambrose Bierce sent an ominous letter to his niece Lora. The old writer was planning to go to Mexico and never come back to the United States. "Good-bye," he wrote. "If you hear of my being stood up against a Mexican stone wall and shot to rags please know that I think that a pretty good way to depart this life. It beats old age, disease, or falling down the cellar stairs. To be a Gringo in Mexico—ah, that is euthanasia!"[6] It sounded like a suicide note.

In November, a neighbor, a man, looked at Carrie in a way no man had in ages and spoke to her with kindness. She had forgotten what that felt like.

Carrie dragged her luggage out and began to pack. George was motoring with Jimmy, escorting a group of ladies to view Frank Powers's latest cooked-up festival: a celebration of Father Junípero Serra. Carmel's 550 permanent residents were joined by over one thousand brothers from the Order of St. Francis of Assisi, who had arrived to recognize the two hundredth anniversary of the birth of Serra, the founder of the Carmel Mission, and thus, in Frank Powers's mind, the ancestral founder of his development. Serra had dedicated his life to converting Indians by founding Catholic missions up and down the coast. He persisted when the Indians revolted, burning the San Diego mission to the ground. The mission at Carmel had served as a forced labor camp. And yet, he was considered a hero.

On one of the most beautiful days of the year, the friars made a solemn procession to the mission, where Mass was given. A ribbon of men in brown, singing in unison, walked through the pines. George was to read a poem in dedication to Serra at the festivities. Carrie had told George that when he returned home, she wouldn't be there. With him away at the festival all day, she had enough time to pack her things properly. When she was finished, she went to the Hoppers' house to stay the night. She caught the early bus to Berkeley the next morning.[7]

. . .

STERLING A POET? READ WIFE'S CHARGES IN DIVORCE PLEA

The San Francisco Call

December 16, 1913

George Sterling is a real poet.

It's been proved again—by his wife's divorce complaint, just filed in Monterey county, according to word received here today.

Here are her charges:

Nonsupport
Idleness
Dissipation

Could a list more typical of the traditional poet's faults be made?

Now instead of listening to "The Testimony of the Suns," Sterling will hear the testimony of a prosaic court, probably touching on his consumption of other beverages than "The Wine of Wizardry."

The suit was filed by Mrs. Sterling's attorney, Hiram Johnson Jr., at Salinas, just back of the hills that enfold Carmel, which Sterling helped discover and of whose literary colony he is one of the pillars.

Two weeks ago Mrs. Sterling's sister, Mrs. Harry Maxwell, announced that the poet was to be sued, after several years of marital uneasiness. Since there has been much speculation as to what charges would be made.

Now that they're out, Sterling's friends see that he is more of a poet than ever, even if he was once a real estate agent.

Carrie had learned from Bessie London's mistake: Don't ever sue your famous husband for adultery, lest you become the object of public scorn and conjecture. So she left Vera Connolly's name out of the suit entirely (in the end, why name any one woman?— there had been so many). She would not reveal to the world her humiliation. They would only side with him, anyway, as they had with Jack London. Men were always forgiven their sins, whereas women were tarred with their own—and their husbands'—for life.

George didn't fight the suit. He signed over the deed to the Carmel bungalow to Carrie at the end of December (he had exercised his option to buy years before). Carrie got half his Realty Syndicate stock and all property except his poetry books, some photos, and a few paintings. She sold the bungalow to the Hoppers immediately. She would not need a house in Carmel. She never intended to step foot in the place again.

The money from the sale of the house wouldn't last long, so she began to look for employment in San Francisco. She had no idea even where to start. For the previous two decades, she had had only one job—that of George Sterling's wife—a job she could no longer do. She at last found a position at an art import business on the corner of Grant Avenue and Geary Street. The pay was minimal, but Carrie leapt at it, even though she hated San Francisco and far preferred the East Bay.

She made enough to rent a small apartment at Powell and Clay Streets, from which she could walk to and from the gallery. Financially independent for the first time in her life, free of the disapproving glares from both her mother and Mrs. Havens, she was at first quite happy. The job, moving high-class etchings and engravings by appointment, gave her lots of time at her desk to ponder where in her life she had gone wrong. Was it that she had had too much faith in George or too much faith in the young women she had taken under her wing? On her good days, she decided she could view her marriage to George as "a developer"— an experience that ultimately helped her grow in independence and self-esteem. Since joining the citizenry of divorced women, she realized she could have been kinder toward women whose marriages had failed. At least they had made a definitive choice instead of drifting for years in uncertainty. There was some dignity to be salvaged in walking away.

Carrie now thought of marriage the way she used to think of children: a sure way to ruin a woman's life. She hoped adopting this view would cushion her from any gossip of George's new affairs, but everything she heard about him reopened old wounds. She had been stunned when, only two months after the divorce, *The San*

Francisco Examiner featured George's engagement to a Miss Estelle Tuttle, a common dancing girl. "George is the reincarnation of Dante," Miss Tuttle told the paper's readers. "I know that I lived many years ago in Egypt. The soul of the Italian poet and that of the denizen of the desert have met and commingled."[8]

Carrie almost retched reading that, right onto the photo of Miss Tuttle, who posed with her cat eyes glaring over her fur-draped shoulder. The paper had reprinted George's handwritten poem "The Star of Love," marked "To Stella," with a sketch underneath of George as a half-naked Pan figure rising from the waves and playing his pipes to a far star. This glowing write-up of George's impending marriage to his "muse" took pains to reveal that Stella had inspired George's poetry of love for years, implying their relationship had been going on while the Sterlings were still married. Despite all of Carrie's attempts to keep George's adultery a secret in her divorce suit, it was now publicly celebrated as evidence of his genius.

Next, she heard George was working in New York and was dropping by to see Vera Connolly. When, in a weak moment, she wrote him to ask whether they were still involved, he responded cruelly that if she desired the particulars of those meetings, she could get them from the Hoppers.[9]

Vera and Miss Tuttle might share George's body, but Carrie was sure they did not have his heart. That, she could see from the new volume of poems he had published, still belonged to Nora May French. His verses were riddled with images of dead and drowned women:

> I knelt below the stars; the sea put forth a wave;
> The moon drew up the captive tides upon her shining grave.[10]

There was no poem mourning Carrie in the volume. No lament for their lost love and squandered years. She sighed. The only women who were ever truly loved were the dead ones.

Mary Austin sent her a letter of condolence a year after the split (Mary's own husband had finally sued her for divorce in 1914). Carrie wrote back immediately, thanking her for writing. She conceded that of late she had been persuaded to embrace Mary's views on the failure of marriage as an institution. Carrie mused that perhaps marriage could be salvaged someday in the future, but that wouldn't happen until after equality between the sexes had been fully achieved—and she didn't see that happening for a long time. "We are too near cave-man state yet to have a perfect or even near-perfect state. Women much more so because they have been forced to be so through centuries by their stronger mate. However, in a thousand years we may have it."[11]

While Carrie was expelled from society for her divorce, George suffered not at all. He was invited to write the opening ode for the Pan-Pacific Exposition of 1915. In a bid to outdo Chicago's famous World's Fair of 1893, San Francisco had erected a mini-city on six hundred acres of the waterfront. The papers described the highlights, including a two-mile-long Palace of Machinery, modeled after the Roman baths of Caracalla, so vast a plane had flown through it. The colonnades of the Bernard Maybeck–designed Palace of Fine Arts would be reflected in a lagoon. But most enchanting would be the Tower of Jewels, rising over four hundred feet and adorned with one hundred thousand colored crystals.

All this to boost California as a land of opportunity and unlimited horizons. When at last the exposition opened and Carrie walked through it, she couldn't help but be impressed. She watched the Ford company assemble an automobile, listened to a recording of the first four-way transcontinental telephone call (completed the month before the gates opened), and gaped at the fourteen-ton typewriter. The message was clear: San Francisco had fully recovered from the earthquake and was ready to assume its place as the Western hub of commerce and industry.

As California boomed, Carrie's own poverty deepened. She began spending less of her time with Blanche Partington and Charmian Kittredge. Blanche and Charmian saw each other more frequently as they still traveled in the social circles where money was assumed. Occasionally, the pair would invite her to join them at the theater, but Carrie could almost see them wince as they climbed their way to the cheap seats and visibly strained to see the stage, as if from a very great distance. They were sitting there for her, the charity case. Their pity was palpable. She knew now what it must have been like for Kate Partington, trying to pretend you weren't as desperately poor as you were to make your richer companions feel comfortable.

Nonetheless, when Jack London died suddenly in November 1916, Carrie immediately sent a telegram of condolence to Charmian. Surprising her, Charmian asked Carrie to come to Beauty Ranch. When Carrie arrived, she found Charmian in grief but also in trouble. It seemed Charmian wasn't as well-off as Carrie had imagined. In the years before his death, Jack had sunk all their capital into a spectacular mansion in the deep woods of their property. Wolf House, as he called it, was to be fifteen thousand square feet with a central vacuuming system. Even Jack couldn't write fast enough to fund construction. To generate cash, he launched himself as a brand, putting his name on grape juice. The stationery of the Jack London Grape Juice Company featured a sketch of Jack in his ranch hat and riding boots, one hand in his pocket, the other arm casually slung around the neck of a human-size bottle of grape juice.[12]

Just before its completion, Wolf House burned down. Jack never seemed to rebound after the fire. His health, long poor, plummeted. His last nights were spent with his teeth clenched in pain, battling uremia, rheumatism, and several other conditions brought on by a lifetime of alcoholic drinking.

Charmian was left buried by his debts. As Carrie walked with Charmian around the ranch in the crisp autumn afternoons, she felt finally that the two of them were equal. They had both had husbands who put their vanity before their duty to provide for their wives. She reflected that there had been only one marriage among the Bohemian set that had prospered, the one that had seemed least likely at first: that of Elsie and Xavier Martínez. Elsie had been sixteen when she fell in love with Marty, who was more than twice her age. Her father, Jim Whitaker, had forbidden her to go out with Marty unless she had a chaperone, like Vera Connolly, present. Vera of course, had made sure that Marty and Elsie had plenty of time to themselves. Finally, Elsie announced she would run away if her father didn't let her marry Marty. The pair had been inseparable ever since, even though she continued to attract admirers, which drove Marty to the brink of insanity. Once, after a visiting writer had overstepped in praise of Elsie, Marty went outside and nailed a piece of paper to a tree. He picked up his revolver and shot at it repeatedly, shouting over the blasts, "I am going to keel that son of a beech!"[13]

Carrie tried to imagine George threatening to kill someone over her. Not in a million years. Nor, for that matter, did she see any evidence that Jack had loved Charmian any more than he did his pigs or his drink. And now Charmian was alone and destroyed.

George made sure Carrie was gone from Beauty Ranch before he came to pay his respects. He had told Charmian that he didn't dare risk seeing Carrie while he had so little to offer her.[14] In other words, he had already spent his money on other women.

By 1917, the art gallery had closed and Carrie was left with only $70 to her name. Unable to find employment, she asked her sister for help. Mrs. Havens grudgingly gave Carrie the job of looking after the Piedmont art gallery and allowed her to live in a small house in the Japanese garden of Wildwood. Saved from destitution, Carrie was nevertheless made to feel a burden every moment. She was now obliged to sit in the Havens mansion and listen to her sister's financial woes. Just before Frank Havens died in February, he had paid a huge fee to the government in penance for cooking the books.[15] The Realty Syndicate had been forced to liquidate completely. Its stock, valued just ten years before at over $300 a share for the purposes of securing a loan for water company acquisitions, was now worth little more than a dollar a share.[16] The Havenses even had to sell Cormaria in Sag Harbor.

Carrie sympathized, but it was difficult to feel sorry for someone who still drove limousines around town. Her own days passed quietly, broken up by visits from Elsie Martínez, who lived nearby and frequently came to chat. Carrie often found herself reviewing her life with George during these afternoons, reflecting on how blind she had been. For years she had naively thought that his attraction to other women would pass. The affair with Vera had jolted her badly, she could admit to Elsie, who had broken off communication with Vera and now thought of her as a schemer. Carrie felt at least she had one true friend.

In May, Charmian reached out to Carrie with an invitation to dine with mutual friends at the St. Francis Hotel.[17] Carrie loved the St. Francis. Built on Union Square with the fortune left by deceased railway magnate Charles Crocker, it was one of the few hotels to emerge from the earthquake with negligible structural damage; a smaller version of the hotel had been erected in the park to house guests while the original hotel, gutted by fire, was re-modeled.[18] George had taken Carrie to the St. Francis shortly after it had opened in 1904, and she had dragged him onto the dance floor. Now she would need to scrimp to afford coffee and dessert.

Charmian embraced Carrie warmly when she arrived in the hotel lobby. The two entered the Tapestry Room arm in arm, greeted by the strains of Ferdinand Stark's orchestra. The hostess showed them to a table next to the dance floor. It was a Saturday evening, and the hall was full. Carrie sat for a moment and looked at the murals on the walls by the artist Albert Herter. Colorful and elaborate scenes paid homage to Mexico, Persia, the Orient, and the American Indian. "Booful, booful," Charmian pointed and exclaimed. The scenes were also printed on the menus.

Like all restaurants, the St. Francis had trimmed its offerings to reflect the austere times. America had entered the Great War just months before, so no more caviar. Carrie was pleased to see they still had filet mignon, pheasant with truffles, and lobster thermidor. Surrounded by live music and in congenial surroundings, Carrie felt like her old self. Sometimes it was good to pretend you weren't poor, that you didn't spend half the day worrying about where tomorrow's meal was coming from. She and Charmian left and went to the Alcazar Theater to take in a melodramatic movie. By the time it let out, it was late enough that Carrie invited Charmian back to her house to stay with her.

Looking out from the streetcar, Charmian couldn't believe how much the Piedmont had changed. The houses had proliferated. She tried to spot Bessie London's old house but couldn't figure out which one it was. She had not been there in so many years. They walked through the gardens at Wildwood until they arrived at Carrie's home.

The surroundings only seemed to inspire Charmian to drone on and on about her struggles replacing her Japanese cook, who had just left.[19] Selling off chunks of Jack's unpublished manuscript, Charmian had managed to keep the ranch going. But finding good people to cook for her at fair rates exhausted her.

Carrie was annoyed. Did Charmian think that looking for a new cook counted as financial difficulty? Tempted to yell at her, she tried the indirect approach of suggesting that she herself was up against it, as George had refused to pay any form of alimony for years. So they had both been left high and dry by their men in some way.

Carrie invited Charmian back for tea two weeks later. They were midway through their second cups when Charmian announced she had had a splendid idea. She could solve both their problems at once. Charmian needed a cook, and Carrie needed a steady income. Carrie could come to work for her as a cook at Beauty Ranch. Her room and board would be taken care of, and she would earn enough to put away a little for retirement.

For a moment, Carrie was speechless. She stared at Charmian, who was grinning, awaiting an answer. She realized Charmian had walked into her little Japanese house and saw a maid's house. She saw Carrie not as a friend but as a potential new servant, someone to take orders, leave and enter through the back door, and sleep in the rear end of the house. Of all the jabs Carrie had endured from this woman over her life, this one was the most revealing of Charmian's true colors. Charmian was not the strong, modern, liberated woman she claimed to be at all, but a kept princess whose greatest panic was that she might have to clean up after herself. She at last proved herself to be the spoiled parasite Carrie knew she was at first glance.

Carrie quickly made up an excuse of things to do and said farewell to her guest. After the door shut, she burst out in angry tears. But after her tears dried, she felt triumphant. She had been right about Charmian after all, and now she never had to see her again.

She began to limit her social engagements. She had a man of sorts—Frank Helfricht, her former neighbor in Carmel. He would come over now and again, and together they would enjoy a quiet night listening to classical music on the phonograph. Helfricht was a humble but cultured man with a steady if poorly compensated security position. George had suggested through friends that Carrie should marry him, but she had no intention of hooking herself to a man for life just to spare George the expense of supporting her according to his legal obligation.

Another year came and went without George paying her the $100-a-month court-ordered alimony. By the summer of 1918, George owed her nearly $5,000. Carrie engaged a lawyer to threaten him with a levy on his book royalties if he didn't pay up. This had scared George enough that he'd accepted a job writing for a light opera in New York.[20] He considered that assignment demeaning. Well, nobody had asked him to be their cook.

It was August, and she had still heard nothing from George. Her calendar marked the date of her planned final communication with him, and she slashed "x's" through the days leading up to it.[21] She gave Elsie a photograph of herself when she left after one of their long afternoon visits. The next morning, she wasn't sure if she had remembered to say goodbye. She picked up the phone and called Elsie.

"I just wanted to say goodbye."

She realized her mistake immediately. "Carrie, 'Goodbye' sounds rather ominous!" Elsie exclaimed.[22]

Carrie laughed it off as a joke. But Elsie knew something was up. That afternoon, she came into the gallery, clearly suspicious. Carrie acted lighthearted. She had always been a better actress than people gave her credit for.

When Elsie left, Carrie closed the gallery and went home to her cottage. It was 4:00 p.m. Everything was prepared. She had written her note detailing to whom her possessions should be given and tacked tags to each piece of furniture to facilitate dispersal. Then she wrote another note so nobody would have to wonder.

"All the beauty is gone out of life," she scribbled. She addressed it to Mrs. Maxwell (not to Mrs. Havens), posted it outside her bedroom, and then shut the door.[23]

She removed her day dress and hung it up carefully. She pulled out a lacy nightgown and put it on, selecting her most elegant dressing robe to wear over it. Sitting in front of the vanity mirror, she took her time with her hair—it was still thick but now half-gray—pinning it up on top of her head. She ran her hand under her jawline, which had begun to sag. She avoided looking at herself in the eyes.

She put Chopin's *Funeral March* on the phonograph and sat down on her bed. Unscrewing the cap from a tiny bottle, she poured cyanide into a glass of water and stirred.

. . .

Caroline Rand Sterling was dead before Chopin's march ended. According to newspaper reports, she was found looking more peaceful than she had in years. The funeral was quiet, with few mourners. Elsie Martínez and Lora Bierce attended. Carrie's mother made a brief appearance. She walked into the church and made her way directly to the coffin. Standing at its head, she rendered her final criticism, "Carrie, you've done a terrible thing and you're no daughter of mine."[24] She turned on her heel and walked out.

Newspapers coast to coast reported the death of "Mrs. George Sterling": in all the California papers; in the *Jackson's Hole Courier* of Wyoming; the *Beaver County News* of Mitford, Utah; and the *Buffalo Enquirer.* The *Harrisburg Tribune* of Pennsylvania printed a large photo of her and mentioned George's "A Wine of Wizardry." The *Brooklyn Daily Eagle* reported she had spent "summers" in Sag Harbor.

The Oakland Tribune reprinted George's poem "To My Wife as May Queen," which subtly seemed to call her bossy:

> But grant us, we that love thy dear decrees
> To know thy sway—solicitous to please
> With coronals and sacrificial wine

The paper also cited George's poem, "To One Self-Slain":

> Nay! Tho' I hunger, I in nowise hark
> The fleeting music scatter with thy dust,
> Nor call thy shadow from the House of Dread[25]

George had published "To One Self-Slain" in his book *Beyond the Breakers* in 1914, four years before Carrie died. He had written it for Nora May French.

Much of what we know about Carrie's death comes through Elsie Martínez, who lived long enough to become the voice of the Bohemians of Carmel. It's always nice to have a firsthand retrospective account, but I don't quite trust Elsie—and for reasons other than that many of the dates she offers are incorrect (common in interviews with elderly subjects). My greater concern is that she seemed almost infatuated by George. He may have won her favor at an impressionable age by dubbing her "the Blessed Damozel"— a name that stuck in their circles. Or maybe she shared Marty's high opinion of him. Whatever the cause, when Elsie talked about the disasters that continually unfolded around George, he was never to blame.

According to Elsie, Carrie and George would have remained married happily if it hadn't been for Carrie's meddling sisters. Carrie never wanted to divorce, Elsie maintained, but was forced to by Mrs. Havens, who thought the affair with Vera was bad press for the entire family. As for the affair itself, Elsie blamed Vera entirely. In her view, Vera had been twenty-two and was old enough to know what she was doing. (Remember, Elsie herself had run away with Marty when she was a teen.)

Elsie also said Jimmy Hopper was a horrible person and everyone hated him. Harry Lafler? She thought him "very likable."[26]

So I do take what Elsie says with more than a grain of salt— particularly her account of where Carrie's cyanide came from. George's sister Alice told the papers that Carrie had bought the cyanide from the Piedmont grocer with her sister Mrs. Maxwell present, using the excuse that she needed it to kill a cat.[27] Carrie's sister had suspected nothing. But Elsie said that Carrie's cyanide had been the remainder of what had been left in Nora May French's bottle.[28]

Every death had to be Nora's fault. Still.

. . .

George Sterling was in New York trying to rustle up some writing gigs during the last weeks of Carrie's life—so in fear was he of being sued by Carrie. On weekdays, he worked to develop librettos for off-Broadway musicals. Weekends, he tried to escape the heat of the city, hiking in the Palisades of New Jersey or heading to the beaches of Connecticut. He hoped to make enough connections out east that he could return to San Francisco and continue writing from there.

The trip to New York had taken him away from his latest flame, a Mrs. Rose Travis (his affair with Estelle Tuttle had fizzled out years before—they never did marry), to whom he wrote every day and sometimes twice a day while away. His letters reveal that he was preoccupied with the specter of being forced to turn over income to Carrie, and—worse—to create that income in the first place. Harry Lafler had sent him a clipping reporting that judges in San Mateo had sentenced men to go to work to support their families. George fretted to Rose: "I wonder if I'll get the same sentence, over in Oakland, when I get back to 'God's country'—and Carrie's?"[29]

So nervous was George about Carrie's plans for him that he implored Rose to go visit her in the Piedmont to find out what her "designs" were. If Carrie was going to take him to court the moment he stepped foot in California, he would hide in Seattle instead.[30] He must, he explained to Rose, to get any writing done. How could he create while being hunted by the law?

It's unlikely Rose had the chance to visit Carrie on the errand of investigating her intentions. George wrote just a week later that he had read of Carrie's death in the newspaper. The news, if we are to believe him, destroyed him. His letter to Rose, sent from the Lambs Club (the Stanford White–designed hotel for the theatrically inclined on Forty-Fourth Street), read:

Dearest! Dearest! I have just read of Carrie's suicide in the morning "American" and am sick at heart. The poor *thing! The poor thing! If I had but known she was so unhappy! I could not have lived with her again, in the full sense of the word, but I might have brought <u>some</u> happiness into her life. Ah! God! I was a bad man—and "the wages of sin is death," and not always the sinner's death. Now "the blinded eyes shall pay."[31]*

The next morning George took a train to Madison, Connecticut, as he had planned. Hosted by Mrs. Putnam, an artist who had let him use her apartment in the Washington Square Mews years before, he was going to have a dip in the Long Island Sound. He wrote Rose again.

I had an awful night, all tears and rending remorse. It had to be, I suppose. But I shudder to think how I must have made that poor woman suffer. If I had known she felt so deeply! . . . Be very near to me in the days to come, Love, for I have been hard hit, and feel so guilty! Were it not for you I think I should die just as she did. I suppose that even now the funeral is going on—or the cremation. Poor body that I held so often in my arms, in tenderness! Change is a terrible thing! May it not be so with us! Oh! Love me <u>forever!</u>[32]

Wait, it gets better. The next day, Sunday, 4:00 p.m.:

I cried half the night, for I feel a crushing weight of remorse. If only I had seen more clearly! But I was not to know the beauty and mystery and holiness of womanhood until I met you. And then—it was too late for anyone <u>except</u> you.

The silver lining for George was that he could now return to San Francisco, untroubled by pending legal threat. He told Rose that he would stay at her place for a while, but not before stopping at the Bohemian Club: "I shall have to go to the club to get my key to the studio, but of course I'll not remain there. For one thing, I cannot as I owe them $70, and am now 'suspended.'"[33]

. . .

The news of Carrie's death reached Charmian the same day it happened. She noted it dispassionately in her diary: "Carrie Sterling kills herself." It did not seem to upset her greatly. Her entry for August 9, 1918, was "Warm but wonderful. Take a holiday, and amuse myself. . . . Shock of poor Carrie's suicide makes me glad of something to take up my mind. It's so awful."[34]

Three days later, she noted reading in the papers that the second Mrs. Lafler—Gladys, whom Harry had married in haste after Nora May French's death but who had since remarried—had shot and killed her own child.

Charmian hadn't seen Carrie in more than a year. The records at the Huntington suggest why. First, it's important to note that most of Jack London's papers made it to Huntington only by passing through Charmian's hands. Conditioned by years of negative press, Charmian enacted damage control wherever possible; before she turned over the letters to the archives, she penciled in her commentary throughout. Many of her notes are helpful, for example, clarifying last names in letters where only first names appeared.

But one note goes way over the line of clarification and into the realm of the editorial. Where George wrote Charmian of Carrie, "Someone said she was 'furious' at you for offering her a job as your cook! I can't believe you did such a thing," Charmian scribbled in pencil next to it: "I didn't."

Oh, but she did. The Huntington has Charmian's diaries for virtually every year from 1900 to 1947 (missing are the diaries from 1902 and 1903, exactly those years that might have proved her affair with Jack was in full swing while she pretended to be friends with his wife, Bessie). Her diary from 1917 records the last weeks of her relationship with Carrie Sterling. Two days after her June visit to Carrie's house for tea, Charmian wrote:

> *June 18: "Hoping Carrie Sterling may come up and keep house for me."*

Her urgency to fill the position during this time is recorded two days later:

> *June 20: "Strange with no servant. Feels nice and <u>private</u> but that's the only advantage."*

Carrie had either told her no definitively, or she got a better offer, because two days after that:

> *June 22: "New cook (a Swedish woman!!!) comes in $50!"*[35]

But back to the letter where Charmian wrote "I didn't" in the margins. She also wrote where George had observed that Carrie had left her phonograph and some real estate stock to Helfricht, but nothing for either her mother or him, "Carrie was unbalanced near her end."[36]

It's not just the men who bring the shovels when it comes to burying women.

George wrote to Charmian a week after Carrie died, the two

seeming to form a pact that they would not succumb to the early deaths their spouses had: "Yes, Charmian, let us both see it through! I too have that fast hold on life, and am prey to illusion. I know it's illusion; but it seems worth while to me even at that."

He added, quoting Nora May's phrase for death, "It will be time enough to open 'the outer gate' when one is old and feeble."[37]

George had already decided on his end. It was just a matter of time.

Chapter Eighteen

൧ᴍᴍ൭

Phantom

THE YEARS FOLLOWING CARRIE'S SUICIDE HAD BEEN FOR GEORGE
one long and expensive bacchanalia, punctuated by fleeting attempts at sobriety.

He wrote mostly to H. L. Mencken. Their friendship had
begun in 1914 during George's post-divorce sojourn in New York
and continued through correspondence after his return to San
Francisco. Mencken had since scaled the crag of literary criticism
and emerged at the top. No longer the book reviewer for *The Smart
Set: The Magazine of Cleverness*, he had become a co-editor, sharp-
ening the magazine's satirical edge. The circulation of *The Smart
Set* grew to fifty thousand—considerable for a literary publication.
Mencken became the kingmaker of American literature, publishing
Dorothy Parker, Eugene O'Neill, and F. Scott Fitzgerald. He also

remained a savage critic. He took Bierce's place in decrying Jack London as a talentless hack (Bierce had never returned from Mexico and was presumed dead). He declared Charmian London's book on the adventures aboard the *Snark* on par with "a high-school girl's essay on the subconscious."[1]

And Mencken took Jack London's place as George Sterling's closest confidant. Many years George's junior, Mencken shared with him the priorities of drink, women, and literature. In a Prohibition-era letter to George, Mencken triumphantly reported his purchase of a case of 39-percent-alcohol Fernet-Branca, which the Italians were sneaking into the country by labeling it as a prescription for menstrual cramps.[2] Mencken had also amassed seven hundred bottles of ale in his basement and knew where to get enough hops and malt that he could keep distilling indefinitely.

Mencken was a racist and a bigot. In 1920, Mencken wrote to George gleefully of race riots in Washington's streets: "At last my dream comes true! No matter the result—the extermination of the coons or the murder of all the Southern whites—I shall give thanks." He ended the letter without apparent irony, "Yours in Xt."[3] Whatever horrible thought George might nurse about the world, he could be comforted that Mencken would have thought worse.

George wrote to Mencken of his own struggles to stay drunk. As Prohibition had constricted the supply of booze to the Bohemian Club, George's haunt in town had become an Italian restaurant called Bigin's, where the grappa flowed freely. Bigin's had become the new place artists gathered. Dinner and wine was sixty cents, or free if the artist was hungry.[4] George helped the owner figure out how to keep the hooch moving—for example, having the cook keep a maximum of ten gallons of grappa in a bucket at a time, so that he could kick it over in case of a raid without losing everything.[5]

When he and Mencken weren't sharing their booze stories, they were crowing over their exploits with women. George, who tried to balance his drinking with dancing so he wouldn't suffer too much in the morning, usually left a club with a girl on his arm or at least a phone number tucked into his pocket. Older women were better in bed than younger ones, George told Mencken, because they didn't take their ability to attract a man for granted: "I've tried this many, many times in the past thirty years, and I know what I'm talking about."[6] He tried to entice Mencken to visit by promising him that San Francisco girls were the easiest to get in bed. They lived for sex, George assured him. It was probably the climate. Mencken put in his order for his next visit. He wanted a polite girl, and one who was on the bigger side: "I am somewhat heavy, and it takes muscle to get me in bed when I am in liquor."[7]

In return for such services, Mencken published the occasional work of George's. He disdained George's love sonnets—just as Bierce had—but he liked "The Killdee," George's poem to Carrie:

> I hated her—that bird
> Whose wild, reiterant word
> Was but the burden of the conscious heart.[8]

Nagging Carrie, always warning that the party must end. George had transformed her into a bird sounding a "reiterant word" to interrupt his joy. The poem ended with the call of suicide, beckoning all unhappy souls to follow where it would go.

Carrie was gone, but as George grew older, he found her admonishing call only seemed to get louder until it became inescapable.

. . .

By the time "The Killdee" was published, George Sterling had moved into a small room in the Bohemian Club, gifted to him by an admirer. Within the dark-paneled rooms of the club, time stood still. Invitations to Yule dinner were still addressed in calligraphic script to "Bohemian" and signed, "By ye mandate of ye Owl." The motto, "Weaving Spiders Come Not Here"—a warning not to abuse the club's artistic purpose by using it as a site for business deals—was still embossed on the stationery, if utterly ignored in practice.

Outside, the relentless march of progress continued. Two decades after the catastrophe of the earthquake, San Francisco's chamber of commerce bragged that the average city resident enjoyed almost twice the prosperity of the average American. Inside the club, men who pretended to have little to do with such matters played dominos and smoked cigars. George had become the club's penniless mascot, its last Bohemian; Willard Huntington Wright—the *Los Angeles Times* reporter who had dubbed Carmel a "vortex of erotic erudition"—declared in the *San Francisco Bulletin*, "The Bohemian Club would have to change its name should Sterling resign from membership."[9]

George played his role as the last Bohemian ably enough; he was cited in the papers for swimming naked with a beautiful woman in Golden Gate Park's Stow Lake, for example.[10] But in between high-profile escapades, George sat in his small room at the club, which he furnished with little more than a table and pallet bed. He stared out the window. He peered into the faces of people who passed below, looking for resemblance to one only.

Nora.

He wrote more poems than ever, the kind of stuff that Bierce would have hated—all about love and regret. It was as if a wellspring of remorse had been tapped, and the resulting gush was unceasing.

He sent "The Strange Bird" to *The Outlook* in 1923. In it, Nora takes the form of a rare bird who has been sighted by a group of men:

> We are not done disputing yet
> Which of us heard its singing first. . . .
>
> Unsolved, ethereal, rain-pure:
> One of us killed it with a stone,
> The story goes. We are not sure.[11]

To the *New York Post Literary Review* in 1924, "Infusion," in which Nora becomes seafoam:

> She is strewn along a league of changing surf
> that those who search for her won't find her
>   tomb in marble.
> But you shall know that with the sea's
>   turquoises
> She mingles, and the silver of the sands,—
> In ocean-echoes find her startling voice,
> And in the foam the flashing of her hands.[12]

In 1926, he sent "Lost Companion" to *Overland Monthly*. He'd previously sent a draft to the poet John Neihardt without telling him who the companion was.

> You that on the heavens look,
> Tell us which way Daphne took.
> Daphne laughed, but when she died
> We who burnt her body cried. . . .
> Marvelling she laughed so well,
> With so much she dared not tell.
> Half it seems we might have known
> Sought by all she walked alone,
> For the tears she would not shed
> Inward ate and inward bled,
> And songs she left behind
> Hold the sorrows of the wind.
> You that are the first to go,
> Tell her that at last we know.[13]

According to Greek mythology, Eros makes Apollo fall in love with Daphne by shooting a golden arrow through his heart. Apollo pursues Daphne through the woods, but to no avail, because Eros had shot her with a lead arrow so she can never love a man back. Daphne's father turns her into a laurel tree, from which Apollo plucks leaves for a wreath to wear on his head. Her death becomes Apollo's wreath—his branding for eternity. The Bohemian men who chased Nora May French did so for a feather in their cap—or, closer to ancient myth and the poem, for a laurel in their wreath, claiming her love only so they could build their own legacy of genius.

In case people didn't get the references, when Sterling sent "Lost Companion" to *Overland Monthly*, he added a subtitle: N.M.F.[14]

. . .

In November 1926, George was expecting a visit from Mencken. He had arranged a banquet in Mencken's honor at the club. It was to be a gala affair, but even as George amassed an impressive cache of liquor for his friend, he was feeling far from celebratory. The eternal fame he had imagined securing when he first started writing poetry he now knew would never be his. Since 1922, New York's cultured readers had not looked to the west but rather farther east, all the way to England and Paris, where T. S. Eliot's *The Wasteland*, James Joyce's *Ulysses*, and Virginia Woolf's *Mrs. Dalloway* had shattered traditional expectations of poetry and prose. Even the American writers F. Scott Fitzgerald, Ernest Hemingway, and Ezra Pound had rejected their homeland and moved abroad. George wrote his friend Clark Ashton Smith a bitter letter in October 1926, conceding that only "cranks and mental hermits" took his "A Wine of Wizardry" seriously. His "blue-eyed vampire" had become nothing more than an intellectual joke.[15]

He had been a fool. He had built Carmel, and the writers hadn't come. He had brought only one poet to Carmel who could capture life's joy and torment in words. And he had as good as killed her.

On November 12, Mencken wired George Sterling that he would be delayed in getting from Los Angeles to San Francisco to meet him. He excused himself, explaining that he had acquired a cold while his traveling companion, another writer, had acquired a blonde.[16]

George received Mencken's note and supped that night, as usual, in the Bohemian Club's dining room. It was his 110th day in a row of sobriety and the nineteenth anniversary of Nora's death. He had plans to commemorate the occasion, but he would have to continue without Mencken. He scribbled a poem on the back of the dinner menu:

My Swan Song.
By George Sterling

Has man the right
To die and disappear,
When he has lost the fight?
To sever without fear
The irksome bonds of life
When he is tired of strife?
May he not seek, if it seems best
Relief from grief? May he not rest
From labors vain, from hopeless task?
—I do not know; I merely ask.[17]

At the bottom of the menu he wrote, "Send a copy to Mencken!"

He climbed the stairs to his room.

. . .

When Mencken arrived three days later, he found George huddled in his room, in pain, unable to sit up, much less leave his bed. In his later years, when George drank, he got very drunk, and when he got very drunk, he got sick. The doctor had visited and predicted George would recover after some rest.

Mencken expected that his friend would join the party the next evening.[18]

But the next night, when Mencken knocked at George's room to urge him to come down, George refused to open the door at all. Instead, he yelled something uncharacteristically indistinct. Mencken had no choice but to abandon him for dinner once again. He descended the broad stairs to join the distinguished mix of businessmen and authors assembled in the Bohemian Club's dining room. Gouverneur Morris IV, whose pulp novel *The Penalty* had just been adapted into a film starring Lon Chaney, was in attendance. The writer Charles G. Norris, the brother of the more famous Frank, whose novel *The Octopus* had galvanized public sentiment against the rapacious Southern Pacific Railroad, assumed George's duties as toastmaster.

George Sterling never made an appearance at the banquet that night. His friends rose groggily the next morning and knocked at his room. No reply. They rang his phone. Nothing. As club members gathered for breakfast, whispers circulated that no one had seen George leave his room the night before. Mencken had gone back upstairs during the evening to waken him but heard nothing in answer to his calls. He assumed George had fallen asleep and slipped him a note under his door.

A sense of alarm began to spread. The club valet was summoned; he used his passkey to unlock George's door. The members of the Bohemian Club first saw Mencken's note lying on the ground. Then they saw George on his bed, contorted in an almost impossible position, his mouth crammed with the bedsheet. A small glass vial lay in the corner of the room. Neat stacks of his manuscripts and letters were positioned at one end of the desk, next to a pile of ashes. George had burned some of his papers before he poisoned himself.

A poem lay not far from the ashes. It was not in George's hand.

Written on a sheet ripped from a ledger book from 1893, it had escaped the flames:

> Why, what's a flower? a day's delight at best,
> A perfume loved, a faded petal pressed,—
> a whimsey for an hour's remembering.

Signed, "as witness my hand, Nora Phyllis May French."

Police were called, and the coroner, who removed the body. The coroner determined George had perished of cyanide poisoning around midnight the previous evening. With horror, his friends realized that George had been dying upstairs while they were laughing and drinking below.

Looking for a suicide note, the club members sifted through the remaining scraps of paper. One scrap showed George's efforts toward a new poem. He seemed to have been grasping for the right words. "You from me like youth's forgotten music." He had crossed that out. "By the beauty forever true / And the morning star in the stream / and the star of my heavenly dream / that leads forever to you." He had crossed those out, too.

The newspapers quoted one line from this sheet that wasn't crossed out: "I walked with phantoms ye knew not of," as evidence of George's thoughts in his final hours.[19]

This line seems in its directness so unlike anything George Sterling had written before that I searched for its inspiration. It bears striking similarity to a line in Hugh l'Anson Fausset's poems "The Condemned: A Confession" and "The Mercy of God: A Miracle," published together in 1922. George, a keen reader of recent poetry, would certainly have read Fausset's work.

Fausset's "The Condemned" records the thoughts of a prisoner on the last evening before his execution for killing a rival to his love. The prisoner understands that his faith promises him release in the morning, if only he confessed during the night:

> As if I walked straight out of this dark cell
> Into heaven's daylight, and found my vision there
> Waiting to greet me, pure and true and smiling,
> As I once knew you, dreamed you in the flesh.
> I will forget that ever I awoke
> To learn I walked with phantoms.[20]

Did George's final words, "I walked with phantoms ye knew not of," continue Fausset's condemned man's thoughts? Was Nora the vision awaiting him in heaven? Was his statement a confession? And if it was, to what was he confessing?

Fausset's poem perhaps gives more clues. In it, the prisoner accuses his flighty lover of driving him to murder.

> You take the blind world captive, as you snared
> Me and the fool I murdered, in the web
> Of your so cunning frailty. You are black
> With the lust you woke in him, the hate in me.
> You have done a deed more devilish than us all,
> Because you floated like a weed in the stream,
> And, as a magnet, drew the powers of life
> To jig with them for pleasure.[21]

I wonder if George read these lines and heard in them Carrie's chastising voice, the reiterative "killdee" rising from the grave, accusing him of causing the deaths of both her and Nora by his careless treatment of them both.

I wonder if I'm giving him too much credit.

. . .

"One can't well go wrong in burning one's papers. But how few of us have the sense to do so," Bierce once wrote to George Sterling.[22] Clearly, George remembered Bierce's advice. The mound of ashes that greeted George's friends when they opened the door to his room represented only one instance of George's regular practice of burning compromising material. After Jack's untimely death, George asked Charmian to return some incriminating letters he had written his best friend. So relieved was he to be able to destroy them, he even sent Charmian the money for postage.[23] We can only imagine what was in them.

Jack London also burned letters and instructed others to burn his after receiving and reading them. In a letter George wrote to Jack confirming that he thought Carrie was planning to divorce him, he cheekily assured Jack that he had burned a previous letter at Jack's request: "The incriminating evidence has been obliterated. (That's *Atlantic Monthly* for 'the letter has been burnt')."[24]

At the same time, George chose very carefully what he burned and what he kept. He was vain. He wanted to ensure that his life and the lives of his male friends were preserved for history. Not so much the lives of women. While the bulk of his correspondence with Bierce, London, and other friends made it to the archives, none of his letters from Vera Connolly survived that I could find—though they are referred to in other correspondence. None of the letters Carrie wrote to him either before or after the divorce appear to have survived, either, though correspondence with Charmian makes clear these also existed. They would not have made George look good.

What Sterling didn't destroy outright, he carefully edited. As co-editor of a 1922 volume of Bierce's correspondence, he was able to remove any references that would reveal the intimate details of Bierce's life or the lives of anyone he cared for. He edited out Bierce's criticisms of the works of Nora May French and Jimmy Hopper and excised some of Bierce's rants about Jack London and Upton Sinclair. He deleted mention of how much money Bierce made writing for William Randolph Hearst, so that his master's unseemly workaday life would not be part of his permanent record He removed most references to his sister Marian and his attempts to marry her off to Bierce. And yet the letters themselves made it to the Berg archives, mostly unscathed.

I could find no surviving letters between George and Nora May French, if indeed any were written. As the pair lived often in close proximity and as Nora had privileged access to the telephone lines, it's possible few notes were exchanged. George's only memento of Nora, found in his room upon his death, was the original copy on ledger paper of the "Rose" poem—"Ay pluck a jonquil when the May's a-wing"—composed in her hand. Carrie had burned almost every other belonging of Nora's the day after she died. This poem would be all that George would have had left of Nora.

He would have cherished it. It doubtless reminded him of the context of its composition, the two of them together in his office. The "Rose" poem also carries Nora's voice and her themes: a nod to impermanence, the perfect love of nature contrasting with the imperfect—if irresistible—love of men. George and Lafler published it in the collected volume of her poems. Yet George kept the original manuscript copy till his end. He could not bring himself to burn it.

George Sterling died without a will. He had $3.50 cash on hand and less than $20 in the bank according to his estate documents in his papers at the Bancroft Library. The publication rights to 102 sonnets that had been the property of Mrs. Upton Sinclair (formerly Miss Mary Craig Kimbrough) were purchased by Upton Sinclair for $500. Jimmy Hopper, who had never fully paid George back for all his financial support, wrote two checks to settle his debts with the estate the following year. When all of George's assets were totaled, the estate amounted to a little over $700—most of it from Upton Sinclair—and a few contracts with various presses.

There must be more to George's legacy, his friends thought. Perhaps another trove of poetry as yet unpublished. Shortly after his death, his friends discovered that George had maintained his little room on Montgomery Street. They raced over to it, hoping to find more manuscripts. They found nothing but empty bottles and a bed.[25]

. . .

Vera Connolly, working as a journalist in New York City, received a letter from her friend Belle in San Francisco. Belle wrote she had been heading home after work on the evening of November 16 when she heard the newsboys in the street calling out the death of George Sterling. She enclosed a clipping reporting George's end so Vera could read it for herself. Belle had known George since the early days in Oakland, having met him at a salon at the house of Jack London. She remembered how likable all these men seemed at first, but how boring and tragic they became, "possessed with socialism and materialism and cocksureness in those days, and it seems to have led to the same conclusion for all—the game played, the light out, and they all in the dark, depleted, spent, alone."[26]

What a wasted life, Vera must have thought, as she laid down the clipping. Not because George died alone, but because he had accomplished nothing of lasting value. There was nothing wrong with being alone. She had never married and never would. But she had long ago decided to use her life to serve others.

It had taken her many years to reckon with the mistakes she had made in Carmel. She realized, finally, that she had to forgive herself. She had been caught up in the romance of it all. It hadn't been real life. It had just been a dream, and in that dream, she believed George was everything he said he was. He had convinced her that his passion for her was so overwhelming, it transcended common understanding. So when he suggested she dress in a toga and run through the pines until he caught and ravished her, she readily gave him her virginity. He swore his undying love but had given her only lingering pain.

For a while after Vera lost their child, she had wanted nothing more than to make George Sterling pay. She had published stories in which versions of George got their comeuppance for ruining young, stupid girls. Over time, the hurt faded and she began to think more of what she could do for the many unwanted children who had been born to unwilling or unsupported mothers. She traveled from Ohio to Alabama, from Illinois to Canada, and sat in hundreds of courtrooms listening to what passed for juvenile justice, dished out to children whose only crime was being raised in poverty or neglect. She interviewed judges as to why juvenile crime had risen. The reasons, time and again, were broken homes where the parents—most often absent fathers—did not care about their children. She published a report from her investigation, "The Stampede of Youth," in *Good Housekeeping* in 1926.[27]

In the summer of 1927, while the president of the Spring

Valley Water Company (a crony of George's) dedicated a bench to George with the inscription "He was a Roman for friendship" atop the famous Lombard Street, Vera Connolly was living on a Pueblo reservation in Taos.[28] She sat in tribal meetings listening to elders tell horror stories of children who had been taken from their families by force and placed in government-run boarding schools. She took notes as they described wards teeming with infection, children given little more than a crust of bread to eat, boys awoken at midnight to dig ditches, girls tied to the laundry at daybreak, children choked almost to death for not working hard enough. She published a series of articles on the mistreatment of Native Americans in *Good Housekeeping* the following year.[29] Gaining a reputation as a dogged investigative reporter, she commanded $1,000 per article for the next decade, while she continued to expose systemic child abuse in the courts, in adoption proceedings, and in employment.

In 1944, the *San Anselmo Herald* reported that a friend of the Sterling family had found three hitherto unpublished poems written in George Sterling's hand. Among the lines: "One tear of yours has more of truth than all / The dreams and fallacies that could not stay. / Stand close, O Love, 'ere the Great Shadow Fall."[30] The "shadow" was Nora May French's term for the lure of suicide. Vera thought again about the woman she had never met, but whose fate had nearly been her own.

Vera did not regret her own abortion. She did not feel shame, even when she heard people offer their casual condemnation on the subject. They never guessed that Vera, ever in control, had been foolish enough to get in "that condition." Judging women's choices had become a national sport, and women and children were dying from it. Since "therapeutic" or physician-performed abortions had become difficult to secure, hundreds of thousands of women a year—single and married—risked punctured wombs, hemorrhages, sterility, and death to end their pregnancies.

Vera spent the early 1940s interviewing women who had resorted to illegal abortion mills. Her report, published in *Collier's*, ended with a clarion call for freely accessible birth control and generous maternity leave. It was her own story as much as it was that of the women she quoted.

In 1982, the city of San Francisco approved a measure that officially renamed the park that surrounded George's bench "George Sterling Park."

In her later years, Vera Connolly championed working women and wrote of the value to society of women who chose to never have children. She remained unmarried until her death in 1964.

. . .

In 1927, Herman Scheffauer, then living in Germany, stabbed his private secretary (and twenty-three-year old lover) Katherine Von Meyer to death. Moments later, he ended his own life by throwing himself out the window.[31]

. . .

Harry Lafler left Carmel and settled in Big Sur with his third wife and their son. Driving with his son through the fog in January 1935, he leaned his head out the side window and was decapitated by an oncoming vehicle.[32] An Oakland paper carried news of his death (section D, page 5), calling him a real estate broker "known by many as the 'Czar of Telegraph Hill.'"[33] His legacy is ensconced south of Big Sur, however, where Lafler Creek flows through Lafler Canyon in recognition of his settlement there.

. . .

Alan Hiley's second wife filed for divorce in 1919. He married his third wife, Alma Graun, two years later. He was fifty-three. She was twenty.

. . .

On April 13, 1938, Herbert Heron was elected mayor of Carmel, on the platform "Keep Carmel As It Is." He promised to preserve tradition and place a limit on the number of beer taverns in town. Frederick Bechdolt was elected as councilman with Heron's backing. Perry Newberry, a former mayor of Carmel, died eight months later.[34] In 1986, the people of Carmel elected the actor Clint Eastwood as mayor.

. . .

In 1941, the John Breuner Company emptied the entire fifth floor of their massive downtown office building to make room for their sale of Frank and Lila Havens's worldly goods. It had taken Breuner's trucks more than two weeks of back-and-forth trips to move more than seven hundred items from Wildwood to the floor. On offer: Ming dynasty rugs, a two-thousand-year-old Cambodian bronze drum, and hand-carved teak screens.[35] Everything had to go. There were accumulated debts to pay, and the mansion itself had been put up for sale by its mortgage holders.

. . .

Blanche Partington did finally buy land in Carmel, but in the newer "Carmel Highlands" development that Powers had established just south of town. In 1950, she tried to put the lot she had purchased on the market for $10,000. Her real estate agent informed her that while her lot had an excellent view, the most he would be able to sell it for would be $5,000, there being adjoining lots selling for much less.[36] She died the following year.

. . .

Charmian Kittredge London died four years later, in 1955.

. . .

James Hopper spent World War I in France as a correspondent for *Collier's*. Although journalists were supposed to stay behind the lines, in 1918, Hopper embedded with the American infantry for the assault on the Germans at Cantigny. Separated from the battalion during the fury of battle, Hopper stumbled upon a group of dazed German troops. Mistaking Hopper for an enemy soldier, they dropped their weapons and put their hands in the air. He grabbed a rifle and marched them back to the American camp and then returned to the front to help medics evacuate the wounded.[37]

James Hopper survived the war and lived out his days in Carmel, just as he had always intended. His wife, Mattie, died in 1935, and he remarried three years later. During his later years, Hopper could still be seen smoking French cigars on his porch, driving his beloved car, or swimming out at Carmel Beach or Point Lobos. He died in 1956 at the age of eighty, having penned more than four hundred short stories. The town dedicated a rock to him in Carmel Bay: Hopper's Rock.[38] He remains, in my estimation, the most likable of this crowd of otherwise irredeemable men.

. . .

Mary Austin went on to write more than twenty books. She died of a heart attack in 1934 and bequeathed her brain to Cornell

University, presumably for study. For me, she is a vexing figure. Whereas she privately condemned the sexism of Carmel's male writers, in public pronouncements she aligned herself with them wherever possible. Her accounts of her time with them are therefore unreliable. She fabricated a first meeting with George at Coppa's in 1904, even though they didn't meet until 1906. But it was critical for her to put herself at the center of Carmel's founding. When she wrote about Carmel, she stuck to the script of the Carmel Development Company, leaving Frank Powers and any hint of the land game motivating her presence there entirely out of it.

She covered for George Sterling, too. In her autobiography *Earth Horizon*, published two years before she died, she spoke of the Sterling divorce, blaming Vera for it more than anyone: "George was entangled with a young woman, and everybody got to know about it. The young woman talked too much, and people who had kept silent all these years also talked. Carrie got to know things that were better for her not to have known. They should never have been separated; but there was nobody to have held them together. I did what I could by letter, but it was not enough."[39]

Mary Austin was, of course, swimming upstream against history. If she took George Sterling or any of the other men down publicly, she would go down with them. But she lived her truth "out loud," to their faces. And she left her mark. Short of Jack London and Upton Sinclair, her legacy of work has been the most influential of the writers associated with Carmel in its early period—and unlike Upton and London, she at least bought property there and lived on it for longer than a few weeks. Her work inspired women through generations. Feminists through the 1970s would embrace *A Woman of Genius* as a rallying cry for the recognition of creative women.

. . .

I did not spend all my time in libraries and archives while writing this book. On my last trip to Carmel, I tried to re-create the walk that Mary, Nora, Carrie, and the others so often took through the woods near the bungalow. There's a small trail system that starts across the street from the mission. One trail takes the hiker close to the border of Carmel. I chose it for my walk, guessing it would be the way Carrie and George and their friends would have most often hiked. In its current state it is manicured, wide, and surrounded by manzanita trees. As I walked, joggers and dog walkers passed me periodically. I came up a gentle incline and passed a patch of succulents on the left. Behind them and across a gully I could see houses on the edge of Carmel, some of them on the market for $3 to $5 million (I checked Zillow on my phone).

And then, suddenly, at the place where the path diverged and crossed over a small stream, an arresting clutch of calla lilies.

Though I'd never walked there before, I had advance warning that the lilies would be there. Harry Lafler had described a lily in just that spot in his letter to Nora May French on his visit to Carmel in 1906.

One expects perhaps to come across a tree as an enduring landmark, or a canyon, or a rock. But never a flower. Flowers are the stuff of impermanence, valued precisely because they die so quickly. As Nora wrote in the poem discovered with George's corpse: "Why, what's a flower? a day's delight at best."

She was on to something there: how we treat women as a day's delight at best, the stuff of impermanence, so unlike how we treat men. We honor men with weighty material: concrete benches, bronze plaques, and rock islets. We strive through sheer mass to make permanent the equally fleeting lives of men.

And we've been doing it forever. In 1989, while witnessing a commencement at Columbia University, I stared out at the columned main library, where the names of canonical authors of antiquity are engraved in its neoclassical facade: Homer, Sophocles, Plato, Aristotle, Cicero, Vergil. I walked under those names for years as a Columbia College student, when I read the works of each one in the college's mandated curriculum.

Columbia College, bear in mind, only started admitting women in 1983. I enrolled in 1986. Then, the school had seemed unprepared for the onslaught of women. Some of the dorms had co-ed bathrooms that were unlocked, so you were likely to walk in on one of your classmates at the urinal. I began to feel that we women were never really expected—always a surprise, and an unwelcome one at that, as we trod on the intimacy of male spaces.

On that commencement day in 1989, as the president intoned through his speech in a nasal drawl, women trespassed again: a white banner had been unfurled over the names of the men engraved on the library. It presented a competing list of writers—all of them women: Sappho, Christine de Pizan, Brontë, Dickinson, Woolf.

Wow, I thought. Things are really changing.

The banner came down. I headed to graduate school in the freezing upper Midwest, where I took several courses in English literature featuring women writers who had never appeared on syllabi in my Columbia classes. On the job market after finishing my dissertation, I interviewed with a university named after a male saint—let's call it St. So and So's. The interview was conducted in a bedroom of a hotel—standard practice in the late 1990s. There were three people in the room apart from me: a verbose male professor, his increasingly nervous female colleague, and a priest who served as an administrator.

Midway through the interview, the male professor—who sat in a chair just inches from the bed behind him—assured me that "of course" they had to put women on the syllabi "these days." His colleague, the woman, widened her eyes with horror but couldn't bring herself to speak. Sensing that the interview had taken an uncomfortable turn, the priest, who had hitherto been silent, jumped in with a routine question: What had attracted me to apply to St. So and So's?

It had been a long day. I had already done several interviews, my shoes were beginning to chafe, and it had been hours since I had last eaten. It was December and already dark outside; I wanted nothing more than to return to my own hotel room, take off my nylons and bra, and collapse into bed. I decided in that moment that no job was worth this indignity. I paused and replied, "I hear you have an excellent basketball team."

Fortunately—and I do mean *fortunately*—I got a position at another university and spent the next two decades climbing the tenure ladder and then the even steeper slope to full professorship. I became one of the mere handful of women who made up only a quarter of that top rank in my English department, while women in the lower ranks were plentiful. "Backwards and in high heels" was the common congratulations for women who were promoted, after the famous remark attributed to Ginger Rogers that she did everything that Fred Astaire did, "but backwards and in high heels."

In the midst of researching for this book, I went back to Columbia University to access the drastically under-researched Vera Connolly Papers. As I walked toward the library over the familiar cobblestones (hell to walk on in heels—they never saw us coming), I saw there was a new banner—this one correcting the focus on white women of thirty years before. I looked up at the names now fluttering on a long white strip: Angelou, Anzaldúa, Hurston, Morrison, Silko.

By this time, I had become well-acquainted with the lives of Nora May French, Carrie Sterling, and Vera Connolly. This time, I did not look at the banner and think, Well, things are really changing. No. This time I looked at it and thought, When will we stop hanging banners only to take them down again? This is the definition of women's progress: a movement toward visibility, then whisked away for being unable to stand "the test of time"—a game perennially rigged in men's favor if ever there was one. Women remain "a day's delight" at best—a banner of their names hung today, gone tomorrow, forgotten for a century or forever.

I don't know why we don't carve them over the door.

Acknowledgments

✺

This book about extraordinary women would have been impossible without the efforts of two extraordinary women: Anna Sproul-Latimer—my brilliant, kind, *patient* agent—and my editor at Dutton, Cassidy Sachs, who incredibly "got it" from the very start—who got *me* from the very start. I pinch myself daily that I found you both.

Deep appreciation to the Guggenheim Foundation and the Center for Advanced Study at the University of Illinois for fellowships that funded my research.

Early drafts were endured by Justen Ahren, Dennis Baron, Iryce Baron, Alexandra Beaton, Kristin Bock, Sanderia Faye, Stephanie Foote, Maria Gillombardo, Joyce Glynn, Ellen Goldstein, Dara Kaye, Amanda Moon, Sean Murphy, Naomi Reed, Jay Venables, Sweta Vikram, Julia Walker, Ashlee White, and my dear, departed uncle, Bob Prendergast, who urged me to get to the point and keep going. All your voices are in this.

A special thanks to Jean Thompson for advising me to give up on my male characters and to Marcia Gregory for always being there when I stumbled out of the archives.

The best piece of writing I've ever done remains the personal ad I put in Madison's *Isthmus* that John Tubbs answered twenty-five years ago. The research for this book required long and repeated absences from home, during which he did everything: the cooking, the cleaning, the boy and cat wrangling. More importantly, he kept doing half of everything when I was home. Most importantly, he reminded me always: We're a team.

And to my son: Calling me by my first name when I was away more than three days was the most ingenious way of saying "I miss you." Your memes and texts always kept me going. Thanks for putting up with all of this.

Bibliography

The primary documents I collected for *The Gilded Edge* came from the following libraries, referred to by abbreviations in the endnotes.

Abraham Lincoln Presidential Library and Museum: ALL

Bancroft Library, University of California, Berkeley: BAN

Berg Collection, New York Public Library: BER

Columbia University Rare Book & Manuscript Library: COL

Harrison Memorial Library (Carmel-by-the-Sea): HAR

Huntington Library: HUN

Oakland Public Library: OAK

San Francisco Public Library: SFL

Wells College Archives: WEL

Frequent correspondents are abbreviated as follows:

Mary Austin: MA

Ambrose Bierce: AB

Nora May French: NMF

Jimmy Hopper: JH

Harry Lafler: HL

Charmian Kittredge London: CKL

Jack London: JL

H. L. Mencken: HLM

Blanche Partington: BP

Carrie Sterling: CS

George Sterling: GS

Notes

꩜

Prologue

1. American Medical Association, "Nostrums and Quackery," *Journal of the American Medical Association* (1912): 593.

2. "House Falls from Telegraph Hill," *San Francisco Chronicle*, March 28, 1907, 1.

3. NMF to BP, January 16, 1907, Partington Family Papers, BAN.

4. NMF to HL, undated, Henry Anderson Lafler Papers, BAN.

5. Raine Edward Bennett, "Don Passé," *The Literary Review* 15, no. 2 (Winter 1971): 133–47.

6. I am grateful to my colleague Stephanie Foote for this observation.

Chapter One · Working Girl

1. GS to AB, September 18, 1906, George Sterling Collection, BER.

2. National Society, Daughters of the American Revolution, Provo, UT, Ancestry.com Operations, Inc., 2000.

3. Thomas E. Benediktsson, *George Sterling* (New York: Twayne Publishers, 1980).

4. The Realty Syndicate Incorporated, brochure, 1896, OAK.

5. Michael B. Katz, Mark J. Stern, and Jamie J. Fader, "Women and the Paradox of Inequality in the Twentieth Century," *Journal of Social History* 39, no. 1 (2005): 65–88.

Chapter Two · Prodigy

1. NMF to Helen French, February 15, 1899, Helen French Collection on Nora May French, BAN.

2. Edward French to Charles Lummis, January 20, 1900, Charles Lummis Papers, Autry Museum of the American West.

3. Mary Wells French to Cassius Wicker, March 22, 1891, French-Wicker Family Papers, ALL.

4. Mary Wells French to Cassius Wicker, March 6, 1892, French-Wicker Family Papers, ALL.

5. Judith Allen, "The Life and Writing of Nora May French" (master's thesis, Mills College, 1963).

6. Mary Wells French to Cassius Wicker, January 12, 1897, French-Wicker Family Papers, ALL.

7. Edward L. French to Cassius M. Wicker, July 2, 1898, French-Wicker Family Papers, ALL.

8. Edward L. French to Charles Lummis, June 17, 1910, Charles Lummis Papers, Autry Museum of the American West.

9. NMF to Cassius Wicker, July 27, 1899, French-Wicker Family Papers, ALL.

10. Helen French to Cassius Wicker, October 19, 1900, French-Wicker Family Papers, ALL.

11. Nora May French, "Pencil and Brush," *Los Angeles Times Illustrated Weekly Magazine*, April 1, 1900. Sadly, no copies of this article are extant.

12. Nora May French, "Answered," in *Land of Sunshine* 12, no. 6 (1900): 331.

13. Helen (French) Hunt to Temple Hollcroft, October 8, 1960, WEL.

14. Henry Wells to Ezra Cornell, May 22, 1866, WEL.

15. Temple Hollcroft, undated notes, Misc. Wells file, WEL.

16. *The Evening World* (New York), August 15, 1888, 2.

17.   Edward French to Lucy May French, January 16, 1874, French-Wicker Family Papers, ALL.

18.   Nora May French, "The Brook's Story," *Los Angeles Times*, December 3, 1899.

Chapter Three · Homemaker

1.   Roy Morris Jr., *Ambrose Bierce: Alone in Bad Company* (New York: Crown Publishers, 1995).

2.   San Francisco Bay Area Writers and Artists: Oral History Transcript, Elsie Whitaker Martínez, interview by Franklin Dickerson Walker and Willa K. Baum, 1969, http://content.cdlib.org/ark:/13030/hb6j 49p1b8/.

3.   CS to BP, undated, Partington Family Papers, BAN.

4.   "To Man He Owes Jack London Writes," *The San Francisco Examiner*, May 29, 1902.

5.   Macmillan Company, advertisement for *The Call of the Wild* in *The New York Times*, July 25, 1903.

6.   GS to AB, July 25, 1902, George Sterling Collection, BER.

7.   AB to GS, July 10, 1902, George Sterling Collection, BER.

8.   George Sterling, *The Testimony of the Suns and Other Poems* (San Francisco: W. E. Wood, 1903), 7.

9.   Clarice Stasz, *Jack London's Women* (Amherst: University of Massachusetts Press, 2001).

10.   JL to BP, September 1, 1904, Jack London Papers, HUN.

11.   Warren Unna, *The Coppa Murals: A Pageant of Bohemian Life in San Francisco at the Turn of the Century* (San Francisco: The Book Club of California, 1952).

12.   GS to AB, June 6, 1905, George Sterling Papers, BAN.

13.   GS to AB, November 12, 1903, George Sterling Papers, BAN.

14.   GS to AB, February 10, 1904, George Sterling Papers, BAN.

15.   GS to AB, July 22, 1911, George Sterling Papers, BAN.

16.   Kate Partington to CS, undated, George Sterling Papers, BAN.

17.   GS to AB, July 25, 1902, George Sterling Collection, BER.

18.　GS to AB, October 10, 1903, George Sterling Collection, BER.

19.　Sterling, *The Testimony of the Suns and Other Poems*, 45.

Chapter Four · Ragged Robin

1.　NMF to Cassius Wicker, March 28, 1904, French-Wicker Family Papers, ALL.

2.　NMF to Cassius Wicker, March 28, 1904, French-Wicker Family Papers, ALL.

3.　Allen, "The Life and Writing of Nora May French."

4.　Nora May French, "In Empty Courts," *The Smart Set: A Magazine of Cleverness* 13, no. 3 (July 1904): 122.

5.　NMF to HL, August 22, 1905, Henry Anderson Lafler Papers, BAN.

6.　Nora May French, photo by Alan Hiley, Bancroft Photo File, BAN.

7.　Nora May French, "The Spanish Girl," in *Poems* (San Francisco: The Strange Company, 1910), 57.

8.　Nora May French, "Vivisection," in *Poems*, 16.

9.　Helen French's notes on her family mention Nora's "illegal operation." Helen French Collection on Nora May French, BAN.

10.　Barbara Jean Matthews, *The Descendants of Governor Thomas Welles of Connecticut, Volume 1*, 2nd edition (Wethersfield, CT: Welles Family Association, 2013).

11.　French, "The Spanish Girl," in *Poems*, 57.

Chapter Five · Poet's Wife

1.　CS to BP, undated, Partington Family Papers, BAN.

2.　MA to GS, February 20, 1905, Rudolph Blaettler Collection of George Sterling Papers, BAN.

3.　CS to BP, undated, Partington Family Papers, BAN.

4.　JL to CS, September 15, 1905, Jack London Papers, HUN.

5.　CS to Gertrude Partington, April 24, 1905, Partington Family Papers, BAN.

6.　Stasz, *Jack London's Women*.

7. GS to BP, July 5, 1905, Partington Family Papers, BAN.

8. JL to BP, September 21, 1904, in *The Letters of Jack London, Volume One: 1896–1905*, edited by Earle Labor, Robert C. Leitz III, and I. Milo Shepard (Stanford, CA: Stanford University Press, 1988), 445.

9. GS to BP, August 25, 1905, Partington Family Papers, BAN.

10. JL to GS, June 1, 1905, Jack London Papers, HUN.

11. CS to BP, September 5, 1905, Partington Family Papers, BAN.

12. Mary Brownfield, "City-Sponsored Home Mail Delivery Clients Hold Steady," *The Carmel Pine Cone*, March 18, 2005.

13. John Steinbeck, *Travels with Charley in Search of America* (New York: Penguin Books, 1961), 150.

14. Robert Louis Stevenson, "The Old Pacific Capital," *Fraser's Magazine* 12 (November 1880): 647–57.

15. "Facts from Interviews," Clara Nixon Carmel History File, HAR.

16. Frank Powers to James Franklin Devendorf, October 31, 1904, Carmel Development Company Collection, HAR.

17. Minutes from Meeting of the Board of Directors, August 12, 1905, Carmel Development Company Collection, HAR.

Chapter Six · Dear Heart

1. NMF to HL, November 26, 1905, Henry Anderson Lafler Papers, BAN.

2. HL to NMF, November 2, 1905, Henry Anderson Lafler Papers, BAN.

3. Edith Wharton, *The House of Mirth* (New York: Charles Scribner's Sons, 1923), 135.

4. Idwal Jones, "King of Bohemia," *Overland Monthly* 85, no. 11 (November 1927): 332–33.

5. NMF to HL, August 22, 1905, Henry Anderson Lafler Papers, BAN.

6. NMF to HL, August 10, 1905, Henry Anderson Lafler Papers, BAN.

7. NMF to HL, August 22, 1905, Henry Anderson Lafler Papers, BAN.

8. NMF to HL, undated, Henry Anderson Lafler Papers, BAN.

9. HL to NMF, November 5, 1905, Henry Anderson Lafler Papers, BAN.

10. NMF to HL, undated, Henry Anderson Lafler Papers, BAN.

11. HL to NMF, December 28, 1905, Henry Anderson Lafler Papers, BAN.

12. NMF to HL, undated, Henry Anderson Lafler Papers, BAN.

13. Alice Fancher Lafler to HL, June 16, 1905, Henry Anderson Lafler Papers, BAN.

14. HL to Bertha Newberry, December 27, 1905, Henry Anderson Lafler Papers, BAN.

15. Bertha Newberry to HL, undated, Henry Anderson Lafler Papers, BAN.

16. Unsigned to HL, October 24, 1905, Henry Anderson Lafler Papers, BAN.

17. HL to NMF, January 31, 1906, Henry Anderson Lafler Papers, BAN.

18. HL to NMF, February 5, 1906, Henry Anderson Lafler Papers, BAN.

Chapter Seven · Homewrecker

1. Henry Anderson Lafler, "My Sixty Sleepless Hours," *McClure's* 27, no. 3 (July 1906): 275–81.

2. James Hopper, "Our San Francisco," *Everybody's Magazine*, June 1906, 760a–60h.

3. Arnold Genthe, *As I Remember* (London: Reynal and Hitchcock, 1936); John Kuo Wei Tchen, *Genthe's Photographs of San Francisco's Old Chinatown* (New York: Dover Publications, 1984).

4. George Sterling diary, April 18, 1906, George Sterling Papers, BAN.

5. CS to BP, April 9, 1906, Partington Family Papers, BAN.

6. Thomas S. Duke, "Synopsis of the San Francisco Police and Municipal Records of the Greatest Catastrophe in American History," Board of Police Commissioners of San Francisco, 1910.

7. GS to AB, April 30, 1906, Partington Family Papers, BAN.

8. GS to AB, April 30, 1906, Partington Family Papers, BAN.

9. CS to BP, August 6, 1906, Partington Family Papers, BAN.

10. CS to BP, August 6, 1906, Partington Family Papers, BAN.

11. Carrie and Charmian's renewal of friendship is described in Charmian Kittredge diary, March 10–12, 1906, Jack London Papers, HUN.

12. Charmian Kittredge diary, September 6, 1906, Jack London Papers, HUN.

13. Charmian Kittredge diary, September 2–8, 1906, Jack London Papers, HUN.

14. Charmian Kittredge diary, November 6, 1906, Jack London Papers, HUN.

15. CS to Gertrude Partington, December 19, 1906, Partington Family Papers, BAN.

16. Jack London, *The Valley of the Moon* (Orinda, CA: Seawolf Press, 2017), 344.

Chapter Eight · Hello Girl

1. "Diary of a Telephone Girl," *Saturday Evening Post*, October 19, 1907, 8.

2. Kerry Segrave, *The Women Who Got America Talking: Early Telephone Operators, 1878–1922* (Jefferson, NC: McFarland & Company, 2017).

3. "One Big Fish in Frisco Graft Net," *Chicago Tribune*, March 25, 1907.

4. "Diary of a Telephone Girl," 7.

5. Allen, "The Life and Writing of Nora May French."

6. George Sterling diary, December 26, 1906, George Sterling Papers, BAN.

7. NMF to HL, undated, Henry Anderson Lafler Papers, BAN.

8. HL to MA, undated, Mary Austin Papers, HUN.

9. Handwritten notations in the margins of the 1909 *Carmel Whirl* (the author is unclear but is likely Herbert Heron) record that Lafler bragged that he had hit Nora. Rudolph Blaettler Collection of George Sterling Papers, BAN.

10. Nora May French, "Says the Old Year to the New," *The San Francisco Call*, December 30, 1906.

11. Nora May French, untitled poem, undated, George Sterling Papers, BAN.

12. "Murders Sister Then Ends His Own Life," *The San Francisco Call*, January 27, 1907.

13. "Water Merger Is Consummated," *The San Francisco Call*, February 1, 1907.

14. James D. Phelan to W. S. Clayton, Esq., September 12, 1907, James D. Phelan Papers, BAN.

15   GS to AB, April 13, 1907, George Sterling Papers, BAN.

16.   GS to JL, August 21, 1906, George Sterling Papers, HUN.

17.   GS to AB, April 12, 1906, George Sterling Collection, BER.

18.   GS to AB, June 10, 1907, George Sterling Collection, BER.

19.   AB to GS, June 25, 1907, George Sterling Collection, BER.

20.   GS to AB, September 10, 1904, George Sterling Papers, BAN.

21.   GS to AB, July 7, 1907, George Sterling Papers, BAN.

Chapter Nine · *La Bohème*

1.   CS to BP, March 21, 1907, Partington Family Papers, BAN.

2.   GS to AB, April 13, 1907, George Sterling Papers, BAN.

3.   CS to BP, March 21, 1907, Partington Family Papers, BAN.

4.   CS to BP, March 21, 1907, Partington Family Papers, BAN.

5.   CS to BP, June 19, 1907, Partington Family Papers, BAN.

6.   Philip L. Fradkin, *The Great Earthquake and Firestorms of 1906* (Berkeley: University of California Press, 2005).

7.   Genthe, *As I Remember.*

8.   Tim Thomas, *The Abalone King of Monterey: "Pop" Ernest Doelter, Pioneering Japanese Fishermen, and the Culinary Classic That Saved an Industry* (Charleston, SC: American Palate, 2014).

9.   CS to BP, September 19, 1907, George Sterling Papers, BAN.

10.   George Sterling, *The Triumph of Bohemia: A Forest Play* (San Francisco: Bohemian Club of San Francisco, 1907).

11.   Robert F. Bruner and Sean D. Carr, *The Panic of 1907: Lessons Learned from the Market's Perfect Storm* (Hoboken, NJ: John Wiley & Sons, 2007).

12.   George Sterling diary, August 20, 1907, George Sterling Papers, BAN.

13.   David Weir, *Decadent Culture in the United States: Art and Literature Against the American Grain, 1890–1926* (Albany: State University of New York Press, 2007), 147.

14.   George Sterling diary, August 28, 1907, George Sterling Papers, BAN.

15.   CS to BP, August 9, 1907, Partington Family Papers, BAN.

16.   CS to BP, August 9, 1907, Partington Family Papers, BAN.

17. CS to BP, undated, Partington Family Papers, BAN.

18. CS to BP, March 1, 1907, Partington Family Papers, BAN.

19. CS to BP, undated, Partington Family Papers, BAN.

20. CS to BP, March 21, 1907, Partington Family Papers, BAN.

21. CS to BP, September 19, 1907, Partington Family Papers, BAN.

22. "Literary Bohemian Sues 'Affinity' for Divorce," August 6, 1907, *The San Francisco Call*.

23. French, "Bells from over the Hills Sound Sweet," in *Poems*, 74.

24. French, "The Mourner," in *Poems*, 89.

25. George Sterling diary, August 27, 1907, Rudolph Blaettler Collection of George Sterling Papers, BAN.

Chapter Ten · Other Woman

1. GS to AB, August 28, 1907, George Sterling Collection, BER.

2. George Sterling diary, August 30, 1907, George Sterling Papers, BAN.

3. Nora May French, "Ave Atque Vale," *Poems*, 90.

4. GS to BP, August 26, 1907, George Sterling Papers, BAN.

5. George Sterling diary, August 31, 1907, George Sterling Papers, BAN.

6. GS to JL, September 12, 1907, Jack London Papers, HUN.

7. GS to AB, September 16, 1907, George Sterling Papers, BAN.

8. GS to JL, September 12, 1907, Jack London Papers, HUN.

9. George Sterling diary, September 11, 1907, George Sterling Papers, BAN.

10. GS to JL, September 13, 1907, Jack London Papers, HUN.

11. CS to BP, September 19, 1907, Partington Family Papers, BAN.

12. CS to BP, September 19, 1907, Partington Family Papers, BAN.

13. U.S. Census Bureau, "Census of Population and Housing," 1890–1940, https://www.census.gov/prod/www/decennial.html.

14. CS to BP, September 19, 1907, Partington Family Papers, BAN.

15. CS to BP, September 19, 1907, Partington Family Papers, BAN.

16. GS to BP, October 4, 1907, Partington Family Papers, BAN; George Sterling diary, September 24, 1907, George Sterling Papers, BAN.

17. Herman Scheffauer to GS, December 16, 1907, George Sterling Papers, HUN.

18. George Sterling diary, November 1, 1907, George Sterling Papers, BAN.

19. Mary Hunter Austin, *Santa Lucia: A Common Story* (New York: Harper & Brothers, 1908), 336–37.

20. Nora May French, "Between Two Rains," *Sunset* 20 (November 1907): 50.

21. Mary Hunter Austin, "Some Literary Myths," *Sunset* 20 (November 1907): 36–39.

22. Gelett Burgess, "A San Francisco Flirtship," *Sunset* 20 (November 1907): 68–80.

23. Nora May French, "The Panther Woman," unpublished, James Hopper Papers, BAN.

24. GS to AB, February 8, 1908, George Sterling Collection, BER.

25. "Poet David Lezinsky Dead," *The San Francisco Call*, July 5, 1895.

26. William Greer Harrison, "The Degeneracy of Ambrose Bierce," *The San Francisco Call*, October 20, 1895.

27. GS to AB, December 7, 1907, George Sterling Collection, BER.

28. George Sterling diary, November 10, 1907, George Sterling Papers, BAN.

Chapter Eleven · Cover Girl

1. "Mrs. Evelyn Nesbit Thaw Describes How Stanford White Wronged Her," *The Evening World* (New York), February 7, 1907; Simon Baatz, *The Girl on the Velvet Swing: Sex, Murder, and Madness at the Dawn of the Twentieth Century* (New York: Mulholland Books, 2018).

2. George Sterling diary, November 13, 1907, George Sterling Papers, BAN.

3. CS to BP, November 15, 1907, Partington Family Papers, BAN.

4. "Midnight Lure of Death Leads Poetess to Grave," *The San Francisco Examiner*, November 15, 1907.

5. GS to BP, October 4, 1907, Partington Family Papers, BAN.

6.   George Sterling diary, November 14, 1907, George Sterling Papers, BAN.

7.   George Sterling diary, November 18, 1907, George Sterling Papers, BAN.

8.   "Authoress Suicides," *The Plymouth Tribune* (Plymouth, IN), November 21, 1907.

9.   "Midnight Lure of Death Leads Poetess to Grave."

10. "Nora May French, Writer, Ends Life with Poison," *The San Francisco Call*, November 15, 1907.

11. Bruner and Carr, *The Panic of 1907.*

12. "Morgan Can't Get French Bank Gold," *The San Francisco Examiner*, November 15, 1907.

13. George Sterling diary, November 22, 1907, George Sterling Papers, BAN.

14. "To Heed Wishes of Dead Poet," *San Francisco Chronicle*, November 17, 1907.

15. "To Heed Wishes of Dead Poet."

16. Alissandra Dramov, *Carmel-by-the-Sea, The Early Years (1903–1913)* (Bloomington, IN: The Author's House, 2012).

17. George Sterling diary, November 22, 1907, George Sterling Papers, BAN.

18. "Poetess a Suicide," *Boston Daily Globe*, November 16, 1907.

19. "Poetess Ends Her Life with Dose of Poison," *Albuquerque Citizen* (New Mexico), November 15, 1907.

20. "Girl Writer Tires of Life," *The Chicago Daily Tribune*, November 16, 1907.

21. "Poetess Suicides," *The Morning Astorian* (Oregon), November 17, 1907.

22. "Authoress Suicides."

23. JL to GS, October 6, 1908, Jack London Papers, HUN.

24. "By Her Own Hand, Young Woman Ends Life," *Los Angeles Times*, November 15, 1907.

25. GS to JL, November 21, 1907, Jack London Papers, HUN.

26. GS to JL, November 21, 1907, Jack London Papers, HUN.

27. GS to AB, December 7, 1907, George Sterling Collection, BER.

28. CS to BP, November 15, 1907, Partington Family Papers, BAN.

29. GS to JL, undated, George Sterling Papers, BAN.

30. Bruner and Carr, *The Panic of 1907*.

31. CS to BP, November 15, 1907, Partington Family Papers, BAN.

32. CS to BP, November 15, 1907, Partington Family Papers, BAN.

Chapter Twelve · Femme Fatale

1. "'Suicide Poem' Causes Three to End Their Lives," *The Evening World* (New York), April 22, 1908.

2. Herman Scheffauer to AB, January 23, 1908, George Sterling Collection, BER.

3. GS to AB, February 26, 1908, George Sterling Collection, BER.

4. Corrie M. Anders, "Piedmont's 'Taj Mahal' for Sale," *Chicago Tribune*, May 18, 1991; "Piedmont Mansion Treasures to Go on Sale Tomorrow," *Oakland Tribune*, November 9, 1941; "Oakland Empire a Tycoon's Dream," *Oakland Tribune*, December 10, 1967; Frank Havens Clippings File, OAK.

5. GS to AB, February 26, 1908, George Sterling Collection, BER.

6. "Poet Sterling Demands Scalp of a Janitor," *The San Francisco Call*, February 5, 1908.

7. Arnold Genthe, portrait of Nora May French, *Sunset* 20, no. 4 (February 1908): 386.

8. Nora May French, "Ave Atque Vale," *Sunset* 20, no. 4 (February 1908): 386.

9. GS to AB, February 26, 1908, George Sterling Collection, BER.

10. GS to AB, December 7, 1907, George Sterling Collection, BER.

11. CS to BP, March 23, 1908, Partington Family Papers, BAN.

12. CS to BP, February 6, 1908, Partington Family Papers, BAN.

13. Prentice Mulford, *Your Forces and How to Use Them* (New York: F. J. Needham, 1891).

14. JH to GS, May 4, 1908, James Hopper Papers, BAN.

15. Richard Bell, "In Werther's Thrall: Suicide and the Power of Sentimental Reading in Early National America," *Early American Literature* 46, no. 1 (2011): 93–120.

16. "Ends Life Leaving Love Note Series," *The San Francisco Examiner*, October 15, 1908.

17. Joseph Noel, *Footloose in Arcadia: A Personal Record of Jack London, George Sterling and Ambrose Bierce* (New York: Carrick & Evans, 1940).

18. GS to AB, December 7, 1907, George Sterling Collection, BER.

19. AB to GS, June 5, 1908, George Sterling Collection, BER.

20. "Killed by Poetry, Her Friends Say," *St. Louis Post-Dispatch*, November 17, 1907.

21. Helen French, undated notes, Helen French Collection on Nora May French, BAN.

22. GS to AB, August 28, 1907, George Sterling Papers, BAN.

23. GS to BP, September 5, 1907, Partington Family Papers, BAN.

24. Herman Scheffauer to AB, January 23, 1908, Herman Scheffauer Papers, BER.

25. GS to AB, February 8, 1908, George Sterling Papers, BAN.

26. GS to AB, June 18, 1908, George Sterling Collection, BER.

27. GS to AB, June 26, 1908, George Sterling Collection, BER.

28. GS to AB, July 12, 1908, George Sterling Collection, BER.

29. "Victim of Poem on Suicide," *Vicksburg Evening Post*, April 27, 1908; "Victim of Poem on Suicide," *The La Crosse Tribune* (Wisconsin), April 23, 1908; "Poem Claims Victim," *The Palladium-Item* (Richmond, IN), May 17, 1908; "Poem on Suicide Causes Youth to Take His Own Life," *Reno Gazette-Journal*, May 5, 1908.

Chapter Thirteen · Fool Sex

1. GS to JL, May 25, 1906, George Sterling Papers, BAN.

2. Carmel-by-the-Sea brochure, undated, Carmel Development Company Papers, HAR.

3. George Sterling diary, August 16, 1908, George Sterling Papers, BAN.

4. *Old Carmel in Rare Photographs by L. S. Slevin*, produced by Sharon Lawrence with Kathryn Printe (self-published, 1995).

5. Herbert Heron to JL, April 18, 1907, James Henry Papers, HAR.

6. CS to BP, July 20, 1908, Partington Family Papers, BAN.

7. CS to BP, July 12, 1908, Partington Family Papers, BAN.

8. George Sterling diary, November 1, 1908, George Sterling Papers, BAN.

9. Anthony Arthur, *Radical Innocent: Upton Sinclair* (New York: Random House, 2006), 115.

10. George Sterling diary, November 9, 1908, George Sterling Papers, BAN.

11. CS to BP, undated, Partington Family Papers, BAN.

12. "Famous Prosecutor Seriously Wounded by Denounced Felon," *Los Angeles Herald*, November 14, 1908.

13. Upton Sinclair, *Money Writes!* (New York: Albert and Charles Boni, 1927), 163.

14. GS to Frederick J. Bamford, November 17, 1908, George Sterling File, OAK.

15. CS to BP, July 15, 1909, Partington Family Papers, BAN.

16. George Sterling diary, May 23, 1909, George Sterling Papers, BAN.

17. GS to AB, April 11, 1909, George Sterling Papers, BAN.

18. Kate Manne, *Down Girl: The Logic of Misogyny* (New York: Oxford University Press, 2017).

19. AB to GS, May 2, 1909, George Sterling Collection, BER.

20. AB to GS, May 2, 1909, George Sterling Collection, BER.

21. JL to GS, May 2, 1909, Jack London Papers, HUN.

22. JH to GS, September 10, 1908, James Hopper Papers, BAN.

23. JH to GS, October 15, 1908, James Hopper Papers, BAN.

24. George Sterling, "The Apothecary's," in *The House of Orchids and Other Poems* (San Francisco: A. M. Robertson, 1911), 49.

25. JH to GS, October 15, 1908, James Hopper Papers, BAN.

26. JH to GS, April 15, 1909, James Hopper Papers, BAN.

27. Leslie J. Reagan, *When Abortion Was a Crime: Women, Medicine, and Law in the United States, 1867–1973* (Berkeley: University of California Press, 1997).

28. JH to GS, April 15, 1909, James Hopper Papers, BAN.

29. JH to GS, April 15, 1909, James Hopper Papers, BAN.

30. Nora May French, "Happiness," *The American Magazine* 66 (1908): 130.

31. French, "Vivisection," in *Poems*, 16.

32. French, "The Panther Woman."

33. Unsigned, "The Suicide," undated manuscript, James Hopper Papers, BAN.

34. JH to GS, April 15, 1909, James Hopper Papers, BAN.

Chapter Fourteen · Mother

1. Willard Huntington Wright, "Hotbed of Soulful Culture, Vortex of Erotic Erudition," *Los Angeles Times*, May 22, 1910.

2. CS to BP, April 26, 1910, Partington Family Papers, BAN.

3. CS to BP, May 16, 1910, Partington Family Papers, BAN.

4. CS to BP, October 6, 1908, Partington Family Papers, BAN.

5. CS to BP, December 27, 1909, Partington Family Papers, BAN.

6. Carrie describes her writing progress in CS to BP, January 9, 1910; April 26, 1910; June 7, 1910, Partington Family Papers, BAN.

7. George Sterling diary, May 29, 1910, George Sterling Papers, BAN.

8. George Sterling diary, May 30, 1910, George Sterling Papers, BAN.

9. George Sterling diary, June 5, 1910, George Sterling Papers, BAN.

10. CS to BP, August 13, 1910, Partington Family Papers, BAN.

11. CS to BP, August 13, 1910, Partington Family Papers, BAN.

12. CS to BP, September 26, 1910, Partington Family Papers, BAN.

13. GS to AB, January 18, 1911, George Sterling Collection, BER.

14. George Sterling diary, January 1, 1911, George Sterling Papers, BAN.

15. George Sterling diary, February 7, 1911, George Sterling Papers, BAN.

16. Carl A. Starace, "Historic Long Island," *The Suffolk County News*, August 18, 1966, 14.

17. CS to BP, May 11, 1911, Partington Family Papers, BAN.

18. GS to JL, February 27, 1911, Jack London Papers, HUN.

19. GS to JL, February 9, 1911, Jack London Papers, HUN.

20. GS to JL, February 27, 1911, Jack London Papers, HUN.

21. GS to AB, May 3, 1911, George Sterling Collection, BER.

22. GS to AB, July 13, 1911, George Sterling Collection, BER.

23. GS to AB, July 22, 1911, George Sterling Papers, BAN.

Chapter Fifteen · New Woman

1. CS to BP, August 18, 1911, Partington Family Papers, BAN.

2. CS to Lora Bierce, June 8, 1911, Partington Family Papers, BAN.

3. CS to Lora Bierce, June 8, 1911, Partington Family Papers, BAN.

4. GS to John O'Hara, June 22, 1911, George Sterling Papers, BAN.

5. GS to JL, July 25, 1911, Jack London Papers, HUN.

6. "The Havens House," Shelter Island Historical Society, accessed February 3, 2021, https://www.shelterislandhistorical.org /historyofhavenshouse.html.

7. Benediktsson, *George Sterling*.

8. Mary Hunter Austin, *The Arrow Maker: A Play in Three Acts* (New York: Duffield and Company, 1911), xii.

9. GS to MA, June 28, 1911, from T. M. Pearce, ed., *Literary America 1903–1934: The Mary Austin Letters* (Westport, CT: Greenwood Press, 1979).

10. Olive Schreiner, *Women and Labor* (New York: Frederick A. Stokes & Co., 1911), 147.

11. Arthur, *Radical Innocent*.

12. Mary Craig Sinclair, *Southern Belle* (New York: Crown Publishers, 1957), 84.

13. Upton Sinclair, preface to George Sterling, *Sonnets to Craig* (New York: Albert & Charles Boni, 1928), 8.

14. Sinclair, *Southern Belle*, 90.

15. GS to Mary Craig Kimbrough, undated, Ditzler Collection, HAR.

16. GS to AB, January 5, 1912, George Sterling Collection, BER.

17. GS to AB, April 3, 1912, George Sterling Papers, BAN.

Chapter Sixteen · Woman of Genius

1. GS to AB, October 9, 1911, George Sterling Collection, BER.

2. GS to AB, October 19, 1911, George Sterling Collection, BER.

3. GS to JL, December 13, 1911, Jack London Papers, HUN.

4. GS to AB, January 5, 1912, George Sterling Collection, BER.

5. GS to JL, January 30, 1912, George Sterling Papers, HUN.

6. George Sterling diary, March 19, 1912, George Sterling Papers, BAN.

7. "Missing Teacher Leaves No Clews," *The San Francisco Call*, March 19, 1912.

8. GS to AB, May 28, 1912, George Sterling Collection, BER.

9. CKL to BP, August 24, 1912, Partington Family Papers, BAN.

10. GS to JL, April 8, 1913, Jack London Papers, HUN.

11. Herbert Heron to Connie Skinner, March 27, 1910, James Henry Papers, HAR.

12. Herbert Heron diary, June 9, 1912, James Henry Papers, HAR.

13. Herbert Heron to GS, August 11, 1912, James Henry Papers, HAR.

14. Herbert Heron to GS, November 25, 1912, James Henry Papers, HAR.

15. "Literary Ranks Split as Art Is Commercialized," *The San Francisco Call*, November 22, 1912.

16. JH to MA, February 26, 1913, in Pearce, *Literary America 1903–1934*.

17. Susan Goodman and Carl Dawson, *Mary Austin and the American West* (Berkeley: University of California Press, 2008).

18. Herbert Heron diary, April 25, 1913, James Henry Papers, HAR.

19. Genthe, *As I Remember*.

20. MA to GS, March 19, 1910, George Sterling Papers, BAN.

21. GS to MA, September 1, 1910, George Sterling Papers, HUN.

22. Published as Jack London, "The First Poet," *The Century Illustrated Monthly Magazine* 82 (June 1911): 251–55.

23. GS to JL, November 11, 1910, Jack London Papers, HUN.

24. JL to GS, November 16, 1910, Jack London Papers, HUN.

25. GS to JL, November 18, 1910, Jack London Papers, HUN.

26. This squeeze is very apparent in the handwritten version of George Sterling diary, October 17, 1910, George Sterling Papers, BAN.

27. Goodman and Dawson, *Mary Austin and the American West.*

28. Mary Hunter Austin, *A Woman of Genius* (New York: Doubleday, 1912), 460.

29. CKL to BP, June 2, 1913, Jack London Papers, HUN.

30. Jack London, *John Barleycorn* (New York: The Century Company, 1913), 15.

31. GS to BP, April 8, 1913, George Sterling Papers, BAN.

32. Herbert Heron diary, June 25, 1913, James Henry Papers, HAR. To complete this scene of the charades, I have embellished some details. We know from Heron's diary that Mrs. Foster stormed out due to Carrie's impression of her. I'm not sure what embarrassing habit of Mrs. Foster's Carrie performed (I have fabricated the detail about her stockings), but whatever it was, Carrie must have executed it perfectly to secure the result.

33. Herbert Heron diary, June 28, 1913, James Henry Papers, HAR.

Chapter Seventeen · Divorcée

1. "Wife's Divorce Suit Shatters Lafler's Romance," *The San Francisco Call*, July 31, 1913.

2. Bennett, "Don Passé."

3. George Sterling diary, August 25, 1913, George Sterling Papers, BAN.

4. George Sterling diary, September 5, 1913, George Sterling Papers, BAN.

5. Vera Connolly, "The Basic Law," *Young's Magazine* 26, no. 4 (October 1913): 111.

6. AB to Lora Bierce, October 1, 1913, in *Letters of Ambrose Bierce*, edited by Bertha Clark Pope (New York: Gordian Press, 1967).

7. George Sterling diary, November 24, 1913, George Sterling Papers, BAN.

8. "Sterling, Poet Will Mate with Inspirer of Verses," *The San Francisco Examiner*, February 28, 1914.

9. CS to JH, July 8, 1914, George Sterling Papers, BAN.

10. George Sterling, "The Hunting of Dian," in *Beyond the Breakers and Other Poems* (San Francisco: A. M. Robertson, 1914), 82.

11. CS to MA, December 16, 1914, George Sterling Papers, BAN.

12. JL to Jack London Grape Juice Co., October 1, 1914, Jack London Papers, BAN.

13. Genthe, *As I Remember.*

14. GS to CKL, November 29, 1916, Jack London Papers, HUN.

15. GS to JL, January 29, 1913, Jack London Papers, HUN.

16. In re note F. C. Havens at First National Bank of Oakland, 1921, Frank Colton Havens Papers, BAN.

17. Charmian Kittredge diary, May 26, 1917, Jack London Papers, HUN.

18. Charmian Kittredge diary, May 27, 1917, Jack London Papers, HUN.

19. CS to Mattie Hopper, December 14, 1917, George Sterling Papers, BAN.

20. GS to John Neihardt, July 14, 1918, George Sterling Collection, BER.

21. "City's Favorite Bard Fought Tragic Shadow," *The San Francisco Examiner*, September 15, 1946.

22. Elsie Whitaker Martínez interview.

23. "Divorced Wife of Geo. Sterling, Cal. Poet, Ends Her Life," *Los Angeles Herald*, August 9, 1918.

24. Elsie Whitaker Martínez interview.

25. "Poet's Tributes to His Wife Are Recalled," *The Oakland Tribune*, August 25, 1918.

26. Elsie Whitaker Martínez interview.

27. Alice Sterling to Mr. Dumont, August 12, 1935, George Sterling Papers, BAN.

28. Elsie Whitaker Martínez interview.

29. GS to Rose Travis, undated, Rudolph Blaettler Collection of George Sterling Papers, BAN.

30. GS to Rose Travis, undated, Rudolph Blaettler Collection of George Sterling Papers, BAN.

31. GS to Rose Travis, undated (Friday), Rudolph Blaettler Collection of George Sterling Papers, BAN.

32. GS to Rose Travis, undated (Saturday), Rudolph Blaettler Collection of George Sterling Papers, BAN.

33. GS to Rose Travis, undated (Sunday, 4:00 p.m.), Rudolph Blaettler Collection of George Sterling Papers, BAN.

34. Charmian Kittredge diary, August 9, 1918, Jack London Papers, HUN.

35. Charmian Kittredge diary, June 18–22, 1917, Jack London Papers, HUN.

36. GS to CKL, August 24, 1918, George Sterling Papers, HUN.

37. GS to CKL, August 24, 1918, Jack London Papers, HUN.

Chapter Eighteen · Phantom

1. HLM to GS, November 30, 1918, George Sterling Papers, BAN.

2. HLM to GS, May 16, 1921, in S. T. Joshi, ed., *From Baltimore to Bohemia: The Letters of H. L. Mencken and George Sterling* (Madison, NJ: Fairleigh Dickinson University Press, 2001).

3. HLM to GS, July 22, 1920, George Sterling Papers, HUN.

4. Samuel Dickson, *Tales of San Francisco* (Stanford, CA: Stanford University Press, 1992).

5. GS to HLM, August 18, 1920, in Joshi, *From Baltimore to Bohemia*.

6. GS to HLM, August 15, 1921, in Joshi, *From Baltimore to Bohemia*.

7. HLM to GS, May 19, 1920, George Sterling Papers, HUN.

8. George Sterling, "The Killdee," *The Smart Set* 68 (1922): 60.

9. Willard Huntington Wright, "An Authentic Poet," *San Francisco Bulletin*, May 19, 1918.

10. "Poet and Girl Swim Unclad in Stow Lake," *The San Francisco Examiner*, August 27, 1924, 1.

11. George Sterling, "The Strange Bird," *The Outlook* 133 (March 1921), 441.

12. George Sterling, "Infusion," undated manuscript, George Sterling Papers, SFL. Marginal notation indicates it appeared in the *New York Post Literary Review*, December 20, 1924.

13. GS to John Neihardt, November 15, 1924, George Sterling Collection, BER.

14. George Sterling, "Lost Companion," *Overland Monthly* 84 (March 1926): 81.

15. GS to Clark Ashton Smith, October 31, 1926, George Sterling Collection, BER.

16. Bennett, "Don Passé."

17. "Sterling's Swan Song Discovered," newspaper clipping, George Sterling Clipping File, OAK.

18. HLM to John Cowper Powys, December 11, 1926, George Sterling Papers, BAN.

19. "Sterling Keeps Tryst with Death as Friends Await," *The San Francisco Call and Post*, November 23, 1926.

20. Hugh l'Anson Fausset, *The Condemned and The Mercy of God: Two Poems of Crisis* (London: Selwyn & Blound, 1922), 27.

21. Fausset, *The Condemned and The Mercy of God*, 25.

22. AB to GS, September 14, 1909, George Sterling Collection, BER.

23. GS to CKL, November 14, 1917, Jack London Papers, HUN.

24. GS to JL, February 12, 1912, Jack London Papers, HUN.

25. "City's Favorite Bard Fought Tragic Shadow."

26. Belle to Vera Connolly, November 17, 1926, Vera Connolly Papers, COL.

27. Vera Connolly, "The Stampede of Youth," *Good Housekeeping*, August 1926, 36.

28. "Bench Dedicated to Sterling's Memory," *The Fresno Morning Republican*, June 27, 1927, 3.

29. Vera Connolly, "Cry of a Broken People," *Good Housekeeping*, August 1928, 36.

30. "Rupert Tourney Receives George Sterling's Poems," *The San Anselmo Herald*, January 13, 1944, 1.

31. Kevin Starr, *Golden Dreams: California in an Age of Abundance, 1950–1963* (New York: Oxford University Press, 2011).

32. Goodman and Dawson, *Mary Austin and the American West.*

33. "Lafler Rites Set for Friday," *Oakland Tribune,* January 17, 1935.

34. "Former Mayor of Carmel Dies," *Oakland Tribune,* December 6, 1938.

35. "Piedmont Mansion Treasures to Go on Sale Tomorrow."

36. Kenneth J. Smith to BP, March 2, 1950, Partington Family Papers, BAN.

37. Chris Dubbs, *American Journalists in the Great War: Rewriting the Rules of Reporting* (Lincoln: University of Nebraska Press, 2017).

38. Connie Wright, "Old Carmel: Jimmy Hopper—One of the Carmel Gang," *Carmel Residents Association Newsletter,* September 2008.

39. Mary Hunter Austin, *Earth Horizon* (Cambridge, MA: The Riverside Press, 1932), 338.

Index

✿

About the Author

⊙〰〰⊙

Catherine Prendergast, PhD, is a full professor in the Department of English at the University of Illinois at Urbana-Champaign, a Guggenheim Fellow, and a Fulbright Scholar. Her previous scholarly books include *Buying into English* and *Literacy and Racial Justice*. *The Gilded Edge* is her first work of narrative nonfiction.